Leicester–Nottingham Studies in Ancient Society

Volume 4

WAR AND SOCIETY IN THE GREEK WORLD

WAR AND SOCIETY IN THE GREEK WORLD

Edited by

JOHN RICH and GRAHAM SHIPLEY

London and New York

First published 1993
First published in paperback 1995
by Routledge
11 New Fetter Lane, London EC4P 4EE

Simultaneously published in the USA and Canada
by Routledge
29 West 35th Street, New York, NY 10001

Printed and bound in Great Britain by
T. J. Press (Padstow) Ltd., Padstow, Cornwall

British Library Cataloguing in Publication Data

A catalogue record for this book is available from the British Library

Library of Congress Cataloguing in Publication Data

A catalogue record for this book has been requested

ISBN 0–415–06643–3
ISBN 0–415–12166–3 (pbk)

Contents

Illustrations

Plates (between pages 114 and 115)

1a An *ambari* (storage chamber) in the mountains, Methana.
1b Battle scene (left-hand side), from the Alexander Sarcophagus (Archaeological Museum, Istanbul, no. 68). Photo: Hirmer Fotoarchiv, Munich (571.2084).
2a Detail of Alexander the Great, from the Alexander Mosaic (Naples Archaeological Museum, no. 10020). Photo: Alinari (12050 a).
2b Alketas Tomb at Termessos, Pisidia. Sculpted relief of mounted warrior. Author's photograph.
3a Alketas Tomb at Termessos, Pisidia. Grave area with receptacles for offerings. Author's photograph.
3b The Lion Monument at Amphipolis (restored). Author's photograph.
4a The Lion Tomb at Knidos, from the sea (tomb arrowed). Author's photograph.
4b Pyramidal tomb at Turgut in the Rhodian *peraia*. Author's photograph.

Figures

1 Hypothetical reconstruction of the funeral carriage of Alexander the Great. After H. Bulle, *Jahrbuch des Deutschen Archäologischen Instituts*, 21 (1906), 54, Abb. (p. 230)

Contributors

Graham Shipley is Lecturer in Ancient History and Head of the Ancient History Division at the University of Leicester.

Robert Carroll is Professor of Biblical Studies at the University of Glasgow.

Hugh Bowden is Lecturer in Ancient History at King's College London.

Alastar Jackson is Lecturer in Ancient History at the University of Manchester.

Tracey Rihll is Lecturer in Ancient History at St David's University College, Lampeter, Wales.

Edith Hall is Lecturer in Classics at the University of Reading.

Lin Foxhall is Lecturer in Ancient History at the University of Leicester.

Stephen Hodkinson is Lecturer in History at the University of Manchester.

Paul Millett is University Lecturer in Ancient History at the University of Cambridge and Fellow of Downing College, Cambridge.

Michel Austin is Senior Lecturer in Ancient History at the University of St Andrews.

Ellen Rice is Senior Research Fellow at Wolfson College, Oxford.

Preface

'There is and has been a powerful reluctance among historians to discuss ancient warfare and its consequences with a steady eye.' Thus Moses Finley, in one of his last published works (*Ancient History: Evidence and Models* (London, 1985), 71). The present book, and its companion volume *War and Society in Ancient Rome*, constitute an attempt to respond to Finley's challenge.

Like the earlier volumes in the series 'Leicester–Nottingham Studies in Ancient Society', they are the product of seminars jointly organized by the classical departments of the universities of Leicester and Nottingham. 'War and Society in the Ancient World' was the theme of a series of meetings held in Leicester and Nottingham between 1988 and 1990. The two volumes contain substantially revised versions of a selection of papers from that series.

Although the seminars focused mainly on Greece and Rome, they also included papers on other ancient societies, represented in this volume by Carroll's chapter, which brings out similarities and points of contrast with the Greek experience. The other papers in this volume examine various aspects of Greek warfare, and of its impact on Greek society, from Homeric times to the age of Alexander and his successors.

We are very grateful to all the participants in the seminar series, both our colleagues in Leicester and Nottingham and those from further afield, some of whom regularly travelled long distances to take part in the discussions. We also thank those of our colleagues who helped us by reading and commenting on drafts of the various manuscripts. (Graham Shipley was primarily responsible for organizing the present book, John Rich for the Roman volume; but the two volumes have been in the fullest sense a work of collaboration between both editors.) We would also like to thank Adrienne Edwards (University of Nottingham) for valuable administrative help, the catering and library staff of both universities (particularly Peter Woodhead at Leicester), and the Audio-Visual Service at Leicester for their help in arranging and setting up meetings. Graham Shipley particularly thanks Helen Parkins for her assistance in preparing the text. The editors are also grateful to Karen Stears for suggesting the jacket illustration.

June 1992   *John Rich*
                                                                Graham Shipley

Note on the second impression

This reprint is essentially unchanged. The plates have been corrected and a few alterations and additions made to the bibliographies.

October 1994   *J.W.R.*
                                                                        D.G.J.S.

Abbreviations

Abbreviated names of ancient authors are generally in the forms used in *The Oxford Classical Dictionary* (2nd edn, ed. N. G. L. Hammond and H. H. Scullard, Oxford, 1970). Those used include Aesch. (Aeschylus), Alc. (Alkaios), Ar. (Aristophanes), Arist. (Aristotle), Arr. (Arrian), Ath. (Athenaeus), Dem. (Demosthenes), Diod. (Diodoros of Sicily), Eur. (Euripides), Hdt. (Herodotos), Hom. (Homer), Just. (Justin), Pl. (Plato), Plut. (Plutarch), Polyb. (Polybios), Soph. (Sophocles), Theog. (Theognis), Thuc. (Thucydides), and Xen. (Xenophon).

Fragments of lyric poets are normally numbered according to *PMG* and *PLF*, elegiac poets according to West (*Iambi et Elegi Graeci*, Oxford, 1971-2).

AD	*Archaiologikon deltion*, Chron.(ika) and Mel.(etai)
AJA	*American Journal of Archaeology*
AJAH	*American Journal of Ancient History*
AJP	*American Journal of Philology*
AM	*Mitteilungen des Deutschen Archäologischen Instituts, athenische Abteilung*
AR	*Archaeological Reports* (supplement to *JHS*; London)
BCH	*Bulletin de correspondance hellénique*
BEFAR	Bibliothèque des Ecoles Française d'Athènes et de Rome (Paris)
BSA	*Annual of the British School at Athens*
CAH	*Cambridge Ancient History* (Cambridge)

CP	*Classical Philology*
CQ	*Classical Quarterly*
FGH	F. Jacoby (1923–58), *Fragmente der griechischen Historiker* (Berlin)
G&R	*Greece and Rome*
IG	*Inscriptiones Graecae*
Inscr. Lindos	C. Blinkenberg (1941), *Lindos: Fouilles de l'Acropole 1902–1914*, ii: *Inscriptions* (Berlin, etc.)
JHS	*Journal of Hellenic Studies*
JRS	*Journal of Roman Studies*
LCM	*Liverpool Classical Monthly*
LSJ	H. G. Liddell and R. Scott (1940), *Greek–English Lexicon* (9th edn rev. H. S. Jones), with *A Supplement*, 1968 (ed. E. A. Barber, Oxford)
ML	R. Meiggs and D. M. Lewis (1989), *A Selection of Greek Historical Inscriptions* (2nd edn, Oxford)
PCPS	*Proceedings of the Cambridge Philological Society*
PLF	E. Lobel and D. L. Page (eds 1955), *Poetarum Lesbiorum Fragmenta* (Oxford)
PMG	D. L. Page (ed. 1962), *Poetae Melici Graeci* (Oxford)
REA	*Revue des études anciennes*
SEG	*Supplementum epigraphicum Graecum* (Leiden)
SIG^3	W. Dittenberger (1915–24), *Sylloge inscriptionum graecarum* (3rd edn, Leipzig)
TGF	B. Snell, R. Kannicht, and S. Radt (eds 1985–), *Tragicorum Graecorum Fragmenta* (Göttingen)
Tod ii	M. N. Tod (1948), *A Selection of Greek Historical Inscriptions*, ii: *From 403 to 323 BC* (Oxford)

∞ 1 ∞

Introduction: The limits of war

Graham Shipley

'It's going to be a mental warfare out there'
(Martina Navratilova, before the ladies' singles final,
Wimbledon, July 1991)

War is often said to have been central to Greek society. As well as introducing some of the themes running through this volume of papers presented at seminars in the universities of Leicester and Nottingham during 1988–90, this paper aims to suggest, via a brief examination of the real scope and nature of Greek warlike activity as presented in ancient and modern writers, that its importance and effects in 'real' terms have been exaggerated. At the same time, however, it follows from this that war in ancient Greece was (and is) presented as more important than it 'actually' was for a variety of ideological reasons; when these are laid bare, Greek society is better understood.[1]

For modern historians, the issue of war is sometimes posed in terms of the need to understand it in order to help future statesmen prevent it. As Michael Howard puts it, 'war is only a particular kind of social conflict . . . the problem is the control of social conflict *as such*; not simply of war' (1984, 11–12; emphases

[1] This chapter was originally delivered at Leicester in November 1988 as the 'keynote' paper of the series. I am grateful to the participants on that occasion, particularly Tim Cornell, and to those who commented on earlier drafts: Hugh Bowden, Lin Foxhall, Helen Parkins, John Rich, and especially Greg Woolf. I have not always taken their advice, however, so any shortcomings that remain are my own responsibility.

original). It is possible to doubt, however, whether many historians have in fact treated war in the wider social context Howard
advocates; on an earlier page (ibid. 7) he observes that historians
as a profession have tended to take the history of war for granted,
focusing instead on the political techniques used to prevent it.
As ancient historians, we cannot prevent the wars we study;
what, then, should be our aim? Some may regard it as a hallmark
of western 'civilization' that intellectual pursuits can be carried out
in a pure, disinterested spirit; but in reality no historian can be, or
should be, wholly disinterested. There is a sense in which ancient
society can be a test-bed for more widely applicable models of
social interaction; and in the case of warfare, we can study it with
the hope of understanding better the role played by war in human
societies. Equally, since Greece and Rome are often used, and all
too often misleadingly, as *comparanda* for other periods and
places, it is important to question the received understanding of
those societies.

Greek warfare then and now

War, warfare, wartime

To begin at the beginning: there is a need to define terms. To talk
about ancient war as if it was the same as modern war – either
implicitly, by refusing to define war at all and using the word as if
we knew what it meant (as some writers still seem to do), or
explicitly, by defining ancient war in similar terms to modern war
– would be to privilege the ancient world, making it magically
distant and immune from criticism. We would disable ourselves
from making a rigorous examination of ancient concepts of war,
thus legitimizing the socially sanctioned ideology of the times. The
ancient experience of war would be made 'safe'; we would be
treating it as if it was just like the modern experience of war and
could tell us nothing new about the nature of human conflict in
general.

   The usual Greek word for violent inter-communal conflict is
polemos, correctly rendered in English, depending on the context,
as 'war', 'warfare', or 'wartime'. A brief examination of the use of
polemos by classical authors reveals differences between its

connotations and those of 'war'. In early authors *polemos* is mostly a general term – simply, as it were, 'fighting' – apparently without a strong implication of a bounded segment of time; phrases such as 'the Median war' or 'the Ionian war' occur occasionally in Thucydides (*ho Mēdikos polemos*, 1. 90; *ho Ionikos polemos*, 8. 11), but seem to become regular only in the fourth century. A specific war is usually called simply 'the such-and-suches', a neuter plural adjective (*sc.* 'things' or 'affairs'). Thus we see, for example, 'the Trojan affairs' (*ta Trōïka*; e.g. Thuc. 1. 3), or 'the Median affairs' (*ta Medika*; e.g. Herodotos, 1. 1). References to wars in the plural form, *polemoi*, are also rare (they are most common in Homer, where the word rather means 'fighting').

Singular events?

To refer, therefore, to 'the Lelantine war' or 'the Persian wars', as we so readily do, may be to impose surreptitiously the modern usage according to which we regularly speak of *a* war; a definite event, so to speak. It seems possible, indeed, that our habit of giving 'war' a capital W – a distinction ancient authors had no way of making – distances wars even further from generalness, emphasizing the specialness of these 'events'. The Peloponnesian war looks like a particular occurrence of a general social phenomenon; the name makes the reader think, consciously or unconsciously, of other wars. The Peloponnesian War, on the other hand, is a singular event with a name unique to itself, an event that was just waiting to happen; an almost human character in the historical drama, whose individuality cannot be dissolved and whose story is subject to explanation only in its own terms.

I suspect that Greek writers did not (originally, and for the most part) see wars as this kind of event. For Herodotos the 'Median things' were surely far more than just a series of battles. Our usual renderings of the titles of ancient books perpetuate this conceptual elision. Despite the title of the Penguin Classics version, Thucydides did not write a *History of the Peloponnesian War*, but a *Histories* (*historiai*). In fact, no author before Strabo and

Diodoros appears to have referred to what we call the Peloponnesian war as *ho Peloponnesiakos polemos.*[1] Works by late authors, too, such as Appian's *Syriaka* and *Mithridatika* (assuming they were so titled by the author or his contemporaries), become books about wars: *The Syrian Wars, The Mithridatic Wars*, and so on. It may even be that *polemos*, let alone *polemoi*, did not feature in the title of any classical historian's work (in contrast to the Romans; one immediately thinks of Caesar's *De bello Gallico*, Sallust's *Bellum Jugurthinum*, and so on).

Nor should we imagine that the names we give ancient wars are in any sense 'correct'. When we refer to the Peloponnesian war, we are of course seeing it from the point of view of those who fought *against* the Peloponnesians. This does not necessarily betray a preference for Athens; the war has long been known by that name, even by the earlier generations of English scholars for whom Sparta was the ideal state. It does, however, leave us predisposed to see the war only from the point of view of the Athenians who wrote about it. From Sparta's point of view we could just as well refer to the 'Athenian war(s)', as Cartledge does in his history of classical Sparta (1979). Strict even-handedness, in fact, would dictate 'Spartan–Athenian' (which is no harder to say than 'Peloponnesian'). Similarly, should we not attempt to see the wars of 490 and 480–479 BC as Greco-Persian, rather than Persian, wars? It is reasonable to reply that established proper names lose their original semantic connotations; who but a historian immediately thinks of hellenization when someone mentions the hellenistic period? As with period names, historians will undoubtedly continue to use the old names (as the contributors to this volume do) because they are generally recognized and can be helpful in singling out particular conflicts (see below, however, on the dangers of treating wars as watertight compartments of time). Nevertheless, though convenience is all very well, we should consciously deconstruct such names even as we continue to use them.

Beginnings and ends

We often regard a war as a definite, and on the whole short,

[1] LSJ s.v. *Peloponnesos.*

period of time with a beginning and end, two moments between which a particular state of being is supposed to pertain; but we also think of the same war in different ways. We speak of the second world war as an event, but exactly when did it begin and end? Did it cease to be a purely European war only when Japan and America joined in? Or was it a world war from the moment in 1939 when the British government, speaking 'on behalf of' the British empire, deemed that a state of war existed between the United Kingdom and Germany? That might well be the view of citizens of the British commonwealth, who are often irritated to hear that Britain (with Greece) 'stood alone' in 1940; alone, that is to say, but for half the population of the globe.

Declarations of war should not deceive; they are for public consumption. Nothing objectively changes at the moment when war is declared, or officially halted; war may effectively have begun before it is declared, or may not begin until months later, as in the case of the 'phoney war' (phoney only to the British!) of 1939–40. The act of declaring war is primarily a legal, ceremonial, and ideological statement.

Even in the case of antiquity, we are hard put to it to find firm beginnings and ends to 'wars' in a way that would explain anything. Given that the Greeks seem to have had a less strong concept than we do of wars as particular episodes, our use of the term to denote such an episode may not always be the only possible use.

Temporal boundaries within wars are not exactly unproblematic either. Within the second world war, people speak of separate wars: the desert war, the Japanese war. Some episodes defy strict definition; was the 'battle of the Atlantic' (the struggle, over several years, between the merchant convoys of the western powers and their navies on the one side, and the German ships and U-boats on the other) a battle or a war? It all depends how you view it. Similarly with the Peloponnesian war. Thucydides certainly means us to regard the various episodes of warfare between 431 and 403 as a unity and as distinct from what came before and after. We do not necessarily have to agree with him, however; and although we habitually refer to the Peloponnesian war, we often subdivide it into phases such as the Archidamian war and the Ionian war, with a gap in between containing the peace of Nikias and the Sicilian expedition.[1] More importantly, however, we also habitually refer to a 'first Peloponnesian war' in the 450s. Why not, then, refer to 431–404 as the *second* Peloponnesian war? Or, for that matter, to the Peloponnesian war(s) of *c*.459–403?

This is not a flippant point. I mean to show that we do an injustice to the past if we straitjacket events into discrete episodes without recognizing that there are alternatives, and that our choice of dates is itself a statement.

A special state of being

Beginnings and ends of wars are often marked by rituals. Greek wars, to be legitimate, had to be 'heralded'; the Romans had spears cast into enemy territory and opened the temple of Janus. Even what the sociologists call 'primitive' warfare might have a definite end; Sillitoe describes 'primitive' war (i.e. all war before the era of explosive weapons) as 'a state of hostility which may be peacefully settled at some stage' (in Kuper and Kuper (eds) 1989, 890). To this extent we are certainly entitled to believe that the Greeks could think of 'a war' as a certain episode in time. But did the Athenians after 431 think of themselves as being continuously 'at war' with the Spartans, particularly during the close season for hoplites, in the same way that the British people undoubtedly thought of themselves as being 'at war' with Hitler for 24 hours a day, 365 days a year between 1939 and 1945? Did they conceive of a special state of being, governing all other activities? Did the 'government' take special powers to control the population? Were normal civic rights suspended for the duration? Such all-pervading connotations of 'war' are more appropriate to the world of the modern nation state.

Strict limits cannot be imposed on brute reality. Even today our definition of when a war is not a war is not well worked-out. Was there a Falklands war in 1982? Many people now say so; but when did it begin? Was it officially recognized as such? Britain never

---

[1]   Is it Athenocentrism that restrains us from calling the Sicilian expedition the Sicilian *war*? Do we perhaps wish to absolve Athens of the guilt of starting that bloody and disastrous campaign? ('It was only an expedition, not an actual war, you know.')

declared war; indeed, states don't do that any more, chiefly perhaps because of the United Nations charter and the desire not to incur a charge of aggression. To avoid calling the episode a war can now, perhaps, be seen as a strategy for deflecting criticism at home and abroad; at the same time, the British public were not discouraged from seeing the episode as a war, thus enabling all the emotive language of jingoism to be mobilized in support of the British government's actions.

Definitions of the events called 'wars' are relative, and the choice of a particular one carries ideological baggage with it. This will be as true of the Greeks as of modern people; and it is no less true of the nature of civic existence in wartime than of the chronological delimitation of a particular war.

Wars and states

Dictionary-writers often require wars to be waged by states; the *Concise Oxford Dictionary* (Allen (ed.) 1990) gives the primary sense of 'war' as 'armed hostilities between esp. nations'. The archetypal modern war thus involves two states. Garlan (1966, 23) even says, 'By definition, so to speak, it [war] excludes all hostile relations before the formation of states.' Such a definition, strictly applied, would obscure the points of contact between state wars and other kinds, and Garlan himself goes on to discuss 'pre-judicial war' (such as Homeric war) as a species of *war*. In practice we do not use 'war' in the narrow sense, or we would not speak, as we do without any metaphorical intent, of guerrilla wars, the war against terrorism, class war, and so on. (Pure metaphors such as 'the war of the sexes' are another thing altogether; as are jocular appellations like the 'cod war', referring to a dispute between Britain and Iceland over fishing rights, which, though not without violent incidents, was chiefly a 'war of words'.) In speaking of antiquity, too, we use 'war' (as Roman writers used *bellum*, perhaps more readily than Greek writers used *polemos*) to denote violent episodes not involving two states, such as Pompey's war against the pirates, the Bellum Catilinarium, or the Bellum Servile.

Warfare clearly transcends the nation state; there were wars long before the modern states system existed. What is important is to merge the concept of wars into that of social violence in general, and even dissolve the boundaries between particular episodes of peace and war. We need a concept of war that can include not only wars as disparate in size and nature as the so-called Falklands war, the Gulf war of 1991, the Cold War, and the second world war, but also wars of independence, guerrilla wars, terrorist campaigns, and the raids of the Border Reavers.

It may be useful to consider warfare as one part of a larger spectrum of *organized societal violence*. At a given time in a given place, the prevailing level of violence could, in principle, be measured against such a scale. Peaks of activity, or episodes of a particular form (inter- rather than merely intra-communal) or scale (regional rather than local in their impact), would then represent wars. Of course, exactly where we draw the line beyond which we consider an episode to be a war is an ideological question; not all cases will be easy ones (was the Falklands war more than local?), and the dividing lines will be different in different value-systems.

The remainder of the spectrum might be composed of other forms of organized violence, such as those listed above. Many of the studies in this and the accompanying volume deal with such non-orthodox forms of warlike activity, such as piracy (Alastar Jackson, David Braund), banditry (Keith Hopwood), and colonization (Tracey Rihll).

Causes

Accepting, then, that there are episodes that we can usefully, if loosely, class as wars, that to speak of wars is not to divide them absolutely from other forms of violence, and that we ought not to isolate wars temporally from their antecedents and aftermaths, then we should also consider their causes; and not merely 'why' they happened, but with what ends in view they were fought, and why they turned out as they did.

What can we say of 'causes'? To judge from the generality of writing about particular Greek wars, historical thinking about their causes is often extremely unsophisticated. Without getting too deeply embroiled in philosophical niceties, I shall make a few points about the nature of 'causes' and about social processes that lead to wars.

The term 'causes', so often used in connection with ancient wars, can be a misnomer. War in general can reasonably be said to be caused by various factors (take your pick). Particular wars, however, are not 'caused' as volcanic eruptions, eclipses of the sun, or chemical reactions are caused, and we should not write about them as if they were. They are *resolved upon*, by groups or individuals *on each side* (an important point) who take a conscious decision to fight (read: require others to fight) in the belief that more is to be gained by fighting than by not fighting.[1] (It follows that it is better to use the plural ethnic name rather than that of the communal unit. It was Romans and Spartans, not 'Rome' or 'Sparta', that waged wars.) Each decision of this kind is made in the light of what is perceived to be the current situation. Thus, for example, the growing power of Athens, in so far as it was (in Thucydides' famous formulation) the main 'cause' of the Peloponnesian war, was a cause only in this special sense. It did not make conflict inevitable; it was a cause only because it was the Spartans' chief 'reason' for deciding to fight. ('Reason' is preferable to 'motive', another blanket term for what leads to a war, which is much favoured by historians and in consequence by students, but invariably goes unexamined. It serves as a stand-in for 'cause'; but like that other favoured historical catch-all, 'influence', it does not actually explain anything. 'Motive' should be replaced by 'reason', a term that highlights the existence of a decision-making process.)

'Cause', therefore, really means two things: (1) in the case of 'war' in general, the underlying determinants of the societal level of violence; (2) in the case of a particular war, the occasion of, or *inducements* to resolve upon, the waging of that war (this applies to all wars, including those that are *prima facie* defensive).

(1) We need to ground the 'causes' of war not only in ideologies and mentalities, but also in social relations. Not all human societies, and not even all animal communities, are inherently violent, and those that are violent are not violent all the time; but they are acquisitive (as Rihll points out in her chapter). What

[1] Howard 1984, 22; cf. 17–18, where H. argues that not arms, or even arms races, but statesmen's perceptions, cause wars (but see p.10 n. 2).

makes humans fight communally is not simply (in Howard's dictum) 'power'; that is a truism. One might suppose, alternatively, that it is population increases (like those in the geometric and archaic periods examined by Sallares 1991, esp. 50–107), and the resulting changes (actual or anticipated) in the standard of life, that have made many societies warlike over the last few millennia; but this is to reduce the causes of war to such a general level that nothing about actual wars is explained. Rather it is a *desire*, the desire to safeguard, or augment, the enjoyment and free disposition of material goods (land, economic surpluses, etc.). This remains true even if the desire is mediated and perceived as a political, rather than material, goal – most commonly freedom.[1] Aristotle, indeed, classified war as a species of 'acquisitive' activity (*ktetikē*; see Garlan 1989, 27–31); and Finley (1985, 77–9) characterizes war as essentially a profit-making enterprise.

(2) Turning to the inducements: they may either be consciously embraced (and, from our standpoint, either objective or merely subjective); or may be unperceived, 'hidden hand' factors which we, from our privileged viewpoint, can detect, such as economic, climatic, or demographic considerations.[2] Not only can causes, or inducements, be consciously apprehended or else unseen, they can also be a matter of short-term or long-term perceptions, and they can be well- or ill-founded. Equally, ancient writers' perceptions of 'causes' can be judged more or less satisfactory according to the same criteria. Momigliano (1966) argues that ancient writers were interested in causes of wars, not of war generally. Garlan (1989, ch. 2) has reminded us of the many passages in which Plato and Aristotle comment on the origins of war; but Momigliano's proposition remains largely true, since Plato and Aristotle tend to communicate these views in asides or short

[1] See Garlan 1989, 33–40, on politics as subsuming economic and other factors; in Musti's words (quoted by Garlan on p. 36), 'Le politique est ici la *somme* de toute l'expérience sociale et économique' (emphasis original). Cf. ibid. 39, where Garlan emphasizes the role of 'un champ politique relativement autonome'.
[2] Hence arms races, and armaments programmes, *do* make wars more likely. For example, President Reagan's earlier investment in new technology made President Bush's decision to bomb Iraq in 1991 easier to take than it would otherwise have been, and therefore more likely to be taken.

digressions, rather than focusing on war as such. Garlan himself comments on the inadequacy of their appraisal, and grounds this in the prevailing ideology of the polis.

Greek writers were not blind to the interrelation of both conscious and unconscious inducements; the Greek term *aitia* covers both, and Herodotos' *aitiai* embrace both subjective and objective causes. Thucydides, similarly, explores the *prophasis*, 'stated grounds', for Sparta's decision to go to war – or those that might have been stated – but takes too narrow a view of them. He was, however, the first to formulate the parallel distinctions between superficial and underlying causes of wars, between short-term and long-term causes, and between official justifications for going to war and the unstated reasons for doing so.

Both Thucydides and Polybios, as Momigliano remarks, operated with explanations that were for the most part too short-term, though both tried to refine the discussion. Above all it is essential to take the long-term view. Thus, in examining the Peloponnesian war, we should not stress – as is often still done in histories of the late fifth century – merely the events of the mid- and late 430s, such as the Corcyra dispute or the Megarian decrees, but (along with Thucydides in his most lucid moment) the Spartan fear of the Athenians' growing power. Indeed, we should range even more widely than he does. It is hardly ever stated, when Spartan–Athenian hostility is being discussed, that both before and after the Persian wars the Athenians had seen repeated Spartan interferences in their internal affairs, only one of which was a welcome intervention.[1] Any explanation of the Peloponnesian war needs to be grounded in things that happened three-quarters of a century before. Equally, if Athenian 'imperial' ambitions after 479 ultimately provoked the war, an assessment of these ambitions must also be grounded in earlier history, not just in the events of 480–479; it must take into account not only the pre-existing antipathy between the élites of Sparta and Athens, but

---

[1] Hdt. 5. 64–5 (Kleomenes I expels the tyrant Hippias); 70, 72 (tries to expel Kleisthenes and make Isagoras tyrant, but is forced to withdraw); 74–5 (tries again to impose a puppet ruler, and is prevented only by the Corinthians withdrawing support). Hdt. lists the various events at ch. 76, adding another from legendary times. After the Persian wars the Spartans tried to prevent the Athenians building a city wall (Thuc. 1. 90–3).

also the early Athenian expansionist moves such as the takeover of Salamis and several north Aegean islands soon after 600, the aggressions by the Philaidai in the Thracian Chersonese and by the Peisistratids in Euboia, and possibly even the Athenians' enthusiastic support for the Ionian revolt in the 490s.

Did the causes of wars change during Greek history? At the deepest level, clearly not. Wars are always occasioned by a group's perception of where its interest lies, and by its concern for its material well-being. But with changes in military organization, and the development (and then, under the hellenistic kings, suppression) of city politics, the motives for particular episodes of conflict may well have changed. Early poleis fought basically for land; by the fifth century the prizes were greater, including control of the supply of luxuries (famously enumerated in the Xenophontic *Athenaion politeia*). Alexander fought partly for glory and wealth (as shown in Michel Austin's paper in this volume); but in the hellenistic period Greek cities fought against kings for their freedom, and kings fought for the secure enjoyment of empires. An example of the latter is provided by the series of 'Syrian wars' between the Ptolemies and Seleukids. The Ptolemies needed Syria for luxuries with which to live the life of pharaohs, while some of their military needs, like timber and pitch, could be satisfied only by controlling the Levantine coasts (Walbank 1980, 102–3). At the same time, these wars seem to have fulfilled the ritual function of proving the king's martial prowess; it is striking how often a change of ruler in one or other kingdom was swiftly followed by another 'Syrian war'.

In accounting for wars we should also stress cultural predispositions, such as the Spartan preoccupation with security from Helot revolts, which caused them to increase the emphasis on military discipline and training; or the bellicism of the Roman senatorial élite (famously explored in Harris 1979), which led them to seek out, or even manufacture, opportunities for leading military campaigns abroad because this was the only way of enhancing their political status and wealth at home. Even in the case of Athens, a society we tend to think of as less warlike, it is important not to forget that the aristocratic élite had an interest in seeking out opportunities for military success in order to enhance their wealth and political prowess. (Paul Millett, in this volume, offers a corrective to the idea that the fourth century represented a time of decline for Athens, and a carefully nuanced evaluation of the costs and benefits of military campaigns to the élite who provided most of Athens' commanders.) There, as in other city-states, the all-important male bonding ritual of the drinking-party, particularly characteristic of the élite, will have played a major part. If, for Clausewitz, modern war was the continuation of diplomacy by other means, then war in classical Greece was the continuation of the *symposion* by other means.

Aims

If we are to take the long-term view, we must look forward to aims, as well as backwards to causes. Not enough is said, in ancient or modern books, about the 'war aims' of belligerents, beyond simple victory. This may be because the occurrence of wars was taken for granted (peace not being regularly set up as the desirable opposite of war), and because the aims of a community waging war were not felt to need stating; victory or survival were seen as unquestioned goods.

Yet wars are almost never fought for, or by, *whole* communities; nor is the decision to go to war ever resolved upon, literally, by a community. What were the aims of leaders, and what were those of 'ordinary' soldiers, in a Greek war? In this volume Stephen Hodkinson and Paul Millett examine the motives and ambitions of commanders (Spartan and Athenian, respectively) in the classical period. Both investigations transcend the traditional mode of examination, in which commanders are assessed purely in terms of their tactical achievements; instead, these individuals are set firmly in a social context.

If we take up the earlier argument we see that aims *can* be short-term, ill-founded, or unconscious. We should not blithely attribute farsightedness or intelligence to ancient decision-makers as is often done, particularly in the case of the Peloponnesian war. That is, of course, the one case where we have reasonable evidence for what one leading man thought; though even there we have to take what Thucydides says about Perikles with a pinch of salt, since he is writing with hindsight and admires the man enormously. On the other hand, there may often have been ulterior aims which our sources do not state; why, for example, did the Spartans not destroy Athens in 403? For fear of the Corinthians?

Aims, of course, tie in with 'causes' (inducements). The usual ulterior aim of war, then as now, was usually to coerce one's opponents (bend them to one's will). Very rarely was it to destroy them; annihilation was rare and usually exemplary. A list of some of the best-known cases will suffice: Plataia, Melos, Thebes (by Alexander), Kios in Asia Minor (by Philip V), Corinth (by the Romans). However, it usually made more sense to allow the enemy to survive in such a condition that they could pay tribute or soldiers in the future. The aim of a war was thus often no more than the replacement of one ruling group by another in the enemy city. To this extent, then, aims (like immediate causes) can be 'political' matters as well as the result of material interests; though if one digs deep enough one can invariably unearth material interests too.

Outcomes

One of the most important contributions to historical thinking about imperialism in recent years has been made by Paul Kennedy in *The Rise and Fall of the Great Powers* (1988). In a massive examination of 500 years of history, Kennedy argues that *in the long run* and in general, 'economic' factors (in the broadest sense, and meaning much more than just 'commercial' factors) have determined the power enjoyed by a state. The argument that economic factors determine history is not, of course, entirely new; but Kennedy deploys it with unusual subtlety.

Kennedy argues that the economic performance that determines a state's power and military success is always to be measured on a relative, not an absolute, basis; the crucial thing is to be doing better, even if only a little better, than your rivals. However, if wealth is a *sine qua non*, or even a major determinant of the military fortunes of a state, it is for Kennedy only one among many factors. Others include the efficiency or otherwise of revenue-raising (the key example is eighteenth-century France); physical and political geography, and the strategic and diplomatic possibilities these offer (the prime example being Britain, as an island); public and élite morale; special motives influencing the leadership (such as the desire for military glory or dynastic primacy, such as in the case of the Habsburgs, for whom such motives seem to have transcended purely material calculations); and (crucially for empires) the degree to which a state's power is 'over-extended'.

As an explanation of the outcome of wars, the emphasis upon material resources has lain behind many earlier writings. Liddell Hart, for example, spectacularly demonstrates, in a mere two pages (1970, 23–4), that the outcome of the second world war was virtually a foregone conclusion.

> There were some twenty basic products essential for war. Coal for general production. Petroleum for motive power. Cotton for explosives. Wool. Iron. Rubber for transport. Copper for general armament and all electrical equipment. Nickel for steel-making and ammunition. Lead for ammunition. Glycerine for dynamite. Cellulose for smokeless powders. Mercury for detonators. Aluminium for aircraft. Platinum for chemical apparatus. Antimony, manganese, etc., for steel-making and metallurgy in general. Asbestos for munitions and machinery. Mica as an insulator. Nitric acid and sulphur for explosives.
>
> Except for coal, Britain herself lacked most of the products which were required in quantity. But so long as the use of the sea was assured, most of them were available in the British Empire. . . .
>
> In striking contrast was the situation of the Berlin–Rome–Tokyo triangle. . . . Here lay the greatest weakness of all in the war-making capacity of the Axis.

In short, the distribution of the control of raw material sources made the victory of the 'Allies' virtually inevitable – provided, that is, they withstood the first assaults by the Axis powers.

Nearly all the resources listed above were, of course, irrelevant to ancient technology, but we could still make a check-list of sorts, including items such as bronze, iron, and timber for weapons and ships; precious metals with which to pay mercenaries; and pack-animals and agricultural surpluses with which to feed an army, unless it could live off the land. In the absence of motor transport and electronic communications, distance will also be a crucial factor, limiting for example the length of supply lines. To some readers of Herodotos it may seem that he goes some way towards doing a similar job on the Persian wars, by listing the king's revenues and repeatedly enumerating the peoples fighting on each side.[1] However, he almost certainly has a different historical motive, that of demonstrating how spectacular the Greek achievement was, given the imbalance in numbers and resources. None the less, we still have to take seriously the point that the control and location of material resources will heavily influence the outcome of wars, and we should not lightly be dissuaded from looking for them.

To take once more the example of the Peloponnesian war. First, as argued above, we must view it as only a part of a long series of conflicts beginning *c.*460 BC (or even earlier). The final outcome, the defeat of Athens, appears at first sight to contradict Kennedy's model. Sparta's victory will come as a great surprise to anyone who considers only the resources available to the Athenian alliance in 431, especially if it is believed that the Spartans rejected all material wealth. But Spartan austerity (as suggested by the fates of many of its commanders, examined below by Hodkinson) was to a large extent a pose; even more importantly, Sparta was able to rely on the assistance of its perioikic subjects and the armies and ships of powerful cities such as Corinth. Nevertheless it is hard to imagine that the Peloponnesians in 431 had financial reserves and revenues in any way comparable to those of Athens. Why, then, did they win the war?

Possible negative material factors on the Athenian side could include the over-extension of Athenian power (of which the Sicilian expedition is only the most glaring example) and the impossibility for Athens of enforcing tribute-paying on a large number of unwilling subjects. On the Peloponnesian side, the crucial items in the scales must be Corinth's trading revenues and fleet, which were probably more stable assets than Athenian tribute. Even more important, and surely decisive in the later stages of the war, was Persian gold. These, I would argue, are plausible explanatory determinants, or the prime ones, of the outcome of the war, and they explain the outcome far better than such alleged factors as the validity or otherwise of Perikles' strategy or the alleged failings of his successors; let alone the

[1] E.g. 7. 60–98 (Persian forces at Doriskos), 184–6 (fleet and army numbers at Thermopylai), 202 (Greeks at Thermopylai); 8. 1–2 (Greek ships at Artemision).

moral corruption of the Athenian demos. Psychological factors, particularly morale, played their part, but on the whole success and failure depended on practical constraints.

On the same basis we might ask whether the Macedonian takeover of southern Greece in the 330s was, as it might seem, simply the result of Philip II's brilliant generalship and cunning statesmanship, the discipline of the Macedonian phalanx, or their extra-long thrusting spear, the *sarissa* (for which some might be inclined to blame the whole history of Greece and Near East after 350). Undoubtedly all three played important parts, as Kennedy would be the first to agree; and we could, if we wished, add in a psychological factor, the cultural aspirations of the Macedonian dynasty. But what *enabled* Philip to redesign and re-equip his army, in short to revolutionize the military power of his kingdom? Surely it must have to do with the programme of urbanization and development of which Arrian writes (*Anabasis*, 7. 9) in his version of Alexander's speech at Opis: 'Philip', says the king, 'found you wandering about without resources. He brought you down from the mountains to the plains, and made you a match in war for the neighbouring barbarians. He made you city-dwellers and civilized you with good laws and customs.'[1] What, if any, historical reality lies behind this piece of rhetoric only archaeology will show; but it does appear that Philip mobilized a pool of resources that had hitherto lain untapped. Such was the size of the pool that the effect on Macedonian power was very rapid. As with the Peloponnesian war, we need to invoke more than just tactical and strategic weaknesses, or moral or psychological failings, to explain the fall of southern Greece.

The list of examples could be lengthened. Was Sparta's failure after 400 a case of over-extension? Was it not inevitable that Alexander's empire would break apart as soon as it was created? Does not the outcome of the Persian wars suggest that Persia's power was fatally over-extended in relation to its unsophisticated revenue-raising capacities?[2] The Kennedy model could fruitfully

[1] Translation quoted from Austin 1980, 30, with omissions.
[2] I do not think we need to resort to Delbrück's argument (revived by Sallares 1991, 47–8) that the Greek forces must have outnumbered their Persian opponents in the battles of the Persian wars. The demographic explanation applies to general causes, not particular events. If we want a demographic explanation, I would prefer another of Sallares'

be explored further and applied to many examples from ancient history.

The 'importance' of war

Garlan (1966, 16–17), noting the low level of theoretical elaboration of war in ancient writers, has shown that the Greeks did not develop an autonomous concept of war. War was a fact of life; and though peace was different, it was not considered the norm, nor was war seen as an aberration. Certain forms and consequences of war might be abnormal, such as the distortions of normal life identified by Thucydides in his portrayal of civil strife in the Greek cities (3. 82), but war as such is not thought of as intolerable. There was no well-worked-out concept of peace (ibid. 17); indeed, treatises were not devoted to war as such, only to the tactics and technology of war, and least of all to the question of how to prevent war. Peace *is* lauded, but almost as a utopian ideal, for example in Hesiod (Garlan 1989, 7–9; cf. ch. 2 on Plato and Aristotle). The most famous work of Greek literature, the *Iliad*, is set against a wholly military background. One may wish to argue that the poem deconstructs and subverts the values of war even while it appears to celebrate them, as Simone Weil pointed out in 1941 (Weil 1986; cf. Scully 1991); but nowhere is it suggested that war can, or should, be abolished. War is at least accepted, at most celebrated as the manliest of occupations.

There is a temptation for a historian to say that whatever one is talking about was central to the society under scrutiny. Garlan writes of the 'omnipresence' of war (1989, 12–13). Was war really, as is often said, central? Or does it seem so only because of the almost exclusive emphasis placed on military history by ancient writers and, even now, by some scholars? It is often said that the Greek citizen was above all things a soldier. There is no doubt that the ideology of collective fighting bulked large in the mentality of the emerging and developed polis; some of the workings of this ideology are explored in the present volume, such as in the papers

---

formulations (p. 47): 'It is possible . . . that the attack from the Orient failed because it happened to come at a time when Greece was overflowing with manpower.'

by Hugh Bowden (on Homer and the early polis) and Edith Hall (on anti-barbarian ideology in classical Athens). Later, too, it could be said that the hellenistic monarchs were, first and foremost, military dynasts who needed to legitimize their position by all possible means (including public monuments, examined below by Ellen Rice). In other societies, too, the ideology of war performed a social function (see Robert Carroll's paper on the Hebrews).

At the same time, it is possible to question whether Greek society was as warlike as is often made out. There is no denying the importance of military organization for citizens, though it is important not to elevate universal military service into some kind of militarism. Finley's essay on Sparta (1968) is an excellent example of how to keep Greek military organization in perspective; he argues persuasively against the idea that Sparta was a militaristic state in the way that some modern states have been. This view certainly accords with Ceadel's typology of views about war, according to which militarism is 'the view that war is necessary to human development and therefore a positive good', and therefore that 'All wars are justified' (Ceadel 1987, 4). This extreme form of militarism is a distinctively modern phenomenon, chiefly found in the former fascist states; it cannot be detected in any Greek polis, even Sparta.

Finley (1985, 74) stresses the centrality of war in determining the distribution of material goods and the political structures of society, accepting Marx's notion that 'in early societies, war was the basic factor in economic growth and consequently in the transformation of the social structure'. To this extent war affected all members of society, directly or indirectly. In the *longue durée* it was one of the chief mechanisms by which populations moved around; in the short term, warlike activity of all kinds (including for example piracy, banditry, mercenary service, and colonization) was a way of avoiding economic hardship.

However, many aspects of life went on largely unaffected by war. The great continuities of Mediterranean existence identified by Braudel were altered only to a modest degree by the outcomes of individual conflicts. When war did impinge, its effects could be limited in extent and duration. Changes in land ownership and the distribution of surpluses did take place, but they influenced the techniques and practices in the (predominantly agricultural) landscape only in the long term, as in the case of the increase in rich villa farms in the Roman provinces, or the institution of the tied colonate. War was not even the sole, or principal, agent of such changes, which had their origin mainly in social dynamics, including demography. When war took place in the classical period, it was likely to be brief and limited to certain seasons when there was less need for agricultural labour. Even the ravaging of the agricultural landscape, so prominent a feature of historical narratives, can rarely have had any lasting effect, as Lin Foxhall shows in her chapter in this volume.

Even among soldiers, casualty rates were almost certainly very low compared to those in modern warfare. One analyst comments, 'War is getting more dangerous all the time. . . . No more than about 2 per cent of belligerents in war in the Middle Ages lost their lives. The proportion rose to about 40 per cent in the First World War' (J. Galtung, in Kuper and Kuper (eds) 1989, 889). Furthermore, it is far from being the case that all Greeks were soldiers. The Greek male, even if he was at certain times a soldier (and we should not forget that he was at least as likely to be a rower as a hoplite), was also typically a farmer, a craftsman, or both; and not all men will have been able-bodied and fit to bear arms. Finally, it is also worth stressing the obvious fact – all too often obscured in discussions of ancient wars – that not all inhabitants of Greece were citizens, or male. The citizen might go to war; his elders, wife, and children did not. Women in particular, though often grievously affected by war, presumably inherited and transmitted a culture (largely hidden from us) that had little or nothing to do with upholding the values of war.

I suspect that we distort the ancient world by harping on about the 'centrality' of war, just as much as when we over-emphasize the role of religion, agriculture, or the subordinate position of women. All these things are important, but none exclusively so. Furthermore, they do not necessarily locate the specific differences between Greek and modern society; such phenomena are still central to modern life, though they may not always be recognized as such. To take only the case of war: a high value was placed on military training in Britain as recently as the 1950s, to judge from the existence of compulsory national service, which still exists in most Continental states. It would be absurd to deny that 'the military' is still a major force in the structuring of British society, and all the more is this true of some other countries, such as the Middle Eastern states. Until recently it was possible, by ignoring events outside Europe, to believe that the world had entered a new era of relative peace; but the violent aftermath of the fall of the Soviet empire has disabused us of that notion. We may like to think that we, in late twentieth-century Europe, live in a particularly peaceful time and place (the evidence of newspapers and television notwithstanding); but the imagery of war still litters our language (see epigraph).

Until the twentieth century, indeed, war used to be taken for granted in European societies, as an unavoidable (and only sometimes regrettable) part of life. Only after the first world war did most people in Europe and America come to believe that wars began through wickedness or incompetence. Michael Howard (1984, 21) writes that 'For liberal intellectuals war was . . . self-evidently a pathological aberration from the norm, at best a ghastly mistake, at worst a crime.' These views were not only held by intellectuals; but they were relatively novel. Similarly, the equation of the just war with the defensive war, and the categorization of all unprovoked wars as wrong, is a modern phenomenon. In short, to adopt Howard's term, most or all states until very recently may be said to have been 'bellicist'.

> Bellicism is morally neutral and applicable only to the period before the offence/defence distinction came to be widely recognized. . . . Militarism can be understood as a deliberate attempt to moralize bellicist assumptions . . . in a new era . . . in which peace came to be regarded both as the normal state of affairs and as overwhelmingly preferable to war.
>
> (Ceadel 1987, 12)

No ancient writer, *a fortiori*, adopted anything we would recognize as a pacifist or even pacificist position,[1] with the

---

[1] 'Pacificism', the original form of the word 'pacifism', is revived by Ceadel (1987, 5) to denote the view which 'rules out all aggressive wars and even some defensive ones . . ., but accepts the need for military force to defend its political achievements against aggression'. This, he argues (ch. 6), is the position implicitly held by most peace campaigners, even though many call themselves pacifists (true pacifists rule out war under *any* circumstances, a rarely-held position). Indeed, most people today, on Ceadel's fivefold typology (pacifism, pacificism, defencism, crusading, militarism), are either pacificists or defencists. Consequently, advocates of strong defence are not militarists; and militarism (like crusading) is nearly defunct even in policy-making circles.

possible exception of the Cynics. It would therefore have made no
sense to ask a Spartan or an Athenian if they saw themselves as
militaristic; the very concept of militarism presupposes that anti-
militarist positions exist, which has been true only in recent
generations.

If war was taken for granted in Europe before 1919, was it so
taken for granted in classical Greece? It was clearly important in
many ways; but the truth may be that while war affected most
people at some time in antiquity, it probably did so to a lesser
extent than today. The ideological importance of war for ancient
(largely male, civic) culture, pre-selected and handed down to us,
cannot be denied; for example, many of the most famous monuments of antiquity that survive today were paid for from the
profits of violence (rather than, as is often the case today, from the
profits of trade). But despite the predominantly military presentation of civic society in art and literary sources, many areas of
social and cultural practice existed independently of warfare.

War and ideology

In the preceding sections I have tried to cut Greek war down to
size, while retaining some of the specific differences that mark it
off from war in other periods. We have seen that many of our
names for ancient wars are modern inventions, which sometimes
betray our inability to see things from more than one angle. I have
also tried to suggest that the Greeks did not structure their sense
of the historical past, as we do, around discrete events called wars;
nor did they regard 'wartime' as a special form of existence for
non-participants and fighters alike. I have argued that historians
often deal myopically with the 'causes' of Greek wars, ignoring the
facts that not all Greeks were warriors and that the decision to
fight was usually taken by a small number of powerful men. I have
also suggested that the main reasons for which fighting was
resolved upon, and the chief factors that led to the victory of one
side, were – on the whole, and in the long term – material, not (as
in the still standard presentation of Greek history) political and
moral. I have tried to assimilate Greek war to war in other
periods, for example with respect to its causes and the factors that
determined its outcome.

War *was* a frequent occurrence, certainly more frequent than in some other periods and societies, but frequency is not the point; what we have to identify is the particular form taken by war in a given society. We should not imagine that Greek war was as all-involving, destructive, or negatively regarded as war is today; a case could be made, after all, for thinking that we live in a much *more* violent world than the Greeks. Why, then, is war presented to us by ancient art and literature as the central organizing principle of civic society? As with all representations of a society to itself and to others, one must look for the ideological subtext. If war, actual or mythological (for examples of the latter see Vidal-Naquet 1968; 1986), was selected for visual and literary representation to the virtual exclusion of trade, crafts, and domestic activities, and if public religion in the world of the polis was ever more bound up with the military successes of the community (and ever less with the relationship of humans to their natural environment, as argued by Osborne 1987), this says much about the real structures of power in Greek society. The selection of war as the paramount activity can be regarded as an attempt to direct energy towards maintaining a particular social structure, one in which citizen was dominated by aristocrat, non-citizen by citizen, female by male, and barbarian by Greek. It is only by understanding the interplay between these social categories, and the ideological use made of them, that Greek warfare can be understood.

Bibliography

Allen, R. E. (ed. 1990), *The Concise Oxford Dictionary of Current English* (8th edn; Oxford).

Austin, M. M. (1980), *The Hellenistic World from Alexander to the Roman Conquest: A Selection of Ancient Sources in Translation* (Cambridge).

Cartledge, P. (1979), *Sparta and Lakonia: A Regional History 1300–362 BC* (London).

Ceadel, M. (1987), *Thinking about Peace and War* (Oxford).

Finley, M. I. (1968), 'Sparta', in J.-P. Vernant (ed.), *Problèmes de la guerre en Grèce ancienne* (Paris), pp. 143–60; = 'Sparta and Spartan society', in *Economy and Society in Ancient Greece* (ed. B. D. Shaw and R. P. Saller; London, 1981), ch. 2 (pp. 24–40); = 'Sparta', in *The Use and Abuse of History* (2nd edn; London, 1986), ch. 10 (pp. 161–78).

—— (1985), 'War and empire', in *Ancient History: Evidence and Models* (London), ch. 5 (pp. 67–87).

Garlan, Y. (1966), *War in Ancient Society* (London).

—— (1989), *Guerre et économie en Grèce ancienne* (Paris).

Harris, W. V. (1979), *War and Imperialism in Republican Rome: 327–70 BC* (Oxford).

Howard, M. (1984), *The Causes of Wars* (London).

Kennedy, P. (1988), *The Rise and Fall of the Great Powers: Economic Change and Military Conflict from 1500 to 2000* (London, etc.).

Kuper, A. and Kuper, J. (eds 1989), *The Social Science Encyclopedia* (London).

Liddell Hart, B. H. (1970), *History of the Second World War* (London).

Momigliano, A. (1966), 'Some observations on the causes of war in ancient historiography', in *Studies in Historiography* (London), ch. 2 (pp. 112–26).

Osborne, R. (1987), *Classical Landscape with Figures: The Ancient Greek City and its Countryside* (London).

Sallares, R. (1991), *The Ecology of the Ancient Greek World* (London).

Scully, S. (1990), *Homer and the Sacred City* (Ithaca).

Vidal-Naquet, P. (1968), 'The black hunter and the origin of the Athenian *ephebeia*', *PCPS* 194 (n.s. 14): 49–64; revised version in R. L. Gordon (ed. 1981), *Myth, Religion and Society: Structuralist Essays by M. Detienne, L. Gernet, J.-P. Vernant and P. Vidal-Naquet* (Cambridge), ch. 8 (pp. 147–62); = *The Black Hunter: Forms of Thought and Forms of Society in the Greek World* (Baltimore, etc., 1986), ch. 5 (pp. 106–28).

—— (1986), 'The black hunter revisited', *PCPS* 212 (n.s. 32): 126–44.

Walbank, F. W. (1980), *The Hellenistic World* (Glasgow).

Weil, S. (1986), 'The *Iliad* or the poem of force', in S. Miles (ed.), *Simone Weil: An Anthology* (London, etc.), pp. 162–95.

∞ **2** ∞

War in the Hebrew Bible

Robert Carroll

> For everything there is a season,
> and a time for every matter under heaven:
> a time for war . . .
>
> *Ecclesiastes*

On the subject of war much of the Hebrew Bible breathes the same
atmosphere as that expressed in the opening lines of the *Iliad*:

> Sing, goddess, the anger of Peleus' son Achilleus
> and its devastation, which pains thousandfold upon the Achaians,
> hurled in their multitudes to the house of Hades strong souls
> of heroes, but gave their bodies to be the delicate feasting
> of dogs, of all birds, and the will of Zeus was accomplished.
>
> (Lattimore 1961, 59; cf. Murray 1924, 2)

The corpses pile up, humans are put to shame, and the will of the
god is brought to its desired conclusion. This Homeric description
of war reflects a point of view that would hold good for many of
the biblical narratives about war and fighting.

A paradigmatic example from the Bible is the story of the
slaying of King Ahab (1 Kings 22). This could have been scripted
by Homer with very few changes (the names of the gods, perhaps
the use of more adjectives). It tells of preparations for war,
involving performances by groups of prophets, and includes a
narrative that depicts the means whereby the king will be lured to
his death by the machinations of the deity in council with his
cohorts. Similarities may be noted between the biblical story and

the arguments put forward in *Iliad* 1 to explain how the countless woes suffered by the Achaeans are caused by strife among the gods. The biblical narrator does not tell a tale of quarrels between the gods (a theomachy); but allowing for that cultural difference in the style of storytelling, the narrator does show how a conspiracy against the king is engineered by the spirits, under the aegis of the god Yahweh. That conspiracy is brought to a successful conclusion on the battlefield of Ramoth-gilead, by means of the prophetically inspired games that lure the ill-fated king to his appointed death.

Between Hebrew Bible and early Greek writers there is considerable sharing of concepts, including the representation of war and some of its causes (Gordon 1962). However, in the historiographical writings of Herodotos and Thucydides – not to mention the many other Greek and Roman historians – we appear to have a rather different approach to the writing of history from what seems to be the case in the Hebrew Bible.[1] I am rather inclined to agree with Dover (1988, 44) when he writes about the originality of the first Greek historians in terms of

> edging the divine out of the history of human affairs; appreciating, however imperfectly, the differences between myth, tradition and events which admit of serious enquiry; applying criteria of probability and possibility; admitting ignorance and uncertainty; and offering personal opinions on what might have followed if certain events had turned out otherwise.

While it would be unwise to assume that the Greek historians were invariably reliable – unfair as it may be to call Herodotos 'the father of lies' – it must be acknowledged that the qualities discerned by Dover cannot be found among the biblical writers. The biblical narratives are still rooted in the sphere of the mythic, where the gods play an active role in human affairs, and so may be better characterized by Collingwood's category (1961, 14–17) of 'theocratic history'. That is, they are stories determined by a quasi-

---

[1] Questions of history and historiography in the Bible are very vexed, and far beyond the resources of this paper. Useful discussions will be found in van Seters 1983, with different viewpoints expressed in Halpern 1988. For classical sources I have benefited greatly from discussions in Momigliano 1966 and Wiseman 1979.

historical aspect (or a history-like story quality) in their approach to human society, in which the gods, or the single god, play a determining role. A reading of the tales of battles in Exodus or Chronicles demonstrates the point well. The Hebrew god YHWH (conventionally vocalized in contemporary biblical scholarship as Yahweh) is represented as a warrior – a 'man of war' in the eulogy at Exodus 15 – who fights on behalf of his tribes, or on occasion in their place, against their enemies (cf. 2 Chr. 20: 1–30).

The language of the warrior-god cult is not peculiar to the Bible. It is the common language and thought of most of the cultures of the ancient Near East, and reflects a common theology shared by all the nations living there (Smith 1952). The gods go out with, or at the head of, their nations and wreak havoc on the enemy. The nation's enemies are the god's enemies, and vice versa. Occasionally, if the people have offended their deity, the deity fights against his or her own people (Pritchard 1969; Tadmor and Weinfeld (eds) 1984). The conventional descriptions of theocratic history represent the cultural norms of the time, and their use in the Hebrew Bible reflects the period that gave rise to the narratives contained in the collected writings constituting the Bible.

Two important methodological factors have to be kept in mind when reading (i.e. interpreting) biblical texts: (1) the accommodation of linguistic utterance to cultural meaning; (2) the relation of narrated story to the historical events it purports to portray.[1] While neither factor can figure largely in this paper, both are worth keeping in mind as preconditions for understanding the Bible.

The first factor has to do with the notion of the god as the tribal or national warrior. Such a notion may have had a naturalistic or literal meaning for the ancient peoples who told tales of their wars and battles as part of their god's story; but the modern historian cannot take such stories at face value, or there would be a plethora of gods functioning as historical explanations for ancient warfare

[1] The category required here is well described by the technical term 'narratology', which is not a synonym for 'narrative' but shorthand for all the factors and values involved in writing narratives. Narratological factors constitute the subtext of the text. Narratology is the theory of narrative writing (Bal 1985).

in a diversity of ancient cultures. We may record it as a fact that the ancients believed these stories in some sense (some literal sense?), but we cannot incorporate their explanations into our historical accounts, as if their stories were unproblematic or constituted history *simpliciter*.

On the second point, the problem of reading such texts has as much to do with the nature of the texts as with our modern sensibilities and scholarly methodologies. If all the many stories and narratives in the Bible that deal with war and fighting are read together, it quickly becomes clear to the competent reader that the book itself is part of the problem. Reading the Bible today is such a complex interpretative activity that even a relatively simple *topos*, such as 'war in the Bible', is instinct with difficulty and complexity. A few illustrations may substitute for lengthy and dense argumentation.

At times, in the Hebrew Bible, a story of a battle appears to have been overwritten by a somewhat different story of a god's activities, so that we have, as it were, a palimpsest in the text. Thus what looks like a naturalistic or rational account of a military encounter has become, with editing, a miraculous story about a god's triumph. An example of this is Exodus 14–15. Reading between the lines of the story of the crossing of the Red Sea (or Reed Sea, as many moderns would read the text), it is possible to detect traces of a battle fought between the Israelites and Egyptians. The more lightly-armed Israelites fight the border guards of the Egyptian forces (reinforced, perhaps, by chariot divisions), and defeat the more heavily-armed troops because they engage them on marshy ground completely unsuitable for chariot warfare. The Egyptian strategy and tactics are all wrong for that area, and the armed formation of Israelites (Exod. 12: 37; 13: 18) turns the border skirmish into a rout of their ostensibly better-equipped opponents. Retold in the cultus as a liturgical celebration of the wars of the warrior god Yahweh, the story takes on a number of 'supernatural' elements, which foreground the divine activity and play down (or write over) the human, militaristic achievements. What was a border clash in historical terms becomes decontextualized in the service of the god, and is told in a cultic context as yet another episode in the story of the triumphant wars of the Israelite god.

This is just one way of reading Exodus 14–15 in its present state

(Hay 1964). Other ways of reading the text might deny that there was any historical battle behind it, and see in the story only the legendary construction of cult liturgies. Alternatively, the classical critical understanding of the Pentateuch would point to different sources behind Exodus, and see in chapters 14–15 the combination of discrete stories into the one we now have. Whatever interpretation we may choose in reading the story, the text will always partially support different explanations. So every reading of a biblical text becomes an interpretative contest, a site of struggle among exegetes. This is an equally important methodological consideration; all readings of texts are interpretations, and have no greater status than that of being a *particular* reading. Competing readings of a specific text vie with each other, and thus different readings constitute part of the quarrel about how such texts should be read and understood.

A similar set of considerations apply to the competing interpretations of the story of the defeat of Sisera and his Canaanite forces in Judges 4–5. Here, however, there are some differences from the story of the triumph at the Red Sea. In the story of Deborah and Barak's defeat of the Canaanite Sisera, the account of the battle is kept quite separate from the song celebrating the battle. Also, in the song of Deborah and Barak the action of the clans fighting the enemy *is* the triumph of Yahweh.

The prose story in chapter 4 tells of the activities of the prophetess and military leader (*šōfṭāh*, 'judge') Deborah, with some religious elements in the story, and the actual battle is described in verses 12–16. In some respects the military strategy of the Israelites under Barak is similar to the battle account detectable in Exodus 14. The more lightly-equipped Israelites encounter the heavily-armed chariot force of Canaanites under Sisera on the mountain slopes of Tabor. Naturally the infantry is better situated, in terrain favouring the foot-soldier against chariots. The brief prose account of the battle mentions the river Kishon (4: 13), but does not relate it to the defeat of the chariots, whereas the poem celebrates the victory as having taken place by the waters of Megiddo and the torrent of Kishon (5: 19–21). The combination of mountain slope and river-bank would be fatal to any army relying on chariot formation.

In both accounts the victory is achieved by Yahweh or attributed to him (4: 15; 5: 11). Military action of a highly co-operative nature among the tribes yields a triumph which *is* (or is equivalent to) the victory of Yahweh, and the enemies of the tribes are seen as his enemies (5: 31). While there need be no necessary connection between the prose and poetic accounts (Whallon 1969, 139–210), both texts are about the same battle, involving the same characters, and so differ from the Exodus story: there is never less than a human struggle going on, whatever status is accorded to the imagery of divine activity. Whatever the prehistory of Exodus 14–15 may have been, its present form presents a story closer in spirit to the kind of stories told about battles in the books of Chronicles than to the spirit of the stories in Judges 4–5.

The military historian reading Judges 4–5 as material pertaining to the historical reconstruction of Israelite society may find the text frustrating, because it focuses much more on the activities of the women than the fighting men. Now war is men's work, so a battle story told in terms of what various women did to win it is odd by any standard of military history.[1] The story of the defeat of Sisera and his army concentrates on the activities of the women (Deborah, Jael, Sisera's mother). Within the context of the book of Judges this female focus may not be so strange (see e.g. 9: 50–7; 11: 34–40; 13–16; 19–21), but given the normal social conditions of warfare in ancient Israel (to say nothing of our own time) the roles of women in the defeat of Sisera remain extremely noteworthy (Bal 1988b; Rasmussen 1989). As irony also appears to be a dominant mode of representation in Judges (Klein 1988), we may read these tales as an ironic reflection on the competence of the menfolk of tribal Israelite society. But if irony is so present in the text, the historian would be well advised to consider abandoning the quest of reconstructing 'history' from the text and leave the

[1] I know of no comprehensive account of war in the Bible, or good theoretical treatment of the subject with respect to the Hebrew Bible. Yadin 1963 is uncritical in its use of illustrations from cultures other than Israel to underwrite the biblical text (this is a constant failure of large-format introductory books on the Bible for general readers). Hobbs 1989 is currently the most useful book on war in the Bible (see Carroll 1989 for further reflections). On war in general see A. Jones 1987; Scarry 1985 is also most interesting (esp. pp. 60–157; shrewd observations on the Bible at pp. 181–243). V. D. Hanson 1989 is useful on classical sources; Nettleship *et al.* 1975 is informative across a wide spectrum of discussion on war.

Bible to literary critics. For an ironic representation of military conflict that extols the efficacious stratagems of women at the expense of rather pusillanimous men – stratagems that sometimes require gender to be brought into play (see the stories of Ruth, Rahab, Judith, Susanna) – suggests that military history is not the primary category of these stories. And that factor may be a central problem for the reading of biblical texts, in terms of the light they may throw on social and historical features of ancient Israel.

This does not mean that nothing of value can be discerned in the stories. It just means the writers' primary aims were not to furnish basic social information. They had other, more pressing ideological concerns to communicate than mere facts for the future archaeologists of texts to uncover in their readerly explorations. The wise modern reader of the Hebrew Bible will take due cognizance of those concerns when perusing its pages in search of hard information about life in ancient times. In many cases the biblical stories may tell us more about the writers' concerns, especially about the time of writing, than about the substance of the stories told. The case is very much as stated by Liverani (1973, 193): 'the problem is the usual one: the text as source of knowledge of its author, and not (or previously to being) source of knowledge of narrated events'.

With these remarks as preamble and prolegomenon, it may now be possible to offer some general observations on war in the Hebrew Bible.

The general social context of military life reflected in the biblical stories is that of tribal existence in territories fiercely contested for living-space and food production, or of national existence under monarchies in which opposing nations go to war for territorial gain or to impose hegemonic control on their neighbours (the books of Joshua, Judges, and Samuel tend to reflect the former scenario, Kings and Chronicles the latter). In the period of the Assyrian, Babylonian, Persian, and Greek empires, when political hegemony lay in the hands of irresistible military powers, the biblical stories tend to reflect coalition forces seeking to curb imperial power, or the inevitable sieges of cities by which imperial might forces itself on the weaker nations.

Much of the language embodies military concepts and practices, but this may simply reflect linguistic and cultural habits rather than actual social practices of a warlike nature (as may be seen in the use of militaristic metaphors in the New Testament, or in the War Scroll from the Dead Sea scrolls). The war imagery is over-determined by a cluster of ideological factors, having little to do with military practice and much to do with linguistic matters of a liturgical and theological nature. Produced by a community living under the domination of Assyrian, Egyptian, and Babylonian powers, or existing as a minor territory on the periphery of an empire (e.g. part of a Persian satrapy), which nevertheless entertained grandiose ideological notions of superiority based on a mythical relationship with the local deity, the Hebrew writings display an inverse relationship between realism and ideology. A particular set of examples will illustrate the point.

In the prophetic books in particular, there is a genre of material which may be categorized as 'oracles against the nations' (e.g. Isaiah 13–23; Jeremiah 46–51; Ezekiel 25–32; Obadiah; Zephaniah). It consists of many oracles, poems, and discursive haranguings of foreign nations. When these statements of nationalistic fervour and outbursts of Judaean chauvinism are set against the many narratives of defeats, deportations, and national humiliations caused by foreign powers (set out, e.g., in the second book of Kings), some kind of explanation is required to account for the discrepancies between the two types of literary material. A cursory reading of the 'oracles against the nations' reveals a fascinating mixture of xenophobic utterance and magical gesture, as well as celebratory chants over the fall of national enemies. These elements may well represent survivals of ancient war oracles, now transformed into liturgical hymns (Christiansen 1975) and functioning in the collections of prophetical texts as emotional hedges against the winds of foreign domination and domestic humiliation (a kind of dissonance resolution).

Many of the major poems in this genre focus, not on Israelites defeating the enemy, but on the destruction of the national foe by other foes; the prime example is Babylon (Isa. 13–14; 47; Jer. 50–1), with Egypt a close runner-up (Isa. 19; Jer. 46; Ezek. 29–32). These particular poems cannot be read as war oracles instructing the Judaean armies to conquer the empires of Babylon and Egypt, especially as Judah was often a vassal state of one or other empire. They could be read as ritual gestures assisting Judah's enemy's enemy in the conquest of the formidable foe. They may also indicate a practical implication of the belief in a sole, effective god at work in the affairs of empire.

As usual, exegetes and biblical scholars disagree over the significance of these collections of poems and their interpretation. What is important in the context of this paper is that the poems demonstrate that there does not have to be a direct or practical connection between the militaristic language used in the oracles and the world of social action outside the text. In the cult of warrior god Yahweh, the language of war is at home; it does not have to have a social or objective correlate. It may be that originally such oracular poems did have a social context in the life of the tribe or nation, functioning as contributions to local war efforts. But they seem to have survived long after the kings (and people) lost the power to impose their will militarily on their enemies. Perhaps they even survived as reminiscences of an idealized past, or elements of a ritualized celebration of a future aspired to.

The narratives of war in the books of Samuel mostly have as their background the stories of the conflict between the Israelite tribes and the Philistines, and as their foreground the stories of the emergence of the monarchy in relation to Saul and David. Both background and foreground are highly problematic issues in contemporary biblical studies, and raise many questions of interpretation and reference. 'The Philistines' is a name given to a notorious cluster of historical–archaeological problems in modern scholarship about the ancient Near East, so anything said about them is open to dispute and serious questioning. The historicity of the stories of David and Saul is also a contentious issue, as is the dating of the material represented in the books of Samuel. With so many methodological disputations going on, it would be unwise to assume that the stories of wars and the details of military tactics that appear in the text are necessarily reliable as history, or afford any serious insight into the social history of the period in which they appear to be set.

Reliable historical and social information may perhaps be discernible in the biblical narratives of war, but it is very difficult to determine in any specific story which elements may be historical and which purely literary. Investigation is hampered by the lack of corroborative material outside the Bible itself. As literature, the Bible is easier to analyse in a literary manner than to explore in conjunction with the material remains of ancient Palestinian culture.

An example of the technical problems involved in distinguishing the literary from the historical is the story of David killing the Philistine giant Goliath (1 Sam. 17). A note in 2 Samuel (21: 19) attributes the killing to Elhanan; there is thus a formal contradiction between the two books of Samuel. This is harmonized by the Chronicler, who manipulates the text so that Elhanan kills instead Lahmi, the brother of Goliath (1 Chr. 20: 5). Given the length and development of the story in 1 Samuel 17, where the Hebrew text is almost twice as long as the Old Greek version in the Septuagint (Barthélemy *et al.* 1986), it is probable that an original note about Elhanan killing the giant became, in time, a much-expanded story of a heroic exploit attributed to David. Further variations of the story are also found in the later Lucianic Greek version, the Qumran material on Samuel, and Josephus' Greek account in his *Antiquities.* Such fluidity of textual witnesses indicates something of the developmental flux of the biblical story, but does not help in the task of determining its historical reliability.

Another interesting feature of the David and Goliath story is the hand-to-hand or single combat element. Such a duel between two warriors is not a frequent occurrence in the Bible (further examples appear in 2 Sam. 21: 18–21; 23: 20–1; 1 Chr. 11: 21–5; 20: 4–8), in contrast to Greek and Roman literature (Oakley 1985). Does the biblical story represent a historical event of the time of David, when Israel and the Philistines were in constant conflict over territory, and is it therefore evidence for the practice of single combat to resolve military conflicts? Or should it be read as a developing literary legend, derived from a later period and used to tell the story of David for propagandist purposes, so that it is of no historical significance for the time of David? These are matters of dispute among biblical scholars.[1] Whatever the complexities of the textual traditions of the story, some readers

[1] It is a common theme of folklore that tables are turned and fortunes reversed when the small meet the great; historical memory may thus have little to do with the story of David and Goliath (cf. Oakley 1985, 408, for other examples). Biblical commentators tend to divide in their opinions about the story in terms of generic analysis of the text, and often because of *a priori* views about the Bible.

avoid some of them by focusing solely on the Hebrew of the Masoretic text (Miscall 1986; Polzin 1989). This, however, does not resolve the vexed question of whether the story reflects historical practice or the influence of Greek practices known to the writer (whenever the writing of the story may be dated). The story of Saul is told against the backdrop of the Philistine threat. Apart from being a minor theme to the major one of the rise of David, it is presented in terms of Saul the warrior and Saul the religious hypochondriac. There is seldom a clear focus on his warrior role. More often there are stories about Saul in battle, or preparing to fight, which highlight other facets of a character who might well be described as the Macbeth of the Bible. As his story is also interwoven with that of Samuel the prophet, a figure represented as constantly sniping at him and throwing fits of pique, it is rather difficult to evaluate the textual picture of Saul *as* warrior.

Some of the stories represent him as an effective fighter who successfully defeats the enemies of the Israelite clans (e.g. 1 Sam. 11; 13–14; 15; 17: 2–53), though little detail is given of these military encounters. The lapidary statement that 'he fought against all his enemies on every side . . . and delivered Israel out of the hands of those who plundered them' (14: 47–8) indicates the various enemies defeated (Moab, the Ammonites, Edom, the kings of Zobah, the Philistines, and the Amalekites), but gives no account of the military strategies or tactics used. When such details are given, they involve complex, circuitous stories about individual acts of bravado which tell us nothing about Saul's abilities as a military leader (e.g. Jonathan's exploits in 14: 6–15; David's challenge to, and defeat of, Goliath in 17). Such individual actions may be indicative of battle skirmishes where military deadlock is broken by the idiosyncratic tactics of inspired individuals. When Saul defeats the Amalekites (15: 7), the thrust of the story is not the military strategy, but the deteriorating relationship between Saul and Samuel, epitomized by a dispute over ritual observances.

A few shards of general information on military matters may be garnered from the stories about Saul, but it would be unwise to insist on the extent to which this information bears directly on historical matters. The stories have very different foci, and the military aspects are but background noise in the narrative. The raiding tactics of David feature more often than the military campaigns of Saul, and the closing chapters of 1 Samuel, which have as their conclusion Saul's death on Mt Gilboa while fighting the Philistines, devote more attention to David's adventures and Saul's psychological profile than to Saul's final battle (chs 28–31). The conflict with the Amalekites in the story of Saul (1 Sam. 14: 48; 15) has elements of a religious war. It is introduced in terms of Yahweh's punishment of the Amalekites for their past oppression of Israel (15: 2). This motif has links with Exodus (17: 8–15), where war between the Israelites and Amalekites is incorporated into Yahweh's permanent war against the latter. In Deuteronomy (25: 17–19) the blotting out of Amalek is made into a duty of the nation on settling into life in the land of Canaan. Hence the annihilation of the Amalekites – men, women, children, infants, and animals – is enjoined upon Saul. His failure to carry out the genocidal extermination of an ancient enemy is then made the grounds for his failure to continue as king in any legitimate (that is, ideological) sense. As Saul does, in fact, continue as king until his death at the end of 1 Samuel, chapter 15 becomes an ideological critique of him, reflecting the values inherent in the production of 1 Samuel.

The story of the conquest of the land of Canaan (Palestine) in the book of Joshua also owes much to the principle of Yahweh's war. The *topos* 'Yahweh's war' reflects a conflict entailing the complete extermination of various nations indigenous to Canaan (the 'seven nations' of Deut. 7: 1–5). This type of religious war is sometimes called a 'holy war' – not a biblical term as such – and compared to the Islamic practice of *jihad*. Such a notion as 'holy war' introduces us to another cluster of problems in biblical interpretation, because it is hard to distinguish between war and religious war in the biblical narratives. All the wars fought by Israel either belong to Yahweh's wars or are fought by Yahweh against Israel, so they all tend towards the condition of having been 'holy' wars.

In many ways the language of the *topos* 'Yahweh's war' typifies the central problems of understanding the biblical stories of war. The *topos* itself has also confused various biblical scholars, causing them to misread the text. A prime example must be Gerhard von Rad's monograph on the holy war in ancient Israel (1951). He fails to consider the phenomenon of religious war outside the Bible, and so produces a defective analysis of the biblical texts by reading them in isolation from their general social context in the ancient Near East (see Weippert 1972; G. H. Jones 1989; Hobbs 1989, 199–207; Smend 1970).[1] A study of the representation of war in non-biblical ancient texts reveals a range of concepts and language equivalent to anything to be found in the Bible (Weinfeld 1984). Yahweh's association with Israelite wars is to be equated with linguistic descriptions of war in other ancient documents, where the deity is invariably invoked and described as being involved in the national fight; Homer's *Iliad* is full of such language, in which Zeus and Hera participate in the war-making of Agamemnon and others.

All ancient wars had deeply religious dimensions, as well as religious rituals attached to them; so distinctions drawn between secular and sacred wars in those times lack serious differences. A close reading of all the biblical narratives dealing with war and fighting will reveal various subtle distinctions between different stories. In some the details given are of a purely military nature: raids, skirmishes, encounters in battle, melées, routs, armed confrontations, and responses to sieges. In others the gods play a part; either they fight for or against their own troops, or Yahweh does the fighting while his people look on (e.g. Exod. 14: 13–14; 2 Chr. 20: 17). In these latter cases, various stratagems may be used by Yahweh, but they all appear to involve no activity whatsoever on the part of the armies, or nation, of Israel or Judah.

One aspect of the *topos* 'Yahweh's war' concerns itself with making ideological distinctions between different ethnic groups. In Deuteronomy 20 there are statements belonging to an inchoate set of regulations governing the conduct of war. Many of the rules are designed to regulate military behaviour and to weed out slackers and malingerers from the army. Also included are rules for treating cities, according to whether they surrender to the

---

[1]   The literature referred to above is adequate for understanding the holy war *topos* in the Bible. However, it is far from certain that there was ever such a practice in biblical times. It is possible that the narratives in the Bible depicting the annihilation of the ideological enemy are but texts produced in accordance with the ideology of the writers of the Pentateuch. Alternatively, perhaps all ancient wars involving the gods were holy wars (or their equivalent), and the modern distinction between sacred and secular warfare had no force in the ancient world.

Israelites or resist (Oliver Cromwell followed these rules during his savage campaign in Ireland). Those cities that accept terms of peace, surrender and become slaves of Israel; those that resist, and are therefore besieged, suffer the slaughter of their males when they are eventually defeated. The spoils of these defeated cities (women, children, cattle, and everything else) are then to be for the enjoyment of the Israelites. In the rules stated in the next chapter (Deut. 21: 10-14), women taken captive in war become available to Israelite men as wives, provided certain ritual formalities are observed. Such general rules about the appropriation of women taken captive after battles are said to apply to 'cities which are very far' from Israel (20: 15), not to cities of the neighbouring territories where Hittites, Amorites, Canaanites, and other groups live. Local and neighbouring inhabitants must be annihilated (the numbers and identities of these groups vary from list to list), and for them Yahweh's war means extermination of a genocidal nature.

One of the questions for ancient historians must be this: did the ancient Israelites go around annihilating their neighbours and intermarrying with captured female slaves from distant lands?[1] While it may be argued that the rules of Deuteronomy 20 and 21 probably reflect practical procedures for foreign and local wars, it has to be admitted that we really do not know anything about whether such rules were followed in practice, or functioned only as theoretical possibilities limited to the ritual recitations of sacred texts in cultic contexts. We have no evidence either way. An ideology of genocidal extermination may only reflect textual matters, and belong to the legend of the past constructed by ideologues of a later period. Purity and separatist ideology of the second temple period may lie behind the rulings of Deuteronomy, and the regulations may be more formal (that is theoretical) than actual. One must enquire whether there was ever any reality

---

[1]   In contrast to classical scholars, who have a wealth of sources, biblical scholars have only the Bible and virtually no information outside it to provide corroborative evidence for what it says. Commentators on Deut. 20-1 tend to note the idealistic nature of the war regulations, without being able to show whether they were put into practice or honoured in the breach. Deuteronomistic formulations determine the final text more than the pre-deuteronomistic elements contained within it (Mayes 1979, 283-304; Weinfeld 1972, 45-51; 238-9).

outside the text for the ideology of extermination. What evidence is there for the view that the Israelites went to war against the Egyptians, Syrians, Assyrians, Babylonians, Persians, Greeks, and even Romans and collected wives from these groups whenever they achieved a victory over them? Is there any evidence for total war carried on by the Israelites against the local cities of Canaan, with the complete extermination of men, women, and children, and without any intermarriage with the local women?

In other words, what are we to make of such books as Joshua, with its ideological presentation of the Israelite annihilation of the Canaanite cities, with all their inhabitants; or Judges, with its counter-presentation of Israelites living among Canaanites and marrying with them? Are these just the contradictions of different traditions and legends about the past? The Ezra–Nehemiah literature also represents the people of Jerusalem as intermarrying with the locals. Now such a cluster of interpretative problems in the reading of biblical texts makes it very hard to ascertain what reliable historical information may lurk in the Hebrew Bible. We really do not have the means to resolve these vexed questions, and commentators on the text are often driven to accepting it at face value, or exercising scepticism about its historicity in favour of a theory of the text as ideological literature. While assigning all the motifs about war in the Bible to the linguistic conventions of common ancient Near Eastern military and ideological practices may be the wisest course, it does not really answer any of the questions raised by the *topos* 'Yahweh's war'.

There *is* a level of social reality reflected in many of the biblical narratives about war. The tactics of fighting, and the weapons used, are realistically portrayed, and may be corroborated to some extent by archaeological and documentary evidence from other cultures (Yadin 1963; Pritchard 1969, 49–55). The same may be said of the Homeric epics. Realism and convention contribute to the construction of stories, and have important places in the analysis of Homeric and biblical narratives. Such conventions of storytelling give us little or no information about historicity or dating. And the extent to which the conventions of epic and lyrical writing utilize elements of history and realism to produce an ideal or idyllic story, quite detached from realism and history, is a very complex matter worthy of serious analysis. If I appear to favour a more 'conventional' or ideological account of the biblical stories about war, rather than a historical reading of these narratives, it is because I think what little evidence there is for such stories favours such a reading.

Further evidence pointing in this direction may be derived from the material on war in the apocalypses. The 'oracles against the nations' genre shifts easily into the mode of apocalypse, especially where Yahweh is represented as destroying *all* the nations (e.g. Jer. 25: 30–8; Joel 4; Isa. 24). The wars of Gog of the land of Magog (Ezek. 38–9) reflect something of this type of literature. Strange tales of the comings and goings of kings in the pursuit of war, as depicted in Daniel 11–12, may also indicate something of a combination of tales of wars (whether real or imaginary – an open question) and expectations of the end (whether of time, foreign domination, or whatever – best left to the reader to ponder). None of these texts is either an easy read or patient of a simple interpretation. Linguistic imagery has taken over from sense, and hyperbolic representation has crowded out meaning. A reading of the Dead Sea War Scroll found at Qumran, in which the 'sons of light' attack the 'sons of darkness', will introduce the reader to the many problems of interpreting biblical imagery and of determining whether historical reality or ideological expectation better describes what is depicted in that scroll (Yadin 1962).

The War Scroll might make a very good paradigm for understanding biblical texts on war. The scroll provides many details about the disposition of troops in this imaginary or expected war, and many descriptions of the weapons to be used. In many ways it is like a biblical scroll. Much of its language is derived from the Bible, and its obsessive concern with the ordering of the camp and the formations of war is heavily indebted to the *liturgical* material in Exodus 25–31 and Leviticus 1–16. It is a quintessentially intertextual document. Such a mishmash of biblical language reflects the product of a community steeped in that language. One term used for the enemy is *kittim*. Used infrequently in the Bible to describe the Mediterranean coastlands (Jer. 2: 10; Ezek. 27: 6), or possibly the Greeks (Dan. 11: 30),[1] it may have a rather non-specific biblical sense in the War Scroll. But it may also have a quite specific referent if the scroll reflects a real historical situation

---

[1] Cf. Num. 24: 24, where ships of *kittim* are also referred to; Isa. 23: 1, where there is a general reference to the land of the *kittim*.

or background. This point, of course, depends on how the vexed question of the dating of the Dead Sea scrolls is answered. If the identification of the *kittim* with the Romans is accepted, then the historical background to the War Scroll may be their wars against the Jews in the first and second centuries AD (if they are not wars of an earlier period). In that case, the document may be an invaluable piece of evidence for how biblical texts may have come into existence as a mixture of linguistic expression, conventionally determined, and social elements derived from the world of the writers. For the scroll would then be using the terminology of ancient Hebrew writings to describe a military phenomenon of its own time. This would hold good whether we identify the *kittim* with the Romans, the Greeks, or even a mythological enemy quite separate from either.

The more complex questions of the relation of the Qumran writings to a specific historical period need not concern us here; but any consideration of war in the Bible needs to extend its scrutiny to the Qumran literature. Whether the Qumran community was equipped for war, or had any intention of going to war against the occupying Roman (or Greek) forces, raises as many problems of interpretation as does any reading of the Bible. The word *kittim* might just be one more biblical term, used by the writer of the War Scroll to delineate the forces of evil ranged against the forces of good in the ultimate cosmic battle between Yahweh and evil. In other words, the scroll should perhaps be read as a further document belonging to the *topos* 'Yahweh's war'.

This paper has focused on the topic of war in the Bible in terms of the literary nature of biblical narrative, with some recognition of the Bible as an ideological production of ancient communities. While it cannot be denied that the Bible may well contain fragments of valuable social and historical information, it must be admitted that its primary concern does not appear to be the conveying of such information. The linguistic conventions used to narrate stories of war and conflict belong more to the great overarching ideological constructions of the biblical writers than to mere descriptions of war and rumours of war. Different readers and exegetes may read these narratives in a variety of ways, and the yield of socio-historical information will differ with each reading; but the deep symbolic forms of the biblical literature ought not to be ignored in the quest for historical information. A deeper, better, and more complex paper would be required in order to do justice to all the material on war in the Bible, and a much more dialectical treatment would be needed to capture something of the sense of the psalmist's conviction that Yahweh was (also) the one who 'makes wars to cease to the end of the earth . . . breaks the bow, and shatters the spear . . . burns the chariots with fire' (Ps. 46: 9).[1]

Bibliography

Bal, M. (1985), *Narratology: Introduction to the Theory of Narrative* (Toronto).

——— (1988a), *Death and Dissymmetry: The Politics of Coherence in the Book of Judges* (Chicago).

——— (1988b), *Murder and Difference: Gender, Genre, and Scholarship in Sisera's Death* (Indianapolis).

Barthélemy, D., Gooding, D. W., Lust, J., and Tov, E. (1986), *The Story of David and Goliath: Textual and Literary Criticism* (Göttingen).

Carroll, R. P. (1989), 'War', in M. Smith and R. J. Hoffmann (eds), *What the Bible Really Says* (Buffalo), pp. 147–70.

Christiansen, D. L. (1975), *Transformations of the War Oracle in OT Prophecy: Studies in the Oracles against the Nations* (Montana).

Collingwood, R. G. (1961), *The Idea of History* (Oxford).

Dover, K. J. (1988), 'The originality of the first Greek literature', in *The Greeks and their Legacy: Collected Papers*, ii: *Prose Literature, History, Society, Transmission, Influence* (Oxford), pp. 38–44.

Gordon, C. H. (1962), *Before the Bible: The Common Background of Greek and Hebrew Civilisations* (London).

Halpern, B. (1988), *The First Historians: The Hebrew Bible and History* (San Francisco).

---

[1] A further problem with the study of war in the Bible is that many scholars who read the book are theologians seeking normative rulings from the sacred tome. As many of these are also practising pacifists, the work they produce on war in the Bible tends to be somewhat lopsided in its analyses, because the momentum of the writing is designed to arrive at the pre-established goal demonstrating the pacifistic nature of the Bible. Hence there is no modern theological movement devoted to the cult of Yahweh the warrior god, even though there are numerous liberation theology movements and Christian pacifist groups using the Bible to justify a strongly anti-militaristic ideology. (On elements of war and peace in the Bible see P. D. Hanson 1984.)

Hanson, P. D. (1984), 'War and peace in the Hebrew Bible', *Interpretation*, 38: 341–62.

Hanson, V. D. (1989), *The Western Way of War: Infantry Battle in Classical Greece* (London, etc.).

Hay, L. S. (1964), 'What really happened at the Red Sea?', *Journal of Biblical Literature*, 83: 397–403.

Hobbs, T. R. (1989), *A Time for War: A Study of Warfare in the Old Testament* (Wilmington, Del.).

Jones, A. (1987), *The Art of War in the Western World* (Oxford).

Jones, G. H. (1989), 'The concept of holy war', in R. E. Clements (ed.), *The World of Ancient Israel: Sociological, Anthropological and Political Perspectives* (Cambridge), pp. 299–321.

Klein, L. R. (1988), *The Triumph of Irony in the Book of Judges* (Sheffield).

Lattimore, R. (1961), *The Iliad of Homer* (Chicago).

Liverani, M. (1973), 'Memorandum on the approach to historiographic texts', *Orientalia*, 42: 178–94.

Mayes, A. D. H. (1979), *Deuteronomy* (New Century Bible; London).

Miscall, P. D. (1986), *1 Samuel: A Literary Reading* (Bloomington).

Momigliano, A. (1966), *Studies in Historiography* (London).

Murray, A. T. (1924), *Homer: The Iliad*, i (Loeb Classical Library; Cambridge, Mass.).

Nettleship, M. A., Dalegivens, R., and Nettleship, A. (1975), *War: Its Causes and Correlates* (The Hague).

Oakley, S. P. (1985), 'Single combat in the Roman republic', *CQ* 79 (n.s. 35): 392–410.

Polzin, R. (1989), *Samuel and the Deuteronomist: A Literary Study of the Deuteronomic History*, ii: *I Samuel* (San Francisco).

Pritchard, J. B. (1969), *The Ancient Near East in Pictures Relating to the Old Testament* (Princeton).

Rasmussen, R. C. (1989), 'Deborah the woman warrior', in M. Bal (ed.), *Anti-covenant: Counter-reading Women's Lives in the Hebrew Bible* (Sheffield), pp. 79–93.

Scarry, E. (1985), *The Body in Pain: The Making and Unmaking of the World* (Oxford).

Smend, R. (1970), *Yahweh War and Tribal Confederation* (Nashville; English trans. of *Jahwehkrieg und Stammebund*; Göttingen, 1963).

Smith, M. (1952), 'The common theology of the ancient Near East', *Journal of Biblical Literature*, 71: 135–47.

Tadmor, H., and Weinfeld, M. (eds 1984), *History, Historiography and Interpretation: Studies in Biblical and Cuneiform Literatures* (Jerusalem, etc.).

van Seters, J. (1983), *In Search of History: Historiography in the Ancient World and the Origins of Biblical History* (New Haven, etc.).

von Rad, G. (1951), *Der Heilige Krieg im alten Israel* (Zurich).

Weinfeld, M. (1972), *Deuteronomy and the Deuteronomic School* (Oxford).

—— (1984), 'Divine intervention in war in ancient Israel and in the ancient Near East', in Tadmor and Weinfeld (eds), pp. 121–47.

Weippert, M. (1972), ' "Heiliger Krieg" in Israel und Assyrien: kritische Anmerkungen zu Gerhard von Rads Konzept des "heiligen Krieges im alten Israel" ', *Zeitschrift für die alttestamentliche Wissenschaft*, 84: 460–93.

Whallon, W. (1969), *Formula, Character, and Context: Studies in Homeric, Old English, and Old Testament* (Cambridge, Mass.).

Wiseman, T. P. (1979), *Clio's Cosmetics: Three Studies in Greco-Roman Literature* (Leicester).

Yadin, Y. (1962), *The Scroll of the War of the Sons of Light against the Sons of Darkness* (Oxford).

—— (1963), *The Art of Warfare in Biblical Lands in the Light of Archaeological Discovery* (London).

Addendum

Niditch, S. (1993), *War in the Hebrew Bible: A Study in the Ethics of Violence* (Oxford).

Hoplites and Homer: Warfare, hero cult, and the ideology of the polis

Hugh Bowden

The Homeric poems are some of the earliest creations of Greek literature, and were enormously influential on the way in which the Greeks of the archaic and classical periods understood the world in which they lived.[1] It is usually suggested that 'Homeric society' owes most to the 'dark ages' of the ninth century BC, and also contains elements from the Mycenaean period (see e.g. Snodgrass 1974); the polis-oriented world that begins to develop during the eighth century is reckoned to be distinct from the 'heroic' or 'aristocratic' world of Homer (e.g. Murray 1980, 38–40). It seems to me difficult to reconcile the centrality of the Homeric poems in the classical polis with the idea that the society they describe was so different. In this paper I argue that the *Iliad* was in fact the product of a polis-based society, and that its subject-matter – heroes and warfare – had a clear message for all those who lived in the polis.[2]

[1] See e.g. Hdt. 2. 53. The literature on Homer is as vast as it is varied. Nothing I say about the composition or nature of the Homeric poems in this paper is intended to be contentious; it is the nature of the society that produced them that interests me. Any views that fall outside the mainstream of scholarly opinion are, I hope, clearly indicated. On the vexed question of the date of composition, I believe the *Iliad* was probably composed sometime in 750–650 BC, a date that falls within the range favoured by many scholars (e.g. Kirk 1985, 10).

[2] Morris (1986) has argued that the Homeric poems were composed within the context of social conflict that accompanied state formation in the early archaic period. However, his suggestion that they served to

I shall start by examining the evidence for polis-like communities in the poems themselves, and will then turn to two areas which, I believe, are central to the structure of the polis: warfare, in particular hoplite warfare, and religion, in particular hero cult.

The *Iliad* and the polis

It is increasingly accepted that the *Iliad* and *Odyssey* do describe a world in which communities close to the Greek polis of the archaic and classical period may be found (see e.g. Vidal-Naquet 1981; Malkin 1987, 138; Easterling 1989, 5-9; Scully 1990). Any attempt to define the minimum requirements for identifying a polis is bound to be open to criticism. I take a polis to be an independent unit with clearly defined territorial limits, clearly defined citizenship, common cult, and a common political centre or centres. This is in accord with Aristotle's idea that the principal feature of the polis is *autarkeia*, something like self-sufficiency or autonomy (*Politics*, 1252 b). In the *Iliad*, the two cities on Achilleus' shield have some crucial features: the political centre is there, with a judgement taking place in the agora, and the farmed territory is situated around it. The importance of common cult and territory may be indicated in the description of the Athenian contingent in the Catalogue of Ships (*Il.* 2. 546-52):

> But the men who held Athens, the strong-founded citadel,
> the deme of great-hearted Erechtheus, whom once Athene
> Zeus' daughter tended after the grain-giving fields had borne him,
> and established him to be in Athens in her own rich temple;
> there as the circling years go by the sons of the Athenians
> make propitiation with rams and bulls sacrificed;
> of these men the leader was Peteos' son Menestheus.

Evidence of polis society is easier to find in the *Odyssey* than in the *Iliad*, however. We may note two examples. One is the description of the founding of Scheria by Nausithoös (6. 7-10). Here the poet describes the building of walls, houses, and temples and the allotment of land. We thus have all the basic elements of a

---

justify domination by the élite of the newly emergent poleis is a rather different reading from mine.

Greek colony, in the form which started in the late eighth century and continued through to the Hellenistic period more or less unchanged.[1] The second piece of evidence derives from the suggestion that the monsters and societies that Odysseus describes in books 9–12 are all incomplete versions of civilized society (Vidal-Naquet 1981). On this view there is in Homer 'an association between agriculture, family life, and the origin of civilisation', which is the essence of the polis.

There is more to a polis than the physical elements mentioned in the poems. The religious structures of the Greek world were bound up with its social and political organization; that is to say, religious activity was determined by social and political considerations, and vice versa (Sourvinou-Inwood 1989). It is now widely accepted that eighth-century Greece witnessed a major change in social, political, and spatial organization (e.g. Snodgrass 1980; Hägg 1983; de Polignac 1984; Morris 1987; Morgan 1990). This phenomenon, called 'the Greek renaissance' or 'the birth of the polis', laid the foundations for the social order of the archaic and classical Greek world. We shall see that the introduction of the hoplite phalanx and the growth of hero cult were crucial to this change.

The origins of the phalanx

The 'hoplite reform' has been a central subject in accounts of the development of Greek society in the early archaic period (e.g. Andrewes 1956; Snodgrass 1980). The introduction of new armour, it is argued, led to a change in tactics and the inclusion in the fighting force of 'non-aristocrats'; this, in turn, led to pressure for social change, most obviously resulting in the rise of tyrants in many Greek states. This view essentially sees military and social change as being driven by technological change; moreover, its proponents assume the pre-existence of a community from which warriors are drawn. The cost of the technology meant that participation in fighting was restricted within the community, as one recent author argues (Morris 1987, 197):

---

[1] Cf. Alexander's foundation of Alexandria in Egypt, Arr. *Anab.* 3. 1. 5. Both passages are discussed in Malkin 1987, 106–8; 138.

A hoplite had to provide himself with a very expensive bronze panoply, which probably required a considerable outlay. It was rare for as many as half the citizens of any polis to qualify as hoplites, and Aristotle underlines the point that in the fourth century the hoplites came from the ranks of the wealthy, not the poor.

In recent years, however, it has been suggested that hoplite tactics were developed not in response to the new weapons, but in response to the needs of the communities developing in the late eighth century (de Polignac 1984; Detienne 1968). The reliance on hoplite tactics in the countryside of Greece has been described as a 'paradox' (Cartledge 1977, 18); but it is no such thing. The phalanx developed at the same time as the concept of the boundary of the *chora* of the polis (de Polignac 1984, 57), and this explains why, in a mountainous country like Greece, a form of warfare developed that is suitable only for flat places; it served to establish boundaries where the territories of two poleis met on a plain. According to de Polignac, this is why the first major battles we know of are boundary disputes, like the Lelantine war. The phalanx also had a symbolic function; the line of citizen-soldiers standing shoulder to shoulder were there to defend the territory of the polis, and were the visible statement of the boundary of that territory. If this is correct, the phalanx will, initially at least, have included more than just the richer members of the community, and hoplites will have come from as far down the social scale as 'des paysans petits propriétaires' (Detienne 1968, 120). In the seventh century BC this would mean the vast majority of the citizen body. On this view the phalanx is isomorphic with the polis – the ideology of the hoplite phalanx and the ideology of the polis are the same – and this is what is expressed in, for example, the tradition of the Athenian funeral speech (most famously at Thucydides, 2. 34–46).

There is some evidence on the other side, but most of the literary evidence is from the fourth century BC. It may be true that in the fourth century hoplites were rich, but is that true for the seventh? It is probably true that a panoply was expensive; but once it had been bought or made, it would have been passed down from father to son. The growth of hoplite warfare, in fact, appears to coincide with the decline of burial practices involving armour (Kurtz and Boardman 1971, 207). If elements of armour could be won in competition, or stripped from the defeated enemy, it would be possible for a polis gradually to build up a well-armoured phalanx that included poor peasant farmers. Such a process would mean that early phalanxes might look rather motley, with, for example, leather helmets here and there instead of bronze, or shields of different shapes and materials. The better-armed would then fight in the front ranks, the less well-armed at the back. As Salmon (1977, 90) suggests, 'Early phalanx warfare might well have taken a slightly different form without being different in nature. A phalanx has two essential features: its cohesion and its relatively large size; both can be achieved without following the later canonical pattern closely.' By the fourth century BC one would expect greater uniformity of armour; rituals such as the arming of orphans as hoplites at public expense, as at Athens (Aeschines, 3. 154), will have reinforced this uniformity. In periods when the fleet provided military employment for many citizens, the hoplite phalanx may well have been the preserve of the rich; but for the early period we should accept at least the possibility of wider hoplite membership.

The implication of the arguments of Detienne and de Polignac, with their stress on the community defining and defending its territory through warfare, is that the hoplite phalanx was a basic feature of the polis from the beginning. It also follows that hoplite warfare only makes sense in the context of the polis.

Hero cult and the polis

We must now consider the development of hero cult in early archaic Greece.[1] It has been argued that the growth of hero cult in the eighth century BC was a response to the dissemination of the Homeric poems (Coldstream 1976; Burkert 1985); but the connection has now been effectively disproved (Snodgrass 1987, 160–1). It is now generally accepted that there is a significant relationship between hero cult and the development of the Greek polis; it is certainly a phenomenon whose geographical extent is more or less

---

[1] The archaeological evidence has recently been examined in some detail by Coldstream 1977, 346–8; Snodgrass 1980, 38–40; de Polignac 1984, 127–51; Whitley 1988; and Morris 1988.

coincident with that of the polis. I do not intend to give a complete account of the subject, but to draw attention to important aspects of it that are relevant to the argument. We are concerned with when, why, and how hero cult happened.

The date of the introduction of hero cult is fairly straightforward: 'tomb cults go back at least to 950 BC, but after 750 they were redefined and used as a source of power in new ways' (Morris 1988, 750). So far as I am aware, no satisfactory explanation has been offered for very early tomb cult, about which virtually nothing is known; it is the post-750 BC period with which we must concern ourselves. Put simply, around this time in a significant number of places, offerings were left at Mycenaean, or sometimes protogeometric, tombs, and some sort of cult emerged. This coincides with another form of cult, that of the founders or 'oikists' of the Greek colonies, which were being launched at the same time.

In colonies, when the founder (*oikistes*) died he was buried in the agora, the heart of the polis, and was commemorated or worshipped as a hero (Malkin 1987, 190–203). Colonization continued into the fifth century BC, and so did the cult of the founder. Indeed, at Amphipolis the oikist, Hagnon, was treated as a hero while he was still alive, since he left the colony after founding it. It seems clear that the oikist, as hero, remained important in the life of the polis after his death; so important that it was sometimes felt necessary to change founders for political reasons. After the death of Brasidas and the revolt of Amphipolis from its alliance with Athens, the Amphipolitans made Brasidas their new oikist (Thuc. 5. 11) and hence escaped from any respect owed to Hagnon, who, being still alive, might have intervened in the city's affairs. The incident is not unique. The important point is the role of the heroized oikist as guardian of his polis.

How does founder cult in colonies relate to mainland hero cult? Malkin believes that the former predates the latter, and that mainland hero cult was started in imitation or emulation of colonial activity (Malkin 1987, 263). This seems uncertain; the archaeological evidence suggests that the start of the two kinds of cult was more or less simultaneous. The growth of colonization and the development of the polis also seem more or less contemporary, and oikist cult and hero cult seem to occupy parallel positions in these two developments. The local hero may act as guardian of the mainland polis, just as the oikist does for the colonial polis. What is clear is that in early polis society, before the Homeric poems were written, certain figures received hero cult and were perceived as protectors of their polis. In colonies these figures were oikists; in old Greece they were usually the occupants of bronze age graves.

How was the hero perceived to fit into the social structure of the polis? One suggestion is the following (Morris 1988, 757):

> the man who became a hero would normally have children living in the polis, themselves powerful figures. In some Greek colonies, the heroised founder's family even became a royal dynasty. In worshipping the hero, then, the citizens of the polis simultaneously bonded together their community and gave implicit semidivine status to the forebears of some of their aristocrats.

In my view this is wrong. The only case of a founder forming a dynasty in the archaic period is at Cyrene (Herodotos, 4. 159), and this appears to be exceptional. Malkin (1987, 253), after exhaustive study, concludes that 'in none of the cases . . . is there any evidence for specific privileges for descendants of oikists which are due to them on the basis of their genealogy'. This is important, because the oikist is the more able to guard the whole polis since he is not associated with any one group within it. The same can, I think, be said about hero cult. Cult does not develop, as a rule, at tombs of the known dead, but the unknown (Snodgrass 1987, 164); there is discontinuity between burial and cult. The choice of graves of unknown or unrelated figures from the past is important, because it means that in mainland poleis, even more than in colonies, the hero is not related to any group within the polis. Morris suggests that the introduction of hero cult was a strategy by the élite to maintain their control as the polis emerged. He has no support for this, and the evidence he relies on in fact points the other way. He claims (1988, 757) that 'the hero cult could well have been one of the main claims to legitimacy, as it apparently was for the Spartan kings'. But the Spartan kings claimed descent from Herakles (Hdt. 7. 204), while the local heroes of Sparta were Menelaos, Helen, and Orestes; that fact itself emphasizes the distinction between the ruling élite and the heroes. The hero stood outside the social structure of the polis.

What emerges from this discussion is that both the hoplite

phalanx and hero cult are concerned above all with the protection of the territory of those who participate in them. They both developed at a period when the emergent poleis were seeking to define their own territories. One story in particular about the seventh century makes a connection between the three elements: warfare, hero cult, and territory. According to Herodotos (1. 68) the Spartans were for a long time engaged in an unsuccessful war against Tegea. Eventually they discovered and brought from Tegea to Sparta the bones of the hero Orestes, and 'ever since that day the Lakedaimonians, whenever they fought each other, had by far the better of it'.

The nature of warfare in the *Iliad*

Let us now look at the fighting in the *Iliad*, to see how far it is compatible with ideas of hoplite warfare. It does not matter here whether or not the poem provides a coherent or accurate description of a hoplite battle; the question is whether someone whose experience of warfare was of hoplite warfare would recognize the descriptions of fighting in the poem.

A recent attempt to make a coherent picture out of the fighting scenes in the *Iliad* concentrates on the *promachoi*. The word is taken to refer to a group of people fighting in front of the main body of warriors, who join in and retire in the course of the battle (van Wees 1988, 12): 'There is only one kind [of combat in the *Iliad*], the hit and run tactics of the *promachoi*, described from two angles: one offering close-ups of individual warriors, and one offering a panorama of battle.' I do not believe that this theory can work. Not all the fighting in the *Iliad* can be described as 'hit-and-run'; nor do I think that '*promachoi*' will bear the weight van Wees puts on it. The word certainly can refer to people fighting in front of the main bodies of troops, but it may also mean those who fight in the front rank in a traditional hoplite battle. Tyrtaios, for one, saw the ideal death coming *en promachoisi*, but only with the enemy spear coming through shield and breastplate. On the whole I agree with Pritchett, who suggests that the *promachoi* has no technical sense, but is simply a laudatory word for a warrior. Van Wees is unhappy with interpretations of fighting in the *Iliad* which accept that it must be inconsistent; this is reasonable, but I shall argue that the inconsistency is in fact deliberate, because it depicts more than one level of reality. Where I strongly agree with van Wees is in his recognition of the relationship between leader and followers, who form cohesive units on the field. I shall return to this point later.

Let us instead consider what someone who had knowledge or experience of hoplite warfare would make of the fighting in the *Iliad*. The best, and most comprehensive, treatment of the experience of a hoplite battle is that by V. D. Hanson in his book *The Western Way of War* (1989). In classical warfare the opposing armies' troops lined up shoulder to shoulder behind their line of hollow, round shields one metre in diameter, ran at each other, and tried to force their opponents off the field.

> The narrative of the battles of Mantineia, Delion, Nemea and Leuktra, not to mention the accounts of earlier (often nameless) conflicts in the Lyric poets, makes no sense unless we understand that both sides literally collided together, creating the awful thud of forceful impact at the combined rate of ten miles per hour.[1]

It is important to bear in mind that victory was dependent on the sheer strength and cohesion of the phalanx; there was, quite literally, no room for individual acts of valour, and anyone who, before the moment of collision, stepped out of line, weakened his own side considerably. Nor is there any evidence in descriptions of classical hoplite battles for hand-to-hand conflict before the main battle was joined.

It is generally accepted that this is the kind of battle described by Tyrtaios, the Spartan poet most closely associated with warfare. Hanson's account fits closely with passages such as these:

> Let him fight toe to toe and shield against shield hard-driven,
>   crest against crest and helmet on helmet, chest against chest;
> Let him close hard and fight it out with his opposite foeman,
>   holding tight to the hilt of his sword, or to his long spear.
>   (fr. 11. 31–4)

---

[1] Hanson 1989, 157. The alternative view (see most recently Cawkwell 1989), that any pushing occurred only after a period of hand-to-hand combat, is not in my view convincing, nor does it fit well with most of the literary evidence.

> Here is a man who proves himself to be valiant in war.
> With a sudden rush he turns to flight the rugged phalanxes
> of the enemy, and sustains the beating waves of assault.
> And he who falls among the front ranks and loses his sweet life,
>   so blessing with honour his city, his father and all his people,
> with wounds in his chest, where the spear he was facing has transfixed
>   that massive guard of his shield, and gone through his breastplate as
>   well,
> why, such a man is lamented alike by the young and the elders,
>   and all his city goes into mourning and grieves for his loss.
>
> (fr. 12. 23–8, trans. Lattimore)

What would a man who had experienced this kind of warfare make of the fighting in the *Iliad*? A passage from Book 4 describes the opposing armies of Greeks and Trojans coming into contact for the first time:

> As when along the thundering beach the surf of the sea strikes
> beat upon beat as the west wind drives it onward; far out
> cresting first on the open water, it drives thereafter
> to smash roaring along the dry land, and against the rock jut
> bending breaks itself into crests spewing back the salt wash;
> so thronged beat upon beat the Danaan's close phalanxes
> steadily into battle, with each of the lords commanding
> his own men.
>
> Now as these advancing came to one place and encountered,
> they dashed their shields together, and their spears, and the strength
> of armoured men in bronze, and the shields massive in the middle
> clashed against each other, and the sound grew huge of the fighting.
>
> (4. 422–9; 446–9)[1]

Whatever Homer is describing here, it seems clear that a possible reading of the passage is that it describes the beginning of a hoplite battle. Certainly Hanson, who draws evidence for his re-creation of hoplite fighting mainly from later writers, has no difficulty in finding in the *Iliad* images that might be drawn from the hoplite battlefield; and several other writers have recognized the warfare of the *Iliad* as hoplite warfare (Latacz 1977; Pritchett 1985, 7–32; Morris 1987, 198–200). We must now look for knowledge of heroes and hero cult.

---

[1]   Cf. Hom. *Il.* 8. 60–3; 12. 105; 13. 130–5; 16. 210–17.

Hero cult and the *Iliad*

There are no descriptions of religious activity at the tombs of
heroes in the *Iliad*; but that does not mean it has nothing to say
about hero cult. I suggest that the social hierarchy of the poem,
with its gods, *basileis*, and people, can be read as a depiction of the
religious hierarchy of the Greek polis with its three levels: gods,
heroes, and ordinary mortals.

Let us look at the way in which the heroes and gods might have
been understood to act in the archaic and classical period. Two
incidents from Herodotos indicate that participants in a battle
might recognize the involvement of heroes in the outcome. The
first takes place at Marathon.

> During the battle a strange thing happened in this way: an Athenian,
> Epizelos son of Kouphagoreus, was fighting in the melée, and showing
> himself a brave man, when he was blinded in both eyes, although he
> had been struck by neither sword nor missile, and from that moment
> on he remained blind for the rest of his life. I have heard that he told
> the following story about his experience: a huge man in armour
> seemed to come up against him, whose beard overshadowed his shield;
> the phantom passed by him, but killed the man standing next to him.
> This I understand to have been Epizelos' story.
>
> (6. 117)

The second takes place ten years later, when the Persians attack
Delphi.

> The barbarians who returned home told this story, I understand, that
> they saw another divine occurrence: two armed men, of greater than
> human size followed them, chasing them off and killing them. The
> people of Delphi say that these two are the local heroes, Phylakos and
> Autonoos, whose *temenea* are near the sanctuary; that of Phylakos is
> by the road above the temple of Pronaia, Autonoos' is near the
> Kastalian spring under the crest of Hyampeia.
>
> (8. 38–9)

It does not matter whether or not these stories are literally true.
What matters is that Greeks in the fifth century BC, and earlier,
accepted that heroic figures might appear on one side or the other
and influence the course of a battle. It is in this context that we
should understand the frequent translations of the bones of heroes
in archaic and classical Greece; for example, the moving of the

bones of Orestes mentioned above, or Kimon's returning of Theseus' bones to Athens (Plutarch, *Cimon*, 8). The particular association between heroes and warfare is also brought out in the story of Kleisthenes' reforms at Athens. Kleisthenes created ten new tribes in place of four old ones. The tribe was the basic military unit of the Greek city, and clearly importance was attached to assigning a hero to each tribe. It is significant that Kleisthenes is said to have referred to the Delphic oracle the choice (or ratification) of the ten eponymous heroes for the new tribes (Aristotle (?), *Athenian Constitution*, 21). Clearly, then, there was room for heroes in the battles of the hoplite age; but not within the phalanx. They were perceived as fighting alongside the mortal army, supporting a military unit, be it a tribe or polis or whatever.

The gods, too, were understood as taking sides. The most significant example of this in the classical period comes from Thucydides. He relates the response of Delphi to the Spartans when they enquired in 431 BC about whether they ought to go to war with Athens. 'The god replied, it is said, that victory would be theirs, if they fought with all their strength, and he said that he himself would support them, whether he was called to aid them or uncalled' (1. 118). Similarly, before the battle of Delion the Theban general Pagondas can claim, 'We may be sure that the god [Apollo Delios] will fight with us, whose sanctuary the Athenians have fortified and now inhabit unlawfully' (4. 92). How the gods might be understood to act may be seen in Herodotos' description of the aftermath of the battle of Plataia:

> An amazing thing was that in the fighting around the grove of Demeter, not one Persian seems to have entered the *temenos* or to have died there. Most of them fell in the melée around the temple; I suggest, if it is permissible to make suggestions about matters concerning the gods, that the goddess herself would not let them into the *temenos*, because they had burned the *anaktoron* at Eleusis.
>
> (Hdt. 9. 65)

These ideas should not be dismissed as fanciful stories deserving no place in our historical explanations. They are very much part of the way in which warfare was understood in the classical period, as is clear from the importance of religious ritual in all areas of Greek warfare (cf. Pritchett 1979) and from the large-scale dedications made to the gods after victories. Warfare therefore involved three levels of participants: not merely the common soldier and his human commanders, but also divine beings – heroes and gods.

If we look at warfare in the *Iliad*, we again find these three levels. The gods play a significant role; and among mortals, there is a clear distinction between the leading men and the ordinary soldiers; between the *skēptouchoi basilēes*, 'sceptre-holding lords', and the *laoi*, 'masses' (cf. 2. 86).

Traditionally, Homeric *basileis* have been seen as the aristocracy of a pre-polis society. It is taken for granted that they are part of a coherent social order, and that this social order reflects the reality of tenth- or ninth-century Greece (e.g. Murray 1980, 41–4). Against this view it has been argued that Homer's *basileis* have no role in society, and are comparable to the King and Prince in *Cinderella* – part of an entirely artificial world (Geddes 1984; cf. Rihll 1986). I suggest that neither of these views is entirely correct; rather, we can best make sense of the role of the Homeric *basileis* by comparing them to the heroes who received cult in Greek poleis.

The distinction between the *basileis* and the people is one of more than simply rank. The ordinary soldiers are never named, except at those moments when one or another *basileus* kills them in the process of cutting a swathe through the opposing ranks. *Basileis* are only ever killed by other *basileis*, never by the masses; only they use chariots; more importantly, it is only they who can see the gods when they intervene (Achilleus in book 1; Diomedes in book 5). The *basileis* do not fight as part of the phalanx, but always alone, travelling by chariot to reach an opponent. These last points require more investigation, since they must be reconciled with a 'hoplite' reading of the warfare of the *Iliad*.

The poem includes many episodes in which individual *basileis* are presented fighting other individuals in what is clearly not the front rank of a hoplite phalanx. Pritchett attempts to dismiss these scenes by producing evidence of individual duels, in both history and myth, within the context of hoplite battles (Pritchett 1985, 15–21). Thus he mentions Eteokles and Polyneikes at the gates of Thebes, in Euripides' *Phoinissai*; Melanthos and Xanthos on the Athenian–Boiotian border; and the battle between three Tegeans and three Pheneans that so closely resembles the battle between the Horatii and Curiatii (Livy, 1. 24–6). These, however, are false parallels, because they are monomachies *in place of* full-scale battles; they are ways of avoiding a hoplite battle, rather than an element in such a battle. They have their equivalent in the duel between Menelaos and Paris in *Iliad* 3, and perhaps in that between Hektor and Achilleus in Book 22; but most of the contests in the *Iliad* are not like that. Those contests are not single set pieces, but tend to involve a single *basileus* dealing with a string of opponents; they are what are called the *aristeia* of the character, and are introduced in the following way:

> Who then was the first, and who the last that he slaughtered,
> Hektor, Priam's son, now that Zeus granted him glory?
>
> (11. 299–300)

There then follows a list of names.

This kind of fighting is not compatible with the hoplite phalanx; but we can find an equivalent in the experience of classical warfare. This is the kind of behaviour Herodotos attributes to the fantastic figures at Marathon and Delphi. The *basileis*, like the heroes in Herodotos' stories, fight with and for the phalanx, but not in it.

The other problem, the presence of chariots, is a problem even for those who see the *basileis* as ninth-century aristocrats, and it has been explained away by various arguments. The most imaginative solution is to suggest that Homer's chariots are horses in disguise (Greenhalgh 1973, 7–18). For him the *Iliad* describes the society of ninth-century Greece, overlain by a thin layer of archaizing and heroizing designed to make the past seem more glorious than the dark age actually was. The poet makes everybody richer than ninth-century rulers really were (although still underestimating the wealth of bronze age palaces); and although ninth-century aristocrats rode horses, mounting them in chariots makes them grander. This does not get us very far, as the idea of fully armoured men leaping on and off horses in the middle of a hoplite battle is as difficult to comprehend as the use of chariots. There is also the problem that the élite came to be known as *hippeis*, horsemen rather than charioteers, which suggests that horse-riding was accepted as a sign of particular rank, not something that needed to be made more impressive.

The alternative suggestion, that of Latacz, is that chariots in the *Iliad* are not really used for fighting, but only for carrying the wounded and for flight and pursuit. This does not answer the question of why they are introduced to what Latacz sees as a hoplite battlefield in the *Iliad*, when there is no evidence for their use in 'real life'. Homer does not really know what to do with the chariots anyway. Nestor wants massed chariot charges, but it never happens; and in the fighting the heroes fly and pursue on foot as well as on chariots.

Here it is more difficult to prove a connection with later hero cult. However, I suspect that the association between chariots and Homeric *basileis* parallels an association between chariot *processions* and hero cult. Processions are an important feature of major polis cults, and those which lead from polis-centre to boundary are seen as being crucially related to territorial definition (de Polignac 1984, 48). Processions appear in scenes on geometric pottery, and these have been linked to hero cult, or at least to cult of the dead. One thing that points to a role for processions in cult is the iconography of the dead Herakles being driven to Olympos on a chariot, with Athena as charioteer. I suggest that a regular part of the Athenian cult of Herakles involved a procession in which the image of the hero was borne in a chariot to the Acropolis. Such a procession may lie behind not only the iconography of some Attic pots, but also the story of Peisistratos' return to Athens, when he supposedly dressed a girl called Phye as Athena and had her drive him into Athens on a chariot (Hdt. 1. 60).

Other activities that characterize Homer's *basileis* are also found in hero cult. Their feasting is particularly significant, since in the Greek world (at least from the early archaic period onwards) meat-eating happened solely in ritual circumstances; even the élite would eat meat only as part of a sacrifice to the Olympian gods. Heroes, however, to whom animals were sacrificed holocaust, would receive a regular supply of roast flesh. Feasting, sacrifice, and games are the main elements in the cult of Miltiades the Elder in the sixth century (Hdt. 6. 38).

The implication of my argument is this: when the citizen of a polis heard the exploits of a Homeric *basileus* described, he would associate it, not necessarily with his own or anyone else's ancestor, but with the hero of a polis.[1] Such a suggestion is surely not very strange. In the *Iliad* we see the Olympian gods acting like men and women and involving themselves directly in human affairs. They come from high Olympos, and appear to whomever they wish. Occasionally they take part in the fighting, and they can join the fray either as individuals pitted against heroes (e.g. Aphrodite at 5. 318–54, Apollo at 5. 431–46, or Ares at 5. 846–63) or in their own private struggle, which has rather less of a direct effect on the battle on earth below (e.g. 21. 385–513). No one denies that these gods would be identified with the figures to which Homer's audience offered cult; and we may surely therefore regard the *basileis* in a similar way. To say this is not to deny the 'humanity' of the characters in the *Iliad*. The emotions of the *basileus*-heroes are fully human (as, in fact, are those of the gods); but their actions set them apart from other mortals.

The actions of the gods and *basileis* receive much more attention in the *Iliad* than the clash of ordinary soldiers. The divine and the heroic actors are characterized; they are given emotions both petty and grand. I believe, however, that the difference between the presentation of warfare in the *Iliad* and in later writers may be seen as one of perspective rather than anything else.

Conclusion

To say that the *Iliad* is a poem about the polis is not to suggest that that is all it is about – any more than to call Shakespeare's *Othello* a play about jealousy would be to give more than a partial description of it. None the less, I have suggested that the poem did speak to the world of the polis, and it is appropriate to conclude by suggesting what it may have been saying to that world.

Above all, there is the importance of territory. We have seen that the hoplite phalanx was introduced precisely to maintain the

---

[1] I am not suggesting that one could find, in the seventh century, cults of all, or even many of, the Homeric *basileis*. The point is that they occupy the same position as the recipients of cult in the hierarchy of the *polis*. The cult of the gods in individual Greek *poleis* associated them with places other than Homer's Olympos.

territorial boundaries of the polis, and that the hero was offered cult as the guardian of the polis. These elements are central to one of the most important parts of the *Iliad*, the Catalogue of Ships (2. 484–760). There we are given the name of each polis or group of poleis, the number of its warriors, the names of its heroes, and some epithet describing the place: 'the meadows of Haliartos . . . Thebes, the strong-founded citadel, and sacred Onchestos, the shining grove of Poseidon . . . Arne of the great vineyards . . . with Nisa the sacrosanct and uttermost Anthedon' (2. 503–8). These are real places, not stock epithets attached to random names, and they emphasize that behind the warriors lies the land they come from. A similar interest in the territory around the polis comes in the description of Achilleus' shield (18. 490–605), in which the two cities are surrounded by ploughed fields, meadows, and vineyards.

The second theme, also indicated in the Catalogue of Ships, is the close relationship between the *basileus* and his men. The *basileis* of the *Iliad* always act with their soldiers; when Achilleus withdraws from the fighting, so do his Myrmidons (2. 771–9). In other words, we cannot separate the leader from the led. If we ignore the common soldiers, we miss an important element of the poem. It is in this context, perhaps, that we should understand the story that Solon was accused of interpolating the lines about Salamis (557–8) into the Catalogue of Ships, next to those about Athens (Plut. *Sol.* 10). Whether or not the story is true, it suggests that the *Iliad* was read as a charter for communities, not individuals. I suggest that the *Iliad* was not then read, and should not now be read, as a celebration of aristocratic society, but as a presentation of the society of the polis. It looks forward to the world of the citizen, rather than back to a world of dark age tribal chiefs.

Indeed, if the *Iliad* is a poem about the society of the early Greek polis, then we cannot use it as evidence for earlier 'pre-polis' society, or for 'pre-hoplite' fighting. In that case, we ought perhaps to question whether the dark age was 'aristocratic' at all, and to look at other possibilities.[1]

---

[1] See e.g. Rihll 1985; Snodgrass 1987.

Bibliography

Andrewes, A. (1956), *The Greek Tyrants* (London).

Burkert, W. (1985), *Greek Religion* (Oxford).

Cartledge, P. A. (1977), 'Hoplites and heroes: Sparta's contribution to the technique of ancient warfare', *JHS* 97: 11–27.

Cawkwell, G. L. (1989), 'Orthodoxy and hoplites', *CQ* 83 (n.s. 39): 375–89.

Coldstream, J. N. (1976), 'Hero cults in the age of Homer', *JHS* 96: 8–17.

—— (1977), *Geometric Greece* (London).

de Polignac, F. (1984), *La Naissance de la cité grecque* (Paris).

Detienne, M. (1968), 'La phalange: problèmes et controverses', in J.-P. Vernant (ed.), *Problèmes de la guerre en Grèce ancienne* (Paris), pp. 119–42.

Easterling, P. E. (1989), 'City-settings in Greek poetry', *Proceedings of the Classical Association*, 86: 5–17.

Geddes, A. J. (1984), 'Who's who in Homeric society', *CQ* 78 (n.s. 34): 17–36.

Greenhalgh, P. A. L. (1973), *Early Greek Warfare* (Cambridge).

Hägg, R. (ed. 1983), *The Greek Renaissance of the Eighth Century BC: Tradition and Innovation* (Stockholm).

Hanson, V. D. (1989), *The Western Way of War: Infantry Battle in Classical Greece* (London, etc.).

Kirk, G. S. (1985), *The Iliad: A Commentary*, i: *Books 1–4* (Cambridge).

Kurtz, D. C., and Boardman, J. (1971), *Greek Burial Customs* (London).

Latacz, J. (1977), *Kampfparänese, Kampfdarstellung und Kampfwirklichkeit in der Ilias, bei Kallinos und Tyrtaios* (Zetemata, 66; Munich).

Malkin, I. (1987), *Religion and Colonisation in Ancient Greece* (Leiden).

Morgan, C. A. (1990), *Athletes and Oracles: The Transformation of Olympia and Delphi in the Eighth Century BC* (Cambridge).

Morris, I. M. (1986), 'The use and abuse of Homer', *Classical Antiquity*, 4: 81–138.

—— (1987), *Burial and Ancient Society: The Rise of the Greek City-state* (Cambridge).

—— (1988), 'Tomb cult and the "Greek renaissance": the past in the present in the eighth century BC', *Antiquity*, 62: 750–61.

Murray, O. (1980), *Early Greece* (London).

Pritchett, W. K. (1979), *The Greek State at War*, iii: *Religion* (Berkeley).

—— (1985), *The Greek State at War*, iv (Berkeley).

Rihll, T. (1985), *Synoikismos* (unpublished Ph.D. thesis; Leeds).

—— (1986), ' "Kings" and "commoners" in Homeric society', *LCM* 11: 86–91.

Salmon, J. (1977), 'Political hoplites?', *JHS* 97: 84–101.

Scully, S. (1990), *Homer and the Sacred City* (Ithaca).

Snodgrass, A. M. (1965), 'The hoplite reform and history', *JHS* 85: 110–22.

—— (1974), 'An historical Homeric society?', *JHS* 94: 114–25.

—— (1980), *Archaic Greece: The Age of Experiment* (London).
—— (1987), *An Archaeology of Greece: The Present State and Future Scope of a Discipline* (Berkeley).
Sourvinou-Inwood, C. (1989), 'What is *polis* religion?', in O. Murray and S. R. F. Price (eds), *The Greek City: From Homer to Alexander* (Oxford), ch. 12 (pp. 295–322).
van Wees, H. (1988), 'Kings in combat: battles and heroes in the *Iliad*', *CQ* 82 (n.s. 38): 1–24.
Vidal-Naquet, P. (1981), 'Land and sacrifice in the Odyssey: a study of religious and mythical meanings', in R. L. Gordon (ed.), *Myth, Religion and Society* (Cambridge), pp. 80–94.
Whitley, A. J. M. (1988), 'Early states and hero cults: a reappraisal', *JHS* 108: 173–82.

Addendum

Van Wees, H. (1992), *Status Warriors: War, Violence, and Society in Homer and History* (Amsterdam).

∞ 4 ∞

War and raids for booty in the world of Odysseus

Alastar Jackson

In his penetrating study of Homeric society *The World of Odysseus*, M. I. Finley argues that in dark age Greece no war could have been on the scale of Homer's Trojan war. War, he held, was more like raiding for booty; and in support of this he quotes translated extracts from Nestor's account of a raid on Elis (*Iliad*, 11. 670–84):

> Would that I were in the prime of youth and my might as steadfast as when a quarrel broke out between us and the Eleans over a cattle-raid. . . . Exceedingly abundant was then the booty we drove out of the plain together, fifty herds of cattle, as many flocks of sheep, as many droves of swine, as many herds of goats and a hundred and fifty bays, all mares. . . . And Neleus was glad at heart that so much booty fell to me the first time I went to war.

This, Finley writes (1977, 46), was 'a typical "war" as narrated by Nestor, a raid for booty. Even if repeated year after year, these wars remained single raids.' A little later he says, 'Wars and raids for booty, indistinguishable in the eyes of Odysseus' world, were organized affairs, often involving a combination of families, occasionally even of communities' (1977, 63). His view of dark age and later Greek warfare remains similar in his *Ancient History: Evidence and Models* (1985, 76):

> There were many wars, especially petty ones, in which it [the profit motive] was dominant, in which the old 'cattle-raid' quality stressed by

the Homeric Nestor (*Iliad* 11. 670–84) more or less summed up the whole story. These were the wars that received no extended attention in the sources (or the modern literature), and often none at all.

This chapter is not concerned with the historicity of the Trojan war (which cannot yet be proved or disproved), but with the causes and character of war in the society Homer reflects (taken, as by Finley, to be largely the Greek dark age, as argued below).[1] No one would doubt that in that society, as on occasions later, there sometimes occurred warfare in which the main aim was profit and hostilities took the form of plundering rather than of battle – though it must remain impossible to be sure of this in the case of wars that receive little or no attention in the sources. But it is argued here that, to judge from the Homeric poems and some relevant archaeological evidence, since Homeric warfare and heroic values do not always concern profit and plunder, warfare in dark age Greece (and over the 400 years from the fall of the Mycenaean palaces to the opening of the eighth century, there must have been some) was probably (more often than not) clearly distinguishable from raids for booty.

Some arguments in favour of Finley's view (which does not lack foundation), and then some against, will be set out before this conclusion is reached; but a fundamental question about the evidence must first be answered briefly: that of the degree of historical reality behind Homeric society.

A historical Homeric society?

Which historical periods are the society, warfare, and raiding in Homer inspired by (in so far as they do derive from history and not from poetic imagination or folktale): Mycenaean, dark age (as just defined), eighth-century, or an amalgam of all three? If the last is the case, then, I would argue, the dark age component will

---

[1] This is a revised version of a paper given in the University of Nottingham in May 1989. The debate it deals with is an old one; Finley was following, quite closely, the line taken by Friedreich (1851, 356–7); and Andreades (1933, 24–7) stressed that honour was more important than booty. Finley's view is not without its followers today.

be predominant; Finley, Andrewes, and others have argued strongly in favour of this being so.[1]

Briefly, the complicated and wealthy world visible in the Linear B tablets, with their elaborate supply lists, could have appeared in poetic garb in Homer, but does not. Homer's ideas of wealth could have been influenced partly, we can now see, by tombs like that now unearthed at Lefkandi, erected in what was hitherto the most obscure part of the dark age (see Popham *et al.* 1982). Homer's society is virtually illiterate; the dark age was totally so, on present evidence, as both Mycenaean and eighth-century Greece were not. Mycenaean chariots and tower-shields were remembered, it is true, but not the probable use of chariots in war. The huge numbers of men in Homer's armies may be an exaggeration encouraged by memories of Mycenaean armies, or even by impressions of eighth-century predecessors of hoplite ones; but they can just as well have been invented or added to in the dark age.

In any case, the reasons for which, and the heroic code by which, the leading warriors fight in Homer are independent of the numbers, chariots, and so on, and must have made sense to the dark age audiences of Homer's predecessors, influencing and being influenced by them. When war occurred in that period, the causes of it, and excellence and prowess in it, must have been matters of burning interest that no poet could ignore. The society and the warfare that will have been part of dark age Greece must be partially visible to us in the epics, in however exaggerated a form.

The periods reflected in Homer's raids for booty are uncertain, for most raids are timeless. The raid on Egypt from Crete, of which Odysseus tells, is not as datable as it may seem. It may be based partly on memories of the Sea Peoples' attacks in the late

---

[1] *Contra*, Snodgrass 1971, 388–94. The doubts raised by Snodgrass (1974) as to the historicity of Homeric society seem largely answered by Finley 1977, 142–58; Murray 1980, chs 3–4. Even if the Homeric world were entirely a literary construct, this discussion would have value as a comment on war seen in it; but even without Homer we cannot assume that dark age wars were primarily about booty. In any case, the virtual illiteracy of Homeric society and the importance of livestock in it (see below) do seem to link it to the dark age; and why should Homeric war *not* be influenced by several centuries of dark age war?

thirteenth and early twelfth centuries; but it could be based on later Cretan raids, for Crete was not always isolated from the outside world in the dark age;[1] it also makes sense in an eighth-century context.[2] But a strong case for a large dark age component in Homer's cattle-raids can be made, even if Mycenaean reminiscences are also present.[3] Livestock were reared in dark age Nichoria in Messenia (Cherry 1988, 27) – next door, one may note, to Nestor's victims in Elis – and Snodgrass (1987, 193–209) has argued strongly that pastoralism was practised in the dark age in southern and central Greece, and in other parts too, though he believes it grew less common from the tenth century on. We may suppose that where cattle were reared, they would be rustled both in peace and in war, just as they were later in Greece.

The sacking of cities is hard to parallel in archaeology after the earlier part of the dark age, and there is doubtless a Mycenaean element here, as with cattle-raids, and perhaps an eighth-century element too. But the dark age was scarcely thereafter innocent of this sort of plundering. The seizure of a town's property, without the use of fire and the sword, need not have left any archaeologically detectable traces, and seems to be contemplated in the siege scene on Achilleus' shield (*Il.* 18. 509–12). If a town were tidily plundered but not actually burnt, and if its menfolk were butchered outside it (and so outside the area of later excavation), it might seem to us to have been peacefully abandoned. Admittedly, Homeric city-sackings seem to be less genteel affairs; but the dark age now seems to have been less tranquil than some have thought (Snodgrass 1987, 189–93).

To sum up: the warfare and raiding in Homer can be held to derive in large part from the dark age (it would be surprising if no dark age memories were among them), though of course there must be, and in some cases demonstrably are, earlier (or later) elements in them.

Arguments for and against Finley's views, that dark age warfare

---

[1] Snodgrass 1971, 339–42; 350; 407.
[2] *Od.* 14. 243–84. Ormerod 1924, 88–94, argues for a late bronze age date, Braun 1982, 35, for an eighth- or even seventh-century one.
[3] A bronze age cattle-raid may actually be illustrated on a wall-painting from Thera, though this is controversial; see Warren 1979, pl. A *a*.

was essentially identical with raiding for booty, can now be set out.

War as raiding

Some of the arguments in favour of the Finley line are strong ones. (1) Plunder and the profit motive were bound to influence war, since raiding for booty in peace was clearly to the fore, and not just practised but respected. (2) In Homer's picture of heroic warfare, plundering is manifestly significant. (3) The fact that war in Homer does not primarily concern land may have made plundering more important.

These three arguments will now be examined in more detail.

Raiding for booty in peace

Raids for booty in peacetime appear to be an entirely accepted part of life in Homer's picture, just as war is. The great Achilleus can speak of them, with sublime nobility of course, but also with a distinct matter-of-factness (*Il.* 9. 406). Lesser men, too, were interested in them, and Odysseus took care to see that each of his men got his fair share of the spoils of Ismaros (*Odyssey*, 9. 39–42). As Thucydides saw (1. 5), there was no reproach in Nestor's question to his guests at a feast, 'Do you sail on some business (*kata prexin*) or travel the sea on chance like raiders (*leisteres*) who wander at risk of their lives, bringing evil on men of other lands?' (*Od.* 3. 69–74). For his guests took no offence, and from Nestor the wise none could be expected. A raider would be blamed by his own community only if he raided its friends. Penelope tells how Antinoos' father was nearly lynched by the demos of Ithaca for raiding the Thesprotians, but she has to add the explanation 'and they were our friends' (*Od.* 16. 418–27).

There was no religious limitation or objection to raiding, as long as holy places and people were protected; raiders would sacrifice to the gods before sailing off to work (*Od.* 14. 249–51; cf. 9. 196–205). As far as we can see from Homer, only someone like

Eumaios, a victim of kidnappers, a humble man with no lord to protect or avenge him, would believe that raiders faced and feared the wrath of the gods, and even he admitted that Zeus gave them booty (*Od.* 14. 83–8). What is more, raiding could afford a man the chance to display prowess and to win wealth and prestige; Odysseus, posing as a Cretan raider, tells how his nine successful raids brought him all these things and a good match too (*Od.* 14. 210–34; Friedreich 1851, 356–7).

The respectability of raiding in Homer might be thought a mere invention to add excitement; but raiding is generally mentioned in Achilleus' matter-of-fact style. It is entirely credible as a feature of early Greek society, for it was just that later. An Athenian law concerning private associations (attributed to Solon but clearly revised after Kleisthenes' reforms) allows not only *demoi* and other manifestly respectable bodies to make legally valid contracts, but also 'men going after booty or for trade' (Justinian, *Digest*, 47. 22. 4; cf. Ormerod 1924, 67–8). The two alternatives in that phrase closely recall Nestor's 'men on business or raiders', and we are surely dealing with the same two groups. It might be held that the 'men going after booty' are not raiders as such, but men raiding the enemy in war or an offending community in a state of reprisals; but there is no mention of enemies, war, or any of the technical terms to do with reprisals such as *sulai* ('a state of reprisals') or *rhusia* (which can mean 'booty seized in a state of reprisals'). The phrase 'men going after booty' is surely a straightforward description, like Herodotos' 'men sailing out after booty' (*kata lēiēn ekplōsantas*), used of the 'bronze men' who raided Egypt (2. 152). Thucydides notes (1. 5) that raiders could still win esteem in the wild north-west of Greece in his own day; for a later period this is confirmed by the use in hellenistic Aitolia of the proper name Laistas, 'Raider' (*SIG*[3] 539 *a*, lines 6–7).

The role of private raiding in winning profit and prestige in Homeric, and therefore in dark age, society must have been significant, and for this reason wars must have had to promise plunder if they were to be thought worth starting, especially if communities were to be combined in order to fight them. Booty may thus have been a very important aim, and could even be held to have been the chief aim of dark age warfare, both petty and more serious.

The prominence of plunder in Homer

Raiding is certainly important in Homeric warfare. The heroes set great store by wealth, especially in the form of gifts (Finley 1977, 120–3); but booty is also eagerly sought. Agamemnon's greed for gain in the form of booty and prizes from it was excessive, to summarize Achilleus' frank opinion of it; which need not mean that a normal appetite for it was very restrained. Achilleus' own accumulation of gold, silver, bronze, iron, captive women, and other spoils is not as large as he would wish, thanks to Agamemnon (*Il.* 9. 325–33; 365–7). Sometimes, instead of killing beaten opponents, he is ready to sell them to a ransom broker for a mere 100 oxen (21. 76–9). Notably, Achilleus regards a cattle-raid as sufficient cause for war, so in a sense as its equivalent. On his new shield the city at war faces either a sack or the loss of its property, and while it waits, its cattle are stolen; no motive but profit seems apparent for the attack (18. 509–40). It is not only humble men like Dolon who may be thought to plunder dead warriors; the heroes are notoriously keen to despoil their beaten opponents of their arms, which may be valuable (10. 387).

Even if we subtract the gold, silver, and bronze from the booty of actual dark age warriors, deny them their metal armour, reduce drastically the ransoms they charged each other, imagine only rather small walled or unwalled towns under siege, and attribute some of their concern with booty to a literary origin, we may still be sure that greed for booty and ransom flourished in dark age Greece. A dark age audience would surely have no difficulty whatever in at once comprehending why besiegers outside a settlement might be in two minds, as those on Achilleus' shield are, as to whether to rip or squeeze the profit from the wretched prey. Modest only in the scale of the opportunities open to them, the dark age will certainly have had its emulators of Agamemnon and Achilleus.

The invisibility of wars over land

It could be argued that the very character of Homeric warfare tallies with the archaeological evidence for the dark age, and will have incited the warriors of that age to seek profit and spoil. For in Homeric warfare, land is almost totally irrelevant (Friedreich 1851, 356–7; Andreades 1933, 27 n. 1; Finley 1977, 95). One might suppose that in the historical world of Odysseus movable wealth was as important as the land the later Greeks fought over so bitterly. Some archaeological evidence may support this view. First, it appears that there was a steep drop in the number of settlements between the thirteenth and the eleventh century, without a corresponding increase in their size, and this is usually taken to mean that the population fell drastically (Snodgrass 1971, 364–7). If this was so, there could, relatively and overall, have been plenty of land for most people (and their livestock), so that the murderous and long-lasting border warfare of later Greece need have no great dark age precedent. Movable wealth could have been of more importance, in providing temptations to jealousy and greed.

Next comes the evidence for an increase in pastoralism in the early dark age, referred to above. Cattle can be tempting and co-operative booty, and if they were a standard of value in the dark age, as they are in Homer, that would increase their worth and their convenience when it came to sharing out the loot. Thus both the lack of wars for land in Homer and the popularity of livestock raiding could fit in with the archaeological evidence as it now stands. So might the apparent poverty of much of dark age Greece, except possibly for the area that supplied the wealth of gold and other objects found in the great tomb at Lefkandi.[1] If dark age bards preserved embarrassing memories of the wealth of Mycenae, then dark age warrior chiefs could have been goaded (if they needed goading) into plundering each other for whatever wealth there was to plunder. The great man of Lefkandi may simply have been one who stole from the poor to make himself rich.

War as distinct from raiding

But there are arguments of no small weight against the view that plunder was primary, and that war and raids for booty were

[1] Popham *et al.* 1982. For poverty see esp. Snodgrass 1971, 380–6.

indistinguishable. I shall begin with the urge to raid in peacetime, and its effect upon war.

Certainly the profit and honour that raids could bring are not to be belittled, as Nowag tried to suggest (Nowag 1983, 163–70; cf. Jackson 1985); but the idea, which he took rather too far, has at least something to be said for it. Raiding simply does not bulk very large in Homeric society or economic life. The sea is, after all, safe for men on business of various sorts, as well as for raiders. Eumaios' dogs are trained to attack strangers, but that does not mean every stranger is a pig-rustler (*Od.* 14. 29–36). The matter-of-fact tone of some references to raids shows that they are accepted, but also suggests they are not of conspicuous importance. Raiding may supplement a royal household, but never seems to provide its sole income.[1]

Nor do raids for booty match plundering in war, if the two are compared in scale. Achilleus has to be given a tally of twenty-three cities sacked, placing him in quite a different class from the most successful raider Homer sees fit to describe, the Cretan captain Odysseus poses as, who has made a mere nine raids and one attempt on Egypt. Admittedly, this pretended person's successes give him wealth and prestige, and he claims to have shared the command of the Cretans at Troy; but he does not play any memorable role there, though Odysseus could have given him one (*Od.* 14. 199–242). To consider plunder and the warrior next: Achilleus' other booty is none of it as important to him as the one special prize of honour, Briseis. His charges against Agamemnon show that the profit motive can grow greater than befitted the heroic code, and the cities he has sacked were attacked for more than loot, though that was one aim, for all the ones we are told anything about are linked to Troy, as Thebe was through Andromache (*contra* Nowag 1983, 62–73). Achilleus' raids may have been on the grandest scale, but in so far as we know them from the *Iliad* they appear as a sideshow. As for the city on his shield, just because no motive for the attack is included, that does not mean a dark age audience would have supposed that profit was the primary aim. No one would deny that the dark age could have had its greedy *basilées* fighting and sacking and raiding for any profit; but they will not necessarily have been motivated

[1]   On raiding see *Od.* 1. 398; 23. 356–8.

primarily by gain. They could have other, more important motives, which will be explored shortly; in the meantime, even if land was not an important issue (and in a dry summer, which means most summers, quarrels over grazing and watering rights, or sheer greed, may have made it an issue), that would not make movable wealth the most important cause of wars. Neither would pastoralism, neither would poverty; and just because cattle were raised, and surely rustled, that does not turn war into cattle-raids.

But before other possible motives are examined, Finley's use of Nestor's raid on Elis should be examined further, to see whether its use as evidence for dark age warfare is strictly justified. In fact, the use he made of it is quite seriously misleading in more than one way. First, the cattle-raid is clearly the preliminary to a more serious quarrel, as Nestor says in the extract quoted at the start of this paper; and in due course Nestor tells how, following the raid, the Eleians attacked and much more severe fighting took place (*Il.* 11. 706–62). The raid itself was one of a special kind: neither war nor unprovoked raiding, but a raid carried out in reprisal for wrongs done to King Neleus and the Pylians by their arrogant and violent Elcian neighbours (11. 685–705). A clue to this, besides the passage cited, lies in Nestor's words (omitted by Finley) describing himself as 'driving booty seized in reprisals' (*rhusia elaunomenos*). This use of *rhusia* is well paralleled, for example in Polybios, where seizure of livestock, with some accompanying violence, is involved in reprisals (described at 22. 4. 10–17, where *rhusia* is also used to mean 'right of reprisals', or the reprisals themselves). Nestor in his raid killed the Eleian Itymoneus, which is what Homer refers to in the last words cited by Finley, who translates 'the first time I went to war'. But the Greek word used here, *polemos*, can simply mean combat, battle, or fighting (see e.g. *Il.* 1. 226; or 7. 174). In the passage under discussion, it is used of single combat. 'War' could thus be a very misleading translation here, since the reprisal raid seems to precede the quarrel and the Eleian attack.

Seen in the proper context, then, Nestor's raid can clearly no longer be used to show that in Homer, war and raids for booty are indistinguishable. Doubtless booty and profit were the main aims of some wars in the dark ages; but in so far as one can make any worthwhile guesses about warfare in that period, it seems more likely from Homer's evidence that many wars will have concerned other matters. As Finley says (1977, 122), the heroes could set honour above all material goods. No doubt their devotion to the heroic code, so well analysed by Finley, is exaggerated for the purposes of entertaining and impressing the audience. But archaic nobles, too, sought to excel in war and athletics, to be generous hosts, to gain and maintain honour, and to defend it by avenging wrongs and insults; and there is no reason to doubt that their dark age ancestors behaved in much the same way. Thus the interest in vengeance seen in Homer, so important to the plot of both epics, could well reflect the sort of reason for going to war that actual leaders in that period really had; honour would have to be defended if hospitality was violated or some other outrage perpetrated. The war of the Kouretes and Aitolians over the spoils of the Kalydonian boar (*Il.* 9. 529–49), Achilleus' refusal to fight because of his injured pride, and his rejection of the profitable gifts that Agamemnon is forced to offer – so beside the point in relation to his wrath over his prize of honour, Briseis – all show that honour came first. War could break out over it, and material profit could be quite irrelevant. In assessing the dark age, as Desborough says (1972, 353), all kinds of disputes must be allowed for.

One might even suggest that the constant display of heroic prowess in killing, illustrated in about one-third of the *Iliad*, could also (except in its scale) be drawn from dark age life and could be relevant to the point at issue. I am not, of course, suggesting that war at that time was ever caused by a wish to compete in slaughter; there is no evidence of that in Homer. But if the warriors of the time were expected to excel in killing, it might have made plunder and profit a little less urgent as priorities, and war a little less rational a pastime. While the massacres of Homeric battlefields may seem to us no more real than the butchery of extras in spy films today, mere fantastic entertainment, they may have had a real counterpart (on a much reduced scale) in early Greece. In later Macedonia, comparable in many ways to early Greece, the warrior was greatly admired, especially as killer (cf. Plutarch, *Eumenes*, 1; Ellis 1976, 33).

In short, dark age warfare, to judge from Homer, may have been more often about defending one's honour and attacking that of others – about pride and martial prowess – than about greed and profit, though that motive was doubtless often present and possibly at times dominant. To imagine what is suggested here, it may help to consider two peoples of later Greece who lived for honour and plunder, but for honour first. The Maniots of the generations before Greek independence were keen pirates, but keener for prestige and power, for which they pursued their prolonged vendettas (Leigh Fermor 1958, chs 8–9). The second example is that of the Sarakatsani, honour-conscious shepherds who, before the time of the dictator Metaxás, went sheep-rustling not just for extra food and profit but also for pleasure and prestige – and also (as both honour and profit demanded) in retaliation for raids they had themselves suffered.[1]

If these comparisons with Homeric society are fair, and in view of the other reasons given, the picture offered here in place of Finley's can be defended as more realistic than his. But it must be said in conclusion that it is partly thanks to Finley's successful exploration of Homer and of the heroic code that I have been able to present a different picture.[2]

Bibliography

Andreades, A. M. (1933), *A History of Greek Public Finance* (Cambridge, Mass.).

Andrewes, A. (1971), *Greek Society* (Harmondsworth).

Braun, T. F. R. G. (1982), 'The Greeks in the Near East' and 'The Greeks in Egypt', in *CAH* iii. 3 (2nd edn), chs 36 *a–b* (pp. 1–31, 32–56).

Campbell, J. K. (1964), *Honour, Family, and Patronage* (Oxford).

Cherry, J. F. (1988), 'Pastoralism and the role of animals in the pre- and protohistoric economies of the Aegean', in C. R. Whittaker (ed.), *Pastoral Economies in Classical Antiquity* (*PCPS* supp. vol. 14; Cambridge), pp. 6–34.

Desborough, V. R. d'A. (1972), *The Greek Dark Ages* (London).

Ellis, J. R. (1976), *Philip II and Macedonian Imperialism* (London).

Finley, M. I. (1977), *The World of Odysseus* (2nd edn, London).

—— (1985), *Ancient History: Evidence and Models* (London).

---

[1] Campbell 1964, 206–10 and ch. 10, noting the parallel with Homeric society.

[2] It is not possible here to discuss booty and war in later Greece, a controversial subject especially as regards the wars against Persia. The importance of booty as a motive for Greek states in going to war is sometimes held up as their main aim, whereas it was probably only a subsidiary, though important, aim.

Friedreich, J. B. (1851), *Die Realien in der Iliade und Odyssee* (Erlangen).

Jackson, A. H. (1985), review of Nowag (1983), *Gnomon*, 57: 655–7.

Leigh Fermor, P. (1958), *Mani: Travels in the Southern Peloponnese* (London).

Murray, O. (1980), *Early Greece* (London).

Nowag, W. (1983), *Raub und Beute in der archaischen Zeit der Griechen* (Frankfurt am Main).

Ormerod, H. A. (1924), *Piracy in the Ancient World* (Liverpool).

Popham, M., Touloupa, E., and Sackett, L. H. (1982), 'The hero of Lefkandi', *Antiquity*, 56: 169–74.

Snodgrass, A. M. (1971), *The Dark Age of Greece* (Edinburgh).

—— (1974), 'An historical Homeric society?', *JHS* 94: 114–25.

—— (1987), *An Archaeology of Greece: The Present State and Future Scope of a Discipline* (Berkeley).

Warren, P. M. (1979), 'The miniature fresco from the West House at Akrotiri, Thera, and its Aegean setting', *JHS* 99: 115–29.

5

War, slavery, and settlement in early Greece

Tracey Rihll

My wealth is here; the sword and spear;
  The breast-defending shield;
With this I plough, with this I sow;
  With this I reap the field.
With this I tread the luscious grape,
  And drink the blood-red wine;
And slaves around in order wait,
  And all are counted mine.
But he, who will not rear the lance
  Upon the battle field,
Nor sway the sword, nor stand behind
  The breast-defending shield,
On lowly knee must worship me,
  With servile kiss adored,
And peal the cry of homage high,
  And hail me mighty lord.
Hybrias (trans. D. Sandford, in Burges (ed. 1876), 176)

Taking is the primal, natural, animal method of acquisition. Herbivores take plants; carnivores take herbivores and other carnivores; omnivores take plants, herbivores, carnivores, and other omnivores. Some ants take other ants to be their slaves, leaving them (like the Spartans) free to indulge their martial arts. Presumably these slave-making ants do not feel guilty about their behaviour; it took *homo sapiens* about 40,000 years to acquire a bad conscience about taking from his own species, and *homo sapiens* is, apparently, the animal with the quickest intellect.

I do not think the ancients felt guilty about it either. For them, bad conscience attached itself only to taking from one's own kind, and one's own *kind* is a lot less inclusive than one's own *species*. That extraordinary largesse is a gift of modern man, and is an attitude not yet shared by all men, despite formal deference to (the so-called developed world's) public opinion. Nobody uses terms like 'subhuman' any more, but only a fool who listens to a man's blarney and neglects the deed done – to quote Solon, fragment 11 – will believe that there is unanimous support for universal human rights. Nor are the 'uncivilized' attitudes to be found only outside what we are pleased to call the 'civilized' world. As Pritchett observes of glorious Greece, 'methods of warfare, so far from improving, became more barbarous as time went on' (1971, 74).

We may be able to avoid some of the red herrings that plague this subject if we consider the Greeks' use of force as a method of acquisition from the perspective of man as an animal, for whom such behaviour is regarded as normal and natural. To suggest that the Greeks behaved like animals is not to judge them unfavourably, but to suggest that they did what came naturally, without shame and without affectation. Neither emotion is apparent in their words; consider, for example, the following:

> Nature demonstrates that it is right that the better man should prevail over the worse and the stronger over the weaker. The truth of this can be seen in a variety of examples drawn both from the animal world and from the complex communities and races of human beings; right consists in the superior ruling over the inferior and having the upper hand.
>
> (Plato, *Gorgias*, 483)

> Since we do not have the money to buy what we want, nor can we survive without supplies, I suggest that we return to the villages, where the inhabitants, being weaker than we are, do not oppose us.
>
> (Xenophon, *Anabasis*, 7. 3. 5)

> For it is a general rule of human nature that people despise those who treat them well and respect those who make no concessions.
>
> (Thucydides, 3. 39)[1]

[1]   Pouncey (1980, 49), offers an excellent summary of Thucydides' theory of power. 'The practice of exploitation for gain or power is, then, a universal one . . . and whether it is practiced by the individual pirate looking after his family, or Minos building a maritime empire, the basic motivation is the same, and the victims, large or small, have learned to live with it, or even embrace it, weaker cities in their desire for gain endured subjection to the stronger' (cf. Thuc. 1. 8. 3). 'Historical change

In the next section I shall argue that the Greeks considered taking, by force if necessary, to be a normal and legitimate method of acquisition; that the toil of the spear was a valid mode of production. One must not only be *willing* but also *able* to use force, so a consideration of that aspect of Greek life forms the subject of the third section of this paper. In the final section I apply the arguments to the so-called colonization of the Mediterranean and Black Sea littorals by Greeks, and suggest that the principal product taken from these areas was slaves.

In their own words

> From Ilion the wind bore me close to the Kikonians
> at Ismaros. Thereupon I sacked the city and killed them –
> but we took their wives and many of their possessions,
> and divided them between ourselves so that nobody was cheated of his
> fair share.
>
> (*Odyssey*, 9. 39–42)

For most Homeric scholars, this is merely another episode in poor Odysseus' difficult homecoming, a ten-year struggle against nature and a vindictive deity to reach his dear wife and son, hard pressed in Ithaca by overbearing suitors and indifferent neighbours. If they comment on this passage at all, it is to point out the fairness of the division, overlooking the fact that what is divided is spoils, including the women of the town.

Ismaros was popular with another famous Greek:

> By spear is kneaded the bread I eat, by spear is won
> the wine of Ismaros, which I drink leaning on my spear.
>
> (Archilochos, fr. 2)

Archilochos can hardly be said to understate the role of fighting in securing his day-to-day existence. This is overlooked by most commentators on the poem, who deduce instead that Ismaros was famous for its vintage. It may well have been, but Archilochos

---

takes place along a continuum of aggression, beginning with the first bandit, and rising to the concerted and organised violence of an empire.' (Translations are generally based on Penguin or Loeb editions. Fragments of iambic and elegiac poets are numbered as in West's edition (1971–2).)

acquired it by fighting for it, not paying for it, and this claim should not be so consistently ignored. (Achilleus and the lump of iron, *Iliad*, 23. 826–35, is a parallel case.)

The background for the tale of the *Iliad* is a band of Greeks who, having set up camp on a foreign shore, plunder the vicinity; that of the *Odyssey* is a community in the homeland whose warrior menfolk are away plundering overseas. Odysseus and his crew deliberately leave an island which is well supplied with food and water in order to go to another about which they know nothing, except that it is inhabited (they see the smoke from fires). There they find and let themselves into a cave-home, where they proceed to raid the larder. When the owner comes home, they first point out that they are the victorious heroes of Troy, and then ask him for 'gifts', to which, they say, they have a certain 'right'. In this kind of situation the canvassed stranger gives 'gifts' in exchange for freedom and safety. If he refuses 'the hand of friendship', the stranger's 'right' to 'gifts', he will be branded savage, unjust, inhospitable, lawless, and ungodly, as the Kyklops is branded (*Od.* 9. 175–6), and a legitimate natural resource to be plundered at will (see Aristotle, *Politics*, 1333 b–1334 a).

Proffered gifts do not have to be accepted, however. For example, Xenophon reports (*Anab.* 5. 5. 2) that 'the towns [of the Tibarenians] near the sea are not very strong; the generals were inclined to attack them, so that the troops might have some plunder. So they declined the presents which the Tibarenians had sent them.' The niceties of refusing gifts should not be misinterpreted; they intended to attack the Tibarenians and take what they chose. This type of behaviour is not reserved for *barbaroi*; by threat Xenophon and his colleagues persuaded the Sinopeans to supply them with ships and provide for the troops. They then considered taking possession of (read: colonizing) their chosen inhabited part of the Euxine littoral, from where, having appropriated the Sinopeans' ships, they might 'undertake surprise attacks upon any part of the country they liked'. This persuaded the people of Sinope and Herakleia to pay them to leave the Euxine area (*Anab. 5 passim*; see also Burstein 1976, 39–41).

An anonymous poem of about the seventh century BC is less reflective, and suggests more of the immediacy of the event:

Bring fruit and cake from your rich house and offer it to us, and a cup of wine and a basket of cheese. The swallow does not disdain even wheaten bread or pulse bread. Shall we go, or are we to get something? If you give us something, we will go, but if you do not we shall not let you be; we shall carry away your door or the lintel, or your wife sitting inside. She is small; we shall carry her easily. But if you give us something, let it be something big. Open, open the door to the swallow; for we are not old men, but children.

(*PMG* 848, trans. Trypanis)

The word 'children' has prompted interpretations of this poem as an archaic Greek version of 'trick or treat', 'Mischief Night', or 'Mari Lywd'. However, early lyric poetry is not renowned for either comic treatment or juvenile themes. This charitable interpretation of the boast to tear down doors and lintels and carry off women can only be explained in terms of sentimental philhellenism (on which see Borza 1973). What the 'swallows' threaten to do is what Odysseus and his crew did at Ismaros.

Aristotle (*Pol.* 1256 a 35–b 2) identifies five main ways of living by natural, productive labour: the pastoral, the agricultural, the piratical, fishing, and hunting. Four of his categories seem 'natural' to us, at least at the level of category titles; the inclusion of piracy comes as something of a shock. Thucydides' apparent statement of the contrary (1. 5), when he says that in his day piracy was considered disgraceful in 'civilized society' and was confined to the backwoods, is not straightforward historical evidence for his times. Rather, Aristotle's analysis is more abstract, and certainly less partisan.

St Augustine observes (*City of God*, 4. 4):

remove justice, and what are states but gangs of thieves on a large scale? What are robber bands but petty states? A gang is a group of men under the command of a leader, bound by an oath of association, in which the plunder is divided according to an agreed convention. If this villainy wins so many recruits . . . that it acquires a territory, establishes a base, captures cities, and subdues peoples, it then openly assumes for itself the title of state, which is recognized by the rest of the world not because it has renounced aggression, but because it has attained impunity.

He goes on to quote from Cicero (*Republic*, 3. 14. 24) the anecdote of the pirate and Alexander the Great ('because I do it with a small craft I'm called a pirate; because you do it with a great navy you're called an emperor'), and continues (4. 6), 'to attack one's neighbours, to pass on to crush and subdue more remote peoples without provocation, and just from a thirst from domination – what is one to call this but brigandage on the grand scale?'[1] Xenophon (*Symposium*, 5) shares the same sort of view as the august saint, and swallows it without the spoonful of spiritual sugar:

> I have heard of some leaders so greedy for wealth that they were more [note: *more*] notoriously criminal in their search for it than private individuals. For although the latter may sometimes steal, break and enter, and sell free people into slavery in order to support themselves, the former do much worse: they ravage entire countries, put nations to the sword, enslave free states, and all this for the sake of chattels and to fill the coffers of their treasury.[2]

Whether an act of violent acquisition is considered legitimate or not, and whether it is committed by armies or gangs, depends largely on one's point of view and the size of the forces involved. The problem is neither trivial nor confined to ancient history. King Ine of Wessex, attempting to define the different kinds of forcible attack that might be visited upon a householder and his property in Anglo-Saxon England, came up with the following solution: 'if less than seven men are involved, they are thieves; if between seven and thirty-five, they form a gang; if above thirty-five, they are a military expedition' (Grierson 1959, 131). Further progress on the question has been slow. About 1,000 years later (in 1956, to be precise), a special committee set up by the general assembly of the United Nations could not decide whether a definition – *any* definition – of aggression would be useful in international law and order.[3]

[1]   Much later Samuel Daniel shrewdly observed, of both the historical situation and Augustine's views on it, 'Great pirate Pompey lesser pirates quails: / Justice, he sees (as if seducèd), still / Conspires with power, whose cause must not be ill' (*Epistle to Lady Margaret*).
[2]   The speaker's disapproval is evident, but this is not a statement about the morality of conquest in the abstract. His subject is the sad condition of the person who is never satisfied, for whom he feels 'great compassion'.
[3]   This was despite, or perhaps because of, the fact that during these deliberations (8 October to 9 November 1956) war broke out in the Middle East (including an Israeli expedition into Egypt and the Anglo-French invasion of Suez) and the Soviet Union put down the Hungarian popular rising. See Stone 1958.

Historians should be able to make more progress than diplomatists, the latter being concerned with preserving the status quo if their country's conquests were in the past, or upsetting the status quo if their country's conquest was in the past. Thus Blainey (1988, 244), but not the politicians involved at the time, could point out, with regard to Japanese ambitions in the second world war, that

> the vast European empires in the Orient . . . had been won by force or threats, and were held by force and threats. . . . It would not be completely logical for Australia and Britain to argue that any Japanese annexations would be immoral if at the same time they insisted that their own past conquests were decidedly moral.

The philosophical literature seems to have come to the conclusion that things called wars are too complex and diverse to be defined by necessary or sufficient conditions, and that, in the final analysis, whether some conflict is called a war or not is politically, not militarily, motivated. Those on centre stage in the national or international theatre claim for themselves legitimacy and morality; pirates and terrorists are always on the periphery.

We are further blinkered by the international dyslexia which sees only the word 'defence' when armed forces are involved. Greek military activities against the aboriginals of Africa, Asia, and Europe during the so-called colonizing process are regularly described as 'defensive wars against troublesome natives' (though not by Burn 1978, 74). To admit that the Greeks were the invaders, who were fighting to take (not keep) possession of various pockets of land and everything on them, would be incompatible with the status of an ambassador; but we are historians of Greece, not its self-appointed diplomats. Finley demanded a 'steady eye' be applied to the study of warfare, and this in turn demands a certain detachment.

Aristotle possessed such detachment. Besides his specifically designated 'pirate' category, his hunting category also includes significant subcategories (*Pol.* 1255 b–1256 b): game-hunting (of birds and wild animals), people-hunting (i.e. slave-raiding), the hunting of movable goods (i.e. plundering), and the hunting of people and possessions together (i.e. war, 'a natural mode of acquisition'). The different types are linked in an epigram of uncertain authorship: 'hunting is a practice for war; and hunting teaches one to catch a thing concealed; to wait for those coming on; to pursue the fleeing'.[1] For the Greeks in general and Aristotle in particular, man was an animal, and animals were there to be hunted.[2]

Before the emergence of the state, travel outside the settlement was dangerous; after the emergence of the state, travel outside the polis was dangerous. Even if one had a foreign friend or two on the way or at the intended destination, hopping between them could still pose threats to life and liberty. Consider, for example, the story of Theseus. After dispatching Periphetes the club-bearing bandit, Sinis the pine-bending brigand, Phaia the wild sow of Krommyon (either a particularly ferocious wild pig or a murderous and depraved highwaywoman), Skiron of Megara (either a thug with a thing about feet or an archaic Robin Hood), Kerkyon the wrestling ruffian, and Damastes the sadist, Theseus is invited to dinner as a foreign guest by Aigeus and Medea, who, not knowing who he is, intend to poison him at the table (Plutarch, *Theseus*, 8–12).

The hazards of travel, particularly by sea, are well documented in the many poems and epigrams that pray for a safe journey and return, or mourn disappearance or death through shipwreck or at the hands of robbers or pirates, or curse the person or persons unknown who murdered the traveller.[3] Herodotos tells how Arion chose to return from Taras, the Spartan *apoikia* in southern Italy, in a Corinthian ship 'because he had more confidence in the

[1] *Greek Anthology*, Edwards' selection 378, in Burges 1876. The words echo Xen. *Cyr.* 1. 2. 10.
[2] Only one of Aristotle's subcategories is what we now mean and understand by hunting; but ours is a very recent conception. In the eighteenth century Richard Carew (1759, 65) noted that Cornish folk did not much engage in trade, despite a favourable geographical situation, but preferred to 'hunt after a more easie then commendable profit, with little hazard, and (I would I could not say) with less conscience'. He went on to wish them well in their affairs.
[3] E.g. Archil. 8; 12–13; Semon. 1. 15–17; Solon, 13. 43–6; Alc. 34 a, 326 (Lobel-Page); Theog. 671–80; Hipponax, fr. 115. Ibykos is said to have been killed by pirates, Stesichoros by robbers (Suda, s.v. *epitēdeos*).

Corinthians than in anyone else' (1. 24); but 'when the ship was at sea, the crew hatched a plot to throw him overboard and steal all his money'. And that, Herodotos goes on to say, is the story as the Corinthians themselves tell it.

From classical times some effort was made to distinguish between Greek and non-Greek prey; but distinctions in theory are not synonymous with distinctions in practice. Ancient arguments for or against the enslavement of Greeks by Greeks are in fact additional evidence that it happened; and if Greek captives were ransomed back sooner or later, that does not change the fact of their enslavement. Ransom is *purchase*, albeit by someone known to and probably friendly to the enslaved person, who will then be in the ransomer's debt. In the Gortyn lawcode, in fact, the ransomed citizen is to all intents and purposes a *slave* of the citizen who ransoms him, until that debt is paid off.[1] And if the captive awaiting ransom had to wait long, he might acquire an accent or dialect that struck his own people as foreign, as happened to an Athenian captured by the Spartans and sold in Leukas.[2] In that case, establishing one's membership of the polis could be tricky; being Greek didn't count. Taken together with various other facts – that some slaves were born and raised in Greece, that an abandoned infant could be raised as a slave, that slaves could not usually be identified as such by their physical appearance, that a promiscuous Athenian woman could be sold into slavery by her father, that exiles illegally re-entering Attica could be enslaved, and that anyone convicted of falsely assuming the prerogatives of citizenship (such as by marrying an Athenian citizen, or failing to pay the *metoikion* and get a patron) could also be enslaved – it seems hard to avoid the conclusion that there was plenty of room for confusion about whether a Greek-speaking slave was a foreign Greek or a foreigner.

[1]   This was also the case in Athens – see Dem. 11 (Nikostratos) – the only circumstance in which enslavement of one Athenian by another for debt was permitted; Garlan 1988, 15.
[2]   Dem. 57 (Euboulides). Solon's claim to have brought back Athenians who no longer spoke the Attic 'tongue' (what we would call dialect, rather than language) is almost certainly to be seen in this light.

Ways and means

I wish now to make a few simple points about the Greeks' *ability* to use force as a means acquisition. Buried in subsection 8 of chapter 2 of Weber's long chapter on 'Non-legitimate domination' ('the city') is a profound observation. It is the distinction between societies whose armies are self-equipped, and those whose armies are not.[1] In characteristic fashion, Weber elaborates this distinction sporadically through dozens of examples drawn from the scholarship of tens of specialists over hundreds of pages. It is the difference between armed and defenceless citizens; between a leader dependent on the goodwill of the led, and subjects dependent on the ruler's goodwill; between persuasion and command; between military life as a 'trade' and as a 'job'; between negotiators and bureaucrats; between popular and despotic power. This is not the place to undertake a clarification of Weber's model, or a revision of the examples in line with modern scholarship; those would be mammoth tasks. Here I shall simply make a few points about the armed citizen, and about the society in which the citizens constitute the strongest coercive force in the state.

There are no statistics to show whether the incidence of highway, or high seas, robbery in ancient Greece was greater or less than that of mugging in our modern cities; but we can be sure that there was no police force ensuring law and order within the state, and that the only guardian angels were oneself and one's friends. What Oedipus remembered as a fracas at a crossroads on the road to Thebes is reported in Thebes as an attack by bandits (Sophocles, *Oedipus the King*, 122–3; 715–16; 802–13); and many years later Oedipus is concerned about this incident only because of the possibility that his own father was among the four men, including a herald, whom he *slew* in this fracas.

Everyone had to defend himself, in so-called peacetime as well as in wartime. The use of violence by private individuals was not a negation of law and order, but a necessary adjunct to the public legal process (Lintott 1982). The so-called 'police' in Athens were

---

[1] Weber 1978, ii. 1260–2. Weber was concerned with the difference between eastern and western societies, but his distinction also illuminates the differences between Sparta and other Greek states.

essentially 'bouncers' for public meetings and 'muscle' for magistrates. Community or citizen militias, not a standing or paid army, underwrote the safety and freedom of the community's members.

One corollary of citizen self-defence is that weapons of some description will have been in every home, and their owner would be familiar with their use. Another is that weapons will have had a high priority in every household budget (see for example Xenophon, *Poroi* (*Ways and Means*), 4), since personal freedom and survival depended on them; each citizen would be armed as well as possible according to his peculiar talents.[1] A further corollary is that the state's coercive organizations possessed weapons that were only as good as those of the citizens; there were no 'hi-tech' arms that could be used for, or against, the citizens, of either the howitzer or the water-cannon variety.

If there was a government, it had no *dependent* coercive organization (unless it employed mercenaries) with which to cull dissident members or citizens into submission. If it did have a supplied mercenary force, in a political sense those soldiers were simply another armed group supporting one particular faction. The early-established and long-continuing importance of the civil laws is to be seen in the context of – and as an antidote to – the settlement of civil and political disagreements by a resort to arms, *stasis*. People needed faith in their laws and the interpreters thereof, for if the system was not equitable, or if some were seen to be above the law, the obvious method of restitution was a resort to arms – the arms hanging in every house. Failure to respond to inequity in this manner led to the charge that one was in subjection. Alternatively, one could take one's arms and go fight for a new home elsewhere. All this provided a fertile physical, social, and psychological environment for military entrepreneurs: armed insurrectionists, mercenaries, pirates, and adventurers.

The arguments advanced above justify alternative assumptions to those normally made, in the absence of evidence favouring a particular interpretation. For example, if archaeology indicates that a native settlement was destroyed by fire or abandoned at about the time when the Greeks are thought to have arrived, then instead of attributing this disruption to non-Greeks (that is,

---

[1]   E.g. Alkaios' lounge seems to have been bedecked with bronze armour and swords, but no spears (fr. 357).

anyone rather than the Greeks) we should attribute it to the Greeks. If localized versions of Greek names appear in local records, then instead of attributing them to high-status Greeks living with the natives, or high-status natives pretending that they are Greeks, we could equally well attribute them to Greek slaves of native owners. If poor copies of Greek products appear in local contexts, then instead of attributing them to native craftsmen with a poor grasp of Greek style, it might be better to attribute them to Greeks who are poor craftsmen (for example, Greeks who were not making pots before they left home). If Greeks sailed in warships, which had little storage space, then instead of calling these Greeks traders and deducing that they traded goods of small size and large value, I call them warriors and note that goods of small size and large value are precisely the kind of goods that are sought and stolen by the typical thief.[1]

I now turn to the period when governments were young, or merely a twinkle in some settler's eye, when men – unlike the sophisticated Athenians of Thucydides' day – daily carried weapons about their person.

War and expansion

Settlement was preceded by voyages of exploration, adventure, and raiding (see Purcell 1990). One of the favourite motifs on geometric vases is the opposed landing from a ship (Kirk 1949, 144 and n. 61; Snodgrass 1964, 193). Kirk (1949, 145 and 151) points out that

> the central position of the ships in the scenes of land–sea fighting certainly makes the crews (i.e. the pirates), not the shore forces, the heroes of the piece. . . . piratical raids are more what the Geometric scenes suggest . . . they must have been a not uncommon part of the life of any maritime people at this period. In brief, there is nothing in the Geometric ship-scenes to connect them with any specific incident in legend or to show even that they represent any *extraordinary* event of daily life [emphasis original].

[1] Most interpretations are based on the first of each pair of assumptions, usually without any acknowledgement of the alternatives. See e.g. Coja, Bryce, Robinson, and Graham, all in Descoeudres (ed.) 1990.

Eighth- and seventh-century West Greek vases depict similar scenes, suggesting not only 'that the ships which visited or sailed from the Greek colonies of southern Italy and Sicily were of the same type',[1] but also that they were engaged in the same sort of activities.

In another period of expansion, Hakluyt (1903–5, 443) wrote:

> So sondrie men entering into these discoveries propose unto themselves severall endes. Some seeke authoritie and places of commandement, others experience by seeing of the worlde, the most part worldly and transitorie gaine, and that often times by unlawful and dishonest meanes.

Of the same period, Kenneth Andrews (1984, 31) comments:

> it is hardly necessary to dwell upon the more or less crude pursuit of riches which was obviously the main if not the sole motive of most of the ventures in expeditions of trade or plunder, in many colonising projects and even in some exploring voyages, nor on that insatiable thirst for fame and honour which undoubtedly drove Gilbert, Ralegh, Cavendish and some less renowned gentlemen . . . to undertake actions they deemed noble, however sordid their conduct . . . may appear in the eyes of a different generation.

We, unfortunately, have less evidence to work with than early modern historians, and the evidence we do have is sometimes frustratingly vague. People and states just seem to 'acquire' things, and archaeology (to borrow a phrase from A. N. Whitehead) leaves the darkness of the subject unobscured (see e.g. Trillmich 1990). Reading Herodotos, one could be forgiven for thinking that money grew on trees, particularly in Italy, Sicily, and Thrace. Arion, for example, 'felt a desire to sail to Italy and Sicily. This he did, and after acquiring a great many things in those countries, he decided to return to Corinth' (1. 24). There is no indication of *what* he acquired, or how. Thucydides is no better in this respect:

---

[1]   Humphreys 1983, 166; see also Coldstream 1977, 110; 352–6. Note the prone figures in some pictures. Kirk correctly says the interpretation of these as rowers is arbitrary; I would add that interpreting them as corpses is only a little less arbitrary. Is it too fanciful to recall the depictions of slaves in the holds of transatlantic ships, which are too familiar to us, and too similar to these, to require separate illustration? As for seaborne raiders, it is probably not irrelevant that when Alkaios and Theognis seek a symbol and metaphor for stasis and strife, they choose a ship (Alc. 6; 73; 326; Theog. 457–60; 575–6; 619–20; 667–82; 855–6).

'As seafaring became more common and capital reserves came into existence . . .' (1. 7).

In Theognis, similarly, we hear of wealth and its acquisition, but not a single explicit word about the getting of it. There are vague references to making a living at sea,[1] and ships and seafaring are often used as analogies.[2] (By contrast, agriculture is cited only once, lines 1197–202, as a point of nostalgic reference in contrast to the poet's current involvement in a 'most hateful voyage'.) Similarly in Solon, one man roams over the sea risking his life in the hope of bringing home possessions (13. 43–6). Solon himself is said to have brought in a law concerning friendly associations formed for the purpose of raiding and piracy (Gaius, *Digest*, 47. 22. 4; quoted in Ormerod 1924, 68 n. 1).

A few relevant sources are explicit. Odysseus, posing as a Cretan, declares that, before the Greeks embarked for Troy,

> nine times I led men on expeditions in swift ships
> against folk in other lands, and many things came to me.
> I took what I wanted, and much of it I got back in the lottery.
> Soon my house was increased, and from that time on
> I was feared and respected among the Cretans.
>
> (*Od.* 14. 230–4)

Note the sequence: from his successful leadership of raids he acquired much, some of his assets increased and thereafter he was feared (not altogether surprisingly) and respected by his fellow Cretans.

When Greeks like Odysseus first arrived, the natives would have been inexperienced in Greek tactics and usually easy prey. Greek military supremacy is obvious from the extent of their conquests and their popularity as mercenaries. Their general inability to establish and hold settlements in areas controlled by more advanced cultures (such as Assyria, Phoenicia, Egypt, and Carthage) was probably a function of the disparity in organization and numbers, rather than in the military ability each individual could bring to bear; for Greeks were at the same time engaged as mercenaries by these and other peoples. Successful resistance by those more disorganized and acephalous peoples on whom the Greeks preferred to presume demanded the adaptation of military practice, in particular, in order

---

[1] Theog. 179–80; 511–22; 691–2; 1165–6; 1197–1202; 1375–6.
[2] Lines 83–6; 113–14; 457–60; 575–6; 619–20; 855–6; 963–70; 1271–4; 1361–2.

to meet the invaders on equal terms. The Etruscan 'adoption' of hoplite tactics, for example, was probably learnt on the hard field of battle, rather than on the parade ground under the instruction of some anonymous and magnanimous Greek.

Tartessos was probably discovered by Greeks on a long-distance voyage of adventure. Kolaios' record-breaking profit from the voyage (Herodotos, 4. 152) does not bear close scrutiny, as Ormerod saw (1924, 101 n. 1). The word Herodotos uses for the dedication made by Kolaios and his crew after they discovered this previously untouched (in the sense of undamaged, undefiled) *emporion* is *dekatē*, the technical term for one-tenth of the spoils of war (Pritchett 1971, 93–100). The Argive-shaped bowl they dedicated symbolized the event; its legs were formed by three submissive, kneeling figures.[1] Since Kolaios' Samians were reputedly the first to discover this area of Spain and its natives, this was war in the Hobbesian sense, and the spoils are properly considered as plunder or booty, the fruits of military entrepreneurship.

In the process of Greek expansion abroad, if an area was inhabited there were four theoretically possible outcomes. (1) The Greeks could be repulsed; (2) the locals could be expelled; (3) the two could cohabit, willingly or not; or (4) the area could be deserted by everybody – a scenario obviously difficult to document and uninteresting to consider. The first three outcomes, however, will now be examined in turn.

Repulsion of the Greeks

Let us suppose that the Greeks are repulsed, and that native life returns to normal – until the next band arrives. In the process the natives may acquire a few trophies – a piece of Greek armour, perhaps, such as Archilochos' shield or the early seventh-century Corinthian helmet found at Jerez, or some abandoned crockery. If resistance is sufficient, the area remains native. If the Greeks continue coming and cannot be repulsed, native life will not return to normal, but move into one of the other three scenarios.

[1] So, in the fifth century, marble Persian supported a bronze tripod dedicated in the olympieion at Athens (Paus. 1. 18. 7), and the Persian Stoa at Sparta had statues of Persians in place of pillars to support the roof (Vitruvius, 1. 1. 6).

Expulsion of the locals

The Greeks establish a beachhead camp; the natives are expelled, and retreat to defensive positions or seek safety in numbers by combining into fewer, larger settlements. Many Greek camps were established on an offshore island or an easily guarded pro- montory;[1] this helped protect the camp from retaliatory attack by the natives, and helped enforce the captivity of any natives taken in the fighting. Alternatively, or somewhat later, the Greeks could set up camp on the site of the nearest native village.[2]

Sicily is an interesting case. Scholars frequently comment on its mineral poverty and its lack of attraction for Greek settlers; yet some of the settlements established there grew to be among the most powerful and wealthy cities of the Greek world. Not least among these was Syracuse. The richest man in Sokrates' day, according to the pseudo-Platonic dialogue called *Eryxias*, was a Syracusan whose vast wealth was reckoned in land and 'an unlimited quantity of those other things which constitute wealth: slaves, horses, gold, and silver' (392–3). This ordering of chattels, in which land and slaves precede all else, is echoed throughout Greek literature, from Homer ('and I had slaves by thousands and many other good things by which men live well and are called wealthy'; *Od.* 17. 422–3) to Aristotle (besides land, 'wealth may consist of slaves, cattle, money, and in addition movables'; *Pol.* 1267 b).

The usual interpretation of the success of the Sicilian cities, for which Finley (1968, 34) may stand as representative, is that Sicily exported 'wheat, olives, wine, timber, fruit, nuts, and vegetables'. But recent scholarship has shown that Athens, the doyenne of grain-importers according to the modernists, 'was less dependent on foreign grain, and in particular on distant sources of grain, than is generally assumed', and 'became dependent on grain from

[1]   E.g. Berezan (Olbia), Epidamnos, Ischia (off Cumae), Kerkyra, Kyzikos, Ortygia (at Syracuse), Platea (off Cyrene), Saint Kiriak (Apollo- nia in the Black Sea), San Martin (at Emporion, Ampurias in Spain), Sinope, Thasos, and Trotilon (Megara Hyblaia).
[2]   E.g. Berezan, St Blaise (Massilia), Mesembria, Cumae, Pantikapaion, and most settlements in Sicily (Boardman 1980, 189), e.g. Akragas, Gela, Katane, Leontinoi, Naxos, Satyrion, and Selinous. Some of these may be cases of cohabitation (see next subsection).

foreign sources later than is generally assumed'; that is, well after the Persian wars (Garnsey 1985, 74–5; 1988, 107–19). As for fruit and vegetables, market gardening occurs closest to the areas of consumption; until modern techniques of preservation, storage, and containerization were developed, long-distance trade in these was a non-starter. The clue to Sicily's attraction for Greeks lies in Finley's earlier observation (ibid., 34) that 'inter-local trade within Sicily seems largely to have been restricted to traffic from Greek communities to the natives in the interior, rather than between the Greek cities'.

We have records of such 'inter-local trade'. Herodotos (6. 23) tells how Zankle fell to the Samians and Rhegians while 'Skythes, the ruler of Zankle, and all his men were trying to capture a native Sikel town' (see also Thuc. 6. 4). According to Diodoros (5. 6) the native Sikanians 'originally lived in villages, building them on the most defensible hills because of the pirates'. Zankle had originally been settled by Chalkidian pirates ejected from Cumae (Thuc. 6. 4–5; Pausanias, 4. 23. 7). The sequel to the story is also illuminating: the dispossessed Zankleans appealed to Hippokrates, tyrant of Gela, for assistance. On his arrival he betrayed and enslaved them, establishing friendly relations with the new occupants of Zankle while profiting to the tune of 'half of all the movable property and slaves in the town, and all those in the open country'. Those who escaped went on to found Himera, described by Finley (1968, 22) as 'a curious site to choose for, though well protected against attack and useful as an anchorage for ships, it has little else in its favour'. There they were joined by some Syracusan exiles.

It seems they did not change profession. We may imagine some of their descendants joining Dionysios of Phokaia, who, when the Persians defeated the Ionian rebels at Lade in 494, sailed to Phoenicia where he 'caught a number of cargo vessels and took from them property of considerable value, then sailed for Sicily, where he set up a base for piratical raids against Carthaginian and Etruscan ships' (Hdt. 6. 17).

The Phokaians, in fact, had a rather distinguished record for this sort of thing. They transported themselves and any 'wares' they may have carried in pentekonters. (There was no distinction in the archaic period between merchant ship and man-of-war, between merchant crew and warrior crew – they had to extricate themselves from whatever trouble they ran into – but there were distinctions between types of ship, and the pentekonter was the warship *par excellence*.) The Phokaians charted unknown waters, opening up the Adriatic, Tyrrhenian sea, and western Mediterranean as well as the Atlantic seaboard. Justin (43. 3) suggests that they were occupational pirates; Strabo says the same of their most famous colony, Massalia,[1] and their known activities are consistent with this.

When in 545 the growing might of Persia threatened their homeland, some of the Phokaians left to join their *apoikia* on Corsica. 'For five years they lived at Alalia with the earlier settlers, and built temples. Because they plundered and carried off all the people in the vicinity, the Etruscans and Carthaginians made common cause to attack them, each with a fleet of sixty ships' (Hdt. 1. 166). The Phokaians are said to have won this battle, albeit in a Pyrrhic victory. Herodotos tells us plainly that the cause of the battle – not a war, commercial or otherwise – was the Phokaians' predatory behaviour, and there are several important points to note. (1) In the course of five years they succeeded, by plunder and pillage, in aggravating two independent nations sufficiently to unite them, not an easy feat in the ancient world. (2) Their depredations upon the people of Agylla (Caere) were serious enough to drive the latter into stoning to death (rather than ransoming, enslaving, or selling) all Phokaians in their possession after the battle. (3) They were confident and professional enough to defeat 120 warships (assuming the story is true), twice their own numerical strength. As Sir Henry Mainwaring, an early modern pirate-cum-admiral, pointed out, pirates 'are commonly the most daring and serviceable in war'.[2]

A similar story is told of a small band of Samian exiles who, having plundered the Siphnians of 100 talents, established themselves at Kydonia in northern Crete. Like the Phokaians,

---

[1]   Strab. 4. 180: in early times they 'trusted in the sea', by which he normally means 'were pirates'.

[2]   Cited by Andrews 1984, 28, who adds that 'the careers of Drake, Frobisher and many less famous men bear out the truth of this remark'. In this context we should mention the Aiginetans; despite their relatively small fleet (30 ships), Aigina won the individual and team prizes for distinguished service at Salamis, and were commended for their performance at Salamis and Artemision (Hdt. 7. 181; 8. 84–92).

they enjoyed five years of great prosperity and built temples; in the sixth year they were attacked and enslaved by Aiginetans and locals acting in concert (Hdt. 3. 58–9), apparently in another act of joint retribution. Other early pioneers were the Euboeans, about whom all I shall say here is that they were renowned in antiquity as 'far-famed lords of war', not far-famed smiths.

'Trade' is often cited as a vague, catch-all motivation for Greek expansion, with the assumption that the Greeks acquired foreign goods by some form of exchange. Possible foreign goods sought are said to have been manufactured items such as textiles which, partly by virtue of being foreign, would be regarded as luxuries, or primary products such as iron. But if the archaic Greeks had wanted luxury goods, and if they had been prepared to exchange for them, they would have taken their own goods to the established ports of the materially more advanced civilizations, such as Tyre. A few did. Significantly, the sixth-century hell-fire and brimstone prophet Ezekiel recorded (27: 5–25) that while Arabs and Africans were bringing in spices, gems, embroideries, horses (with riders), and so on to exchange in Tyre, the Greeks were shipping in slaves and bronze vessels (not, be it noted, pots). From Joel (3: 6) we learn that what they received in exchange included other slaves; 'the children of Judah and of Jerusalem', he tells the men of Tyre and Sidon, 'have you sold unto the Greeks'.[1]

From the location of their settlements and *emporia*, however, we can fairly infer that the majority of Greek settlers did not want such goods, or were not prepared to pay for them. Literary evidence supports this. For example, the Etruscans of Agylla – the same who stoned the Phokaians – enjoyed a high reputation among the Greeks for abstaining from piracy *despite* the fact that they were strong enough to have practised it (Strab. 5. 220). One gets the distinct impression that Greeks resorted to buying only when other options were closed. Most new settlements (including

[1] See also Amos (1: 6, 9; 2: 6) for the men of Gaza, Tyre, and Israel as slave-traders. What Tyre gave in exchange for the diverse goods she received from north, south, east, and west is never made explicit; the Hebrew word used is of general meaning, like the Greek *chremata*. However, every example of the word's meaning given by van Dijk (1968) involves the buying and selling of people.

emporia) were in 'backward' regions, even those in the east. The potential for plunder in such places was very limited, and the most plentiful, if not the only, commodity for the Greeks to take was people.

Even the famous *emporion* of Al Mina at the mouth of the Orontes in north Syria was not then, or later, on a main route to or from anywhere; swamp vegetation may have covered most of the valley,[1] just as Massalia was surrounded by marshes. If Al Mina was planted with a view to trade, the Greeks displayed inordinate misjudgement. Since they chose to return there time and again after repeated and deliberate destructions, the implication is that it was not their judgement that was unsound, but the hypothesis that attempts to explain their choice with reference to trade. The point can be argued from another perspective. The majority of excavated pots at Al Mina are drinking-vessels rather than storage vessels. Moreover, these drinking-vessels constitute such a small amount in total that 'pottery could have formed only a small proportion of the commodities offered by Aegean visitors and residents, which must have consisted largely of perishable goods' (Coldstream 1977, 95) – perishable goods that did not require containers, and assuming of course that they did offer anything. This is all very cosy, but can we justifiably assume that they were not occupied in the honourable business of man-hunting?[2]

Al Mina is not untypical; the ceramic, metallic, and lithic evidence at a Greek site overseas is usually too meagre to support the idea that goods made from those materials were produced or

---

[1]   As it did before it was drained in 1953–5; van Zeist and Woldring 1980, 112. Baly 1963, 28, is unaware of the recent date of the drainage.
[2]   Greeks and others had raided the coasts of the Levant and Egypt since Homeric times, irritating the centralized powers into whose orbits they came. Assyrian documents speak of *Yawani* (Ionians) raiding the Phoenician coast *c*.730 BC. In 720 Sargon destroyed Hamath and deported the population, resettling the area with some 6,000 Assyrians. Al Mina and Tarsus were bases on the edge of the Assyrian empire from which forays into the interior could be launched and escape made. Ashdod, further south, provided a convenient base at the southern end of the empire, from which Egypt could also be raided by sea. In 712 Sargon marched again and destroyed Ashdod. Al Mina and Tarsus were probably destroyed during his successor Sennacherib's reign, *c*.696.

used for exchange. Consequently, it is usually assumed that the goods in question were perishables, or that what was exchanged was 'invisibles' such as skills; slaves are perishables like wine, oil, foodstuffs, and textiles, and have to be considered as an archaeologically invisible component in the economy. All this is common 'knowledge' and common practice; but two things are often overlooked. (1) This set of beliefs is based on the assumption that the Greeks exchanged with natives, and did not simply take from them. (2) Like wine, oil, foodstuffs, and textiles, slaves were *produced*, by the toil of slavery's counterpart to the plough, the press, or the loom: the spear. 'With this I plough, with this I sow, with this I reap the field' (see epigraph).

Let us, then, consider one of the few individual settlers known to us, Archilochos. 'His fragments leave us in no doubt that [he] was turbulent and fierce', says Rankin (1977, 1; cf. Lefkowitz 1981, 25–31, esp. 31); or, if one prefers to see the 'I' in his poems as representative rather than biographical (as do Miralles and Pòrtulas 1983), we can generalize and say that Archilochos stands for not one but many turbulent and fierce settlers. His father or grandfather had led a Parian expedition to the island of Thasos off the coast of Thrace, whence forays into the mainland continued into and beyond Archilochos' lifetime. The famous shield song (fr. 5), despite what philhellenes are wont to imagine, hardly refers to the defence of his island, since the Saians were mainlanders and landlubbers.

> Some Saian flaunts my shield, which I left by a bush –
> although it was perfectly good – because I had to.
> But I saved myself. What do I care about that shield?
> It's gone. I'll get me another no worse.

Archilochos was not fond of Thasos, to put it mildly (frs. 20–1; 102; 228). He went there because he was in need (fr. 295; see below), becoming a 'soldier of fortune' (fr. 216) and specializing in hand-to-hand combat (fr. 3). His fellow settlers seem to have been in similar straits (fr. 109). What were later called 'necessitous persons', otherwise known as the scum of Europe, were to be found on what was to them the equally unpleasant coast of Africa as slave-traders and factors.

Modern assumption and clever interpretation[1] 'rescue' Archilochos from himself and from his ancient (but not contemporary) Kritias, who cites but does not quote the poem (fr. 295) in which Archilochos states that his mother Enipo was a Thracian slave; there may have been as many as 1,000 of these on Thasos (Rankin 1977, 15). The 'spear song' (fr. 2) quoted earlier strongly suggests that he had a slave woman as attendant (and no doubt bedfellow), acquired, like everything else he mentions, by the spear.[2] Archilochos was hopping mad with one of the Peisistratids for upsetting things in Thrace by offering the natives pure gold (fr. 93 *a*); the third-century inscription quoting this poem adds that they got their just deserts when some of them were killed by Archilochos' Parians and others by the Thracians. This fury is intelligible only if the Peisistratids introduced something new into Greek–Thracian relations; in addition to the offer of goods of real value, Archilochos' sarcastic reference to lyre- and flute-players implies that it is the absence of weapons. The story thus indicates the two main trajectories Greek–native relations could follow: bellicosity or peaceful accommodation.

If military superiority was established in the local area, what began as *ad hoc* raids may have developed into a regular slave-raiding industry, or a system of slave tribute paid by dominated tribes in return for protection (from the settlers as well as from other natives and Greeks). To be paid with plunder, particularly human booty, is a very natural and common reward for such assistance. During his expedition of 1567, Hawkins adopted the tactic of intervening in a tribal war. He accepted POWs in payment for his services, and then shipped these slaves – along with others acquired, in his own words, 'partly by the sword and partly by other means' – to the Caribbean for sale (Andrews 1984,

---

[1] E.g. Gerber 1970, 8; Lefkowitz 1981, 26 (but cf. 31).

[2] Being Thracian was no bar to being perceived by the Greeks as attractive. Rhodopis, sweetheart of Sappho's brother, was a Thracian slave prostitute (Hdt. 2. 134–5). Anakreon knew of another, not yet domesticated: 'Thracian filly, why do you look at me askance, coldly shunning me and taking me for a boor? Know that I could put a bridle on you, and hold the reins, and get you to the finishing-post. But now you graze in the meadows, playing and frisking, for you have no able horseman to mount you' (*PMG* 72, trans. Fränkel 1975, 296, with modifications).

110). Magellan tried the same tactic in the Philippines, but the islanders declined his offer (Dodge 1976, 5).

The natives further from the camp would suffer less regular incursions, and were forewarned about the invaders' presence and their habits. They might offer gifts (asked or unasked) as a natural and spontaneous reaction to the threat of attack; among which slaves (or 'hostages') would again be at or near the top of the list (if not immediately, then as soon as alternatives were exhausted). Villagers would obviously not want to reduce their own members to this condition (except perhaps persistent criminals), and if inter-tribal warfare did not already exist to produce POWs (who may hitherto have been killed, sacrificed, ransomed, exchanged for other POWs, and so on), then it would soon begin. The assertion that the 'primitive' Thracians offered their own kind for sale (Hdt. 5. 6) probably reflects this later stage; 'their own' probably meant other inhabitants of Thrace, not members of their own community.[1] If comparative evidence is a reliable guide, the Greek demand for slaves probably stimulated the war and raiding that were already producing slaves for those tribes who kept them, such as (in the Thracian area) the Ardians, Dacians, and Gardani (Garlan 1988, 104). It will also have encouraged the seizure of other people by any means available; opportunist kidnapping was something of which travellers and hosts alike had to beware. The most reputable sources of income in Thracian thinking were war and plunder (Hdt. 5. 6).

Alternatively, if resistance was or became indomitable, at a certain point it would become easier and cheaper, in lives and effort, to exchange for the desired goods rather than fight for them.[2] This meant that other goods had to be offered in exchange; which may seem obvious to us, but then we do not live in a world in which acquisition by toil of the spear is considered a legitimate occupation and commerce an illegitimate one. Plato, for example, though it is necessary to point out that peaceful

---

[1] Again, recidivist criminals might be the exception. It is not unknown for people in slave societies to pass off slaves as their own children; see e.g. Twaddle 1988, 122. Many negroes were also sold into slavery by other negroes.

[2] See Guzzo 1990, noting that the two known cases of peaceful accommodation between Greeks and natives in southern Italy are late.

exchange required goods to be offered as well as received (*Republic*, 370 e–371 b). Goods had to be produced or obtained from elsewhere to exchange for local items. Native slaves would probably discharge many of the necessary functions – farming, quarrying, smelting, hewing wood, building walls and ships, and rowing the boats they had built which transported them to market. The Peisistratids' gold did not come from Attica; the Peisistratids were not miners.

Cohabitation

The strongest type of cohabitation involves the domination of one group by another; either enforced servitude or voluntary subservience on condition of not being sold abroad. The natives were reduced to some form of tribute-paying servitude; there are many examples of this. Of those in mainland Greece and the islands the Helots of Messenia and Lakedaimon, the Klarotai of Crete, and the Penestai of Thessaly are only the most famous; other possible cases are the Arisbians (at Methymna on Lesbos), Gymnetes (Argos), Konipodes (Epidauros), and Korynephoroi (Sikyon). Known cases abroad include the Bithynoi of Byzantion, the Mariandynoi of Herakleia on the Pontos, and the Kyllyrioi (or Kallikyrioi) of Syracuse; while the same sort of servile populations may have existed at Epizephyrian Lokris, Gela, Sybaris, Taras, Kyzikos, Olbia, Kolophon, Miletos, and Teos.[1]

This is rather a lot in a relatively small area, and the quantity is quite surprising, since the successful enslavement of neighbours or local peoples is historically very rare (Blackburn 1988, 268). The reasons were appreciated by Plato and Aristotle, among others.[2] Slaves are easier to handle when disoriented. Separated from home, family, and community, wrenched from their traditions, history, and self-identity, they are isolated and psychologically

---

[1] See Garlan 1988, 102–5; on Kolophon, add Mimnermos, fr. 9.
[2] 'Slaves who are to submit to their condition quietly should neither be all of one stock, nor, as far as possible, of one speech' (Pl. *Laws*, 777). 'The people who farm [the territory] should ideally, and if we can choose will, be slaves – but slaves not drawn from a single stock, or from stocks of a spirited temper' (Arist. *Pol.* 1330 a).

enfeebled; in their new surroundings they are non-persons, socially dead (Patterson 1982, esp. chs 2–3). This is not so in the case of those enslaved in their own lands, the Helot and serf types; but if they are privately owned, the threat of alienation through sale can be used to control them. One example of such a threat is recorded in the poetry of Meleagros (first century BC):

> Let him be sold, although not yet weaned from his mother's breast. Let him be sold. Why should I raise this bold thing? For he is naturally sly in appearance and fast underfoot, and he scratches the skin with his nails, and frequently laughs in the middle of a burst of tears. In addition he will not shut up, sit still and be quiet; he's wild – even his mother cannot tame him. He is in every respect precocious. Therefore he shall be sold. If any trader, leaving port, wants to buy the boy, let him step forward. But see, now he is supplicating, bathed in tears. Then I will not sell you. Cheer up. Remain here in my house with Zenophila.

What began as equal or willing cohabitation could become unequal or unwilling, and vice versa. For the first and second generations of women the latter was the norm, as Greek colonizing was a male-only affair. Overseas, captive women were taken as 'wives', in the euphemized language of gentle domination upon which Bourdieu (1977, 190–7) has cast so much light.[1] The first daughters were probably regarded more highly than the first 'wives', who were usually seized from the local communities after their menfolk had been killed. Alternatively, there may have been marriages of convenience between native hosts and their Greek 'guests'. One of the legends about the foundation of Massalia concerns the marriage of a local girl whose native, 'maiden' name was Petta, which probably meant something small, furry, and affectionate (Rankin 1987, 38).[2] Her Greek husband was Euxeinos, 'Goodguest' (or -host); her 'married' name was Aristoxene, which goes one better. All three names are, of course, appropriate for the purposes of the legend.

However, the flow of women in such 'marriages' was in one

---

[1] It has to be said that some moderns are more prone to euphemism than the ancients; e.g. Boardman 1980, 190: 'At any rate, it is clear that in most places [in Sicily] the Greeks and Sikels got on well enough, even if only in the relationship of master and slave.'

[2] Arist. *Constitution of the Massaliots* (in Ath. 576 a–b); Just. 43. 3. 4.

direction only; and as one might expect, however well the relationship with the natives began, it probably deteriorated. In the case of the Massaliotes, by the next generation the natives were attempting to rid themselves of their 'guests', and the fighting apparently continued for centuries (ibid.). A similar story exists about the Phokaians at Lampsakos (Plutarch, *Brave Deeds of Women*, 18). However, the reliability of both stories is questionable; the Phokaians seem to have liked and promoted this image of themselves as warmly welcomed friends of barbarians (we have the same type of story for Tartessos). Recent research from the Celtic viewpoint has concluded that Massalia's main trade, more or less from its foundation, was in slaves (Nash 1985, 45–63, esp. 53–4), of whom some were acquired by exchange, particularly with West Hallstatt Celts to the north, others by harvesting the local territory and waters.[1]

The one town singled out by Nash (1985, 53) in connection with the Massaliot slave trade is Gravisca, a port of Agylla in Etruria – the same Agylla that the Phokaians from Alalia plundered. An aniconic Apollo Agyllieus was dedicated by Sostratos (Torelli 1977, 398–458); the dedicator has been identified more or less plausibly with Sostratos of Aigina, or a relative of his. Sostratos of Aigina was the only man in Greek popular mythology who was thought to have been richer than Kolaios, the discoverer of Tartessos (Hdt. 4. 152). He has also, with less certainty, been linked to the Attic black-figured SOS vases, all dated to c.535–505, of which those of known provenance all come from Etruria.[2] Even if this second identification is correct, the rich

[1]   The Ligurians may have been caught between Celts and Massaliotes, and the victims of raids by the former and 'protection' by the latter. It may only be a coincidence, but Hdt. observes (5. 9) that 'the word *sigunēs* is used by the Ligurians above Massalia for "trader" (*kapēlos*), [while] in Cyprus it means "spear" '. Note also the change in west-central Celtic culture around the time of Massalia's settlement, from small, dispersed villages of about 40 or fewer persons, with egalitarian social structure, to hill-forts with populations of hundreds and growing social stratification.
[2]   There is, in fact, a difficulty with the identification. The idea of an Aiginetan trading Attic vases in the late sixth century is at variance with the 'unheralded' war going on between the two states at the time. If the Aiginetans were in the habit of burning Phaleron and raiding the Attic coast, one would expect an Aiginetan to get short shrift in Athenian markets.

Aiginetan Sostratos did not make his fortune selling Attic pots abroad; it is almost an economic law that in pre-modern societies the profit on an overseas venture is made not on the outward, but on the return journey. What, then, did he take back to Greece? What could he acquire in Etruria or elsewhere that realized such a hefty profit in Greece?

The answer is probably to be found in Aigina's reputation. Apart from its open-ended 'trading' fame – and Aigina founded no colonies of either the *apoikia* or the *emporion* variety – there are two exceptional features of the island. (1) It does not seem to have had a significant metic population, power and 'trading' interests notwithstanding (Whitehead 1977, 50–1). (2) It had a phenomenal number of slaves. The actual number does not matter;[1] the point is that in a world without statistics Aigina was seen as a major slave-holder. Aigina is an island with few natural resources in a small territory; yet it was one of the most powerful and wealthy archaic states. Are we to believe that its great wealth was acquired entirely through freight charges and middleman profits? Recent arguments on archaic Greek trade, or rather the dearth of it, suggest that this explanation is no more credible than that offered by Herodotos (9. 80): that Aigina's wealth was founded on the exploitation of thieving Helot booty-collectors who were ignorant of the difference between bronze and gold.

Besides the evolution of scenario (2), expulsion of the locals, to scenario (3), cohabitation, it was also possible for cohabitation and co-operation to follow immediately as a result of the incoming Greeks joining one of the native groups in the vicinity, though one is hard pressed to find examples. We may, however, cite 'permitted' settlements in areas controlled by other powers, such as Abydos (where Gyges of Lydia allowed Milesians to settle) and Naukratis (where Amasis allowed Greeks to settle).

In scenarios (2) and (3), native expulsion, subservience, or co-operation allowed the Greek camp to step down from a permanent war footing. They could then afford to relocate away from the inconvenience (and perhaps discomfort) of the original island or promontory to another more spacious environment, or establish a *peraia* (mainland territory) on the mainland. Once

---

[1]   It is 470,000 according to [Arist.] *Constitution of the Aiginetans*, in Ath. 6. 272 b.

the camp took on some semblance of permanence, territoriality would become important. The surrounding land was allotted to community, deity, and individuals, and efforts began to be directed to future production: ploughing, planting, and sowing for the next harvest. This raises the second oft-cited motive for Greek expansion: land hunger or overpopulation.

A recent discussion amply demonstrates the unjustified and unjustifiable leap that is made when scholars link expansion and settlement abroad with demographic change and land shortage (Podlecki 1984, 32):

> [Kritias] reported that Archilochos 'left Paros because of poverty and need, and went to Thasos' [Archil. fr. 295]. . . . It was the lure of wealth or, put in other terms, the pressure of crowding and overpopulation at home, that drew the Parian settlers northward.

'The lure of wealth' and 'the pressure of crowding and overpopulation' are not semantic equivalents. Putting something 'in other terms', in this case, is not saying something differently, it is saying something different.

Similarly, in the oft-quoted case of the two boatloads of men (no women) who founded Kyrene, a seven-year drought lay at the root of the famine problem (Hdt. 4. 150–8). The most technologically advanced country in the world today has serious problems combatting drought when it occurs; I do not think the inhabitants of sub-Saharan Africa would be impressed by the idea that their chief problem is overpopulation.

No settlement could exist without land; so the fact that land was available and cultivated at a settlement overseas proves nothing. It is only modern methods of food production and processing that allow the divorce (with which we are now familiar) between urban and rural environments; until very recently, every settlement had to have enough land to produce the bulk of its food. Meat came in on the hoof, not in refrigerated trucks; cereals came in on donkey-back, not by juggernaut. This put severe constraints on the viable distance between the point of production and the point of consumption.[1] If land was *not* cultivated, it shows that the

[1] The debate over the grain supply to classical Athens and imperial Rome is irrelevant here. I am dealing with the eighth and seventh centuries BC; more importantly, I am not concerned with those atypical super-cities but with the more common settlements, or settlement clusters, with populations from a few score to a few thousand.

settlement was not permanently occupied, but a staging-post or temporary, seasonal camp.

Concluding remarks

The principal aim of this paper has been to draw attention to the role of fighting and warfare in the Greek 'colonizing' process. I have emphasized the 'naturalness' of the use of force to secure and preserve lives and livelihoods in ancient Greek societies. The essential message of the argument is that warfare in the ancient Greek world was a mode of *production*.

Bibliography

Andrews, K. (1984), *Trade, Plunder, and Settlement* (Cambridge).

Archer, L. (ed. 1988), *Slavery and Other Forms of Unfree Labour* (London).

Baly, D. (1963), *Geographic Companion to the Bible* (London).

Blackburn, R. (1988), 'Slavery: its special features and social role', in Archer (ed.), pp. 142–56.

Blainey, G. (1988), *The Causes of War* (3rd edn, London).

Boardman, J. (1980), *The Greeks Overseas* (2nd edn, London).

Borza, E. N. (1973), 'Sentimental philhellenism and the image of Greece', in E. N. Borza and R. W. Carruba (eds), *Classics and the Classical Tradition* (Pennsylvania), pp. 5–25.

Bourdieu, P. (1977), *Outline of a Theory of Practice* (Cambridge).

Bryce, T. R. (1990), 'Hellenism in Lycia', in Descoeudres (ed.), pp. 531–41.

Burges, G. (ed. 1876), *The Greek Anthology* (London).

Burn, A. R. (1978), *The Lyric Age of Greece* (London).

Burstein, S. M. (1976), *Outpost of Hellenism: The Emergence of Heraclea on the Black Sea* (Berkeley).

Carew, R. (1759), *The Survey of Cornwall*, reprinted in R. C. Richardson and T. B. James (eds 1983), *The Urban Experience* (Manchester), pp. 15–17.

Coja, M. (1990), 'Greek colonists and native populations in Dobruja', in Descoeudres (ed.), pp. 157–68.

Coldstream, J. N. (1977), *Geometric Greece* (London).

Descoeudres, J.-P. (ed. 1990), *Greek Colonists and Native Populations* (Oxford).

Dodge, E. S. (1976), *Islands and Empires* (Oxford).

Edmonds, J. M. (1931), *Elegy and Iambus* (Loeb Classical Texts; Cambridge, Mass., etc.).

Finley, M. I. (1968), *Ancient Sicily* (London).

Fränkel, H. (1975), *Early Greek Poetry and Philosophy*, trans. M. Hadas and J. Willis (Oxford).

Garlan, Y. (1988), *Slavery in Ancient Greece*, trans. J. Lloyd (Ithaca).

Garnsey, P. (1985), 'Grain for Athens', in P. A. Cartledge and F. D. Harvey (eds), *Crux: Essays in Greek History Presented to G. E. M. de Ste. Croix on his 75th Birthday* (London; = *History of Political Thought*, 6 (1–2)), pp. 62–75.

—— (1988), *Famine and Food Supply in the Graeco-Roman World: Responses to Risk and Crisis* (Cambridge).

Gerber, D. E. (1970), *Euterpe* (Amsterdam).

Graham, A. J. (1990), 'Pre-colonial contacts', in Descoeudres (ed.), pp. 45–60.

Grierson, P. (1959), 'Commerce in the dark ages: a critique of the evidence', *Transactions of the Royal Historical Society*, 9: 123–40.

Guzzo, P. G. (1990), 'Myths and archaeology in South Italy', in Descoeudres (ed.), pp. 131–41.

Hakluyt, R. (1903–5), *The Principall Navigations*, viii (first published Glasgow 1589).

Humphreys, S. C. (1983), *Anthropology and the Greeks* (London).

Kirk, G. S. (1949), 'Ships on Greek vases', *BSA* 44: 93–153.

Lefkowitz, M. R. (1981), *The Lives of the Greek Poets* (London).

Lintott, A. (1982), *Violence, Civil Strife and Revolution in the Classical City: 750–330 BC* (London).

Miralles, C., and Pòrtulas, J. (1983), *Archilochus and the Iambic Poetry* (Rome).

Nash, D. (1985), 'Celtic territorial expansion and the Mediterranean world', in T. C. Champion and J. V. S. Megaw (eds), *Settlement and Society* (Leicester), pp. 45–67.

Ormerod, H. A. (1924), *Piracy in the Ancient World* (Liverpool).

Patterson, O. (1982), *Slavery and Social Death* (Cambridge, Mass.).

Podlecki, A. J. (1984), *The Early Greek Poets and their Times* (Vancouver).

Pouncey, P. R. (1980), *The Necessities of War: A Study in Thucydides' Pessimism* (New York).

Pritchett, W. K. (1971), *The Greek State at War*, i: *Greek Military Practices* (Berkeley).

Purcell, N. (1990), 'Mobility and the *polis*', in O. Murray and S. Price (eds), *The Greek City: From Homer to Alexander* (Oxford), pp. 29–58.

Rankin, H. D. (1977), *Archilochus of Paros* (Park Ridge, NJ).

—— (1987), *Celts and the Classical World* (London).

Robinson, E. G. D. (1990), 'Between Greek and native', in Descoeudres (ed.), pp. 157–68.

Snodgrass, A. M. (1964), *Early Greek Armour and Weapons* (Edinburgh).

Stone, J. (1958), *Aggression and World Order* (London).

Torelli, M. (1977), 'Il sanctuario greco di Gravisca', *La parola del passato*, 32: 398–458.

Trillmich, C. B. (1990), 'Elea: problems of the relationship between city and territory, and of urban organisation in the archaic period', in Descoeudres (ed.), pp. 365–71.

Twaddle, M. (1988), 'Slaves and peasants in Buganda', in Archer (ed.), pp. 118–29.

van Dijk, H. J. (1968), *Ezekiel's Prophecy on Tyre (Ez. 26. 1–28. 19)* (Rome).

van Zeist, W., and Woldring, H. (1980), 'Holocene vegetation and climate of north-western Syria', *Paleohistoria*, 22: 111–25.

Weber, M. (1978), *Economy and Society: An Outline of Interpretive Sociology* (ed. G. Roth and C. Wittich; Berkeley, etc.).

West, M. L. (1971–2), *Iambi et Elegi Graeci* (Oxford).

Whitehead, D. M. (1977), *The Ideology of the Athenian Metic* (*PCPS* supp. vol. 4; Cambridge).

6

Asia unmanned: Images of victory in classical Athens

Edith Hall

In the early years after Xerxes had been expelled from Greece, the citizens of Attica began to celebrate their victories over the Persians. Spoils from the battle – triremes, weapons, armour, harnesses and bridles, plentiful gold, a throne – were prominently displayed as material symbols of their ascendancy (Thompson 1956). In addition, however, an enormous programme of cultural production was undertaken. Vases, statues, wall-paintings, epigrams, lyric poetry, and even drama all celebrate the vanquishing of the barbarians and legitimize the war still being waged against them, by the Athenians' newly created Delian league, for hegemony in the Aegean.

Across the centuries, however, the only Athenian with firsthand experience who speaks to us at any length about the Persian wars is Aeschylus. In his *Persae* of 472 BC he traps the Persian court inside the theatre of Dionysos for the inspection of his audience. The long journey to Susa is made instantly in the imagination, the walls of its monumental architecture torn down to reveal their secrets. But those secrets have little to do with any kind of authentic Persian reality; for the Asiatics of Greek poetry and art were invented by the Greek imagination. The secrets exposed in Athenian drama are those of the Athenian mind: its invention of this land called Persia, and the conceptual systems by which the experiencesof the war were encoded in its historical consciousness. The subject of the present investigation is one of those secrets: the determination by gender of much of the imagery

and language with which Aeschylus surrounds his invented
Persians – that is, the feminization of Asia in the Greek imagination.[1]

Orientalism

In 1978 Edward Said published a book called *Orientalism*. The
waves it made have been felt in numerous academic disciplines:
history, politics, anthropology, and literature (Barker 1985;
Kabbani 1986). He argues that the concepts of Europe and the
Orient as polarized entities are socially produced. He shows how
Europeans have represented the Orient in ways that have constructed it as Europe's 'other'; that is, they have invested it with
the negatives of attributes felt desirable in Europeans. Moreover,
Said argues, such representations are inseparable from the historical facts of European imperialism and from Europe's oppression
of the countries to its east. The weakening of the Orient in cultural
discourse is interconnected with the programme which has sought
to keep it under European control in economic and political
terms. Although he is primarily concerned with much later forms
taken by orientalism, he believes that the stereotypes of the Orient
that are still in circulation, especially those of the Arab and
Muslim worlds, inherit much of their vocabulary and imagery
from the earliest surviving European discourse. He writes of
Aeschylus' *Persae*, for example, that 'Asia speaks through and by
virtue of the European imagination, which is depicted as victorious over Asia, that hostile "other" world across the sea' (Said
1978, 56).

Gender as articulator of experience

There was an asymmetry of power in Greek culture between men
and women. Athenian men, for example, controlled their wives
and daughters sexually and economically, and excluded them

[1] I am grateful to Isobel Clark, Richard Hawley, Gerard O'Daly, John
Rich, Alan Sommerstein, Angus Stephenson, and especially Paul
Cartledge for their comments on a previous draft.

from political power. This was a fundamental characteristic of ancient Athenian society. The concept of the hierarchical duality of the human species also came to inform other conceptual hierarchies and polarizations. The Pythagorean table of opposites, 'an explicit expression . . . of much older Greek beliefs' (Lloyd 1966, 49), opposed man, light, right, and good to women, darkness, left, and evil (Aristotle, *Metaphysics*, 1. 986 a 22–6). Myth presents a rich and complex nexus of such antitheses around the polarization of male and female; in Aeschylus' *Oresteia* they include Olympian–chthonic (Apollo–Erinyes), order–chaos, and Greek–barbarian (Zeitlin 1984, 181–2; Hall 1989, 204–9).

Gender is a primary articulator of perception. This paper looks more closely at the assimilation of the male–female polarity to that of Greek over barbarian; in particular, at the metaphorical means by which Athenian thought conceptualized its victory over the Persians as an analogue of the male domination of women. Male supremacy over the female was considered to be natural and right; sexual relations were conceived as hierarchical, with the man coming out on top (Halperin 1990, 266). By drawing a parallel between the asymmetry of power between male and female and the relationship between Greek and barbarian, Greek ascendancy over non-Greek cultures was 'naturalized' and legitimized.

Defeat as sexual union

The Greeks' use of the possession of women, and of victory over them, as metaphors for the defeat of Asia is typical of the way in which the male–female polarity informs and shapes the representation and interpretation of experience in patriarchal societies. Gender is a primary articulator of the social order, of history, and especially of the history of warfare (Porter 1986, 232).

Men active in peace movements are often accused of effeminacy. When Woodrow Wilson was reluctant to take America into the first world war, Teddy Roosevelt accused him of 'lack of manhood' (Wiltsher 1985, 172; MacDonald (ed.) 1987, 21). In military training, gender is one determinant of the language and imagery used both to stimulate men to fight and to identify the enemy. It has been observed that 'In warfare, *per se*, we find maleness in its absurdest extremes' (Gilman 1911, 211; see also Ogden and Florence 1915). The rhetoric of militarism may characterize as homosexuals, or 'womanish', men (whether from among the enemy or on one's own side) who fail to show enough aggression (MacDonald 1987, 16).

A striking image expressing Greek victory over Persia in terms of the sexual domination of one male over another is provided by a red-figured oinochoe probably celebrating Kimon's victory at the river Eurymedon in the early 460s (Schauenburg 1975, 104, with plate 25, 1–3). It portrays a Persian, equipped with standard oriental leggings and quiver, bending over and offering his buttocks for penetration to a naked masculine Greek who approaches him with erect penis in hand. The wording on the vase reads, 'I am Eurymedon. I stand bent over.' As Dover remarks, 'This expresses the exultation of the "manly" Athenians at their victory over the "womanish" Persians . . . it proclaims, "We've buggered the Persians" ' (Dover 1978, 105). But more often the enemy is actually defined as a woman.[1] Such strategies help to imbue the individual combatant with an insecurity about his sexual status and a desire to 'prove' his masculinity. This desire helps to perpetuate not only the imagery of military victory as sexual conquest, but also the actual practice of rape and other violence against women in war. Image and reality are dialectically related, each feeding off the other (Brownmiller 1973).

When the warfare has an imperialist or expansionist purpose, the gender articulation may be extended to accommodate the conqueror–conquered polarization, and the land itself may be feminized (Kolodny 1973; Porter 1986, 232); the winning of new territory is conceptualized as an act of sexual union. One of the imperial reliefs from the Sebasteion at Aphrodisias, for example, depicts a muscular Claudius standing triumphantly over the prostrate figure of Britannia. He pulls her loosened hair and

---

[1] For examples of victory as 'rape' of a woman, see Porter 1986, 232. On the feminization of the defeated in early Greek literature, see Vermeule 1979, 99–105. Seamus Heaney's *Act of Union*, a poem about British imperialism in Ireland (in Heaney 1975), ironically subverts the traditional *topos*.

prepares to strike the death-blow with his spear; she, semi-naked, struggles to prevent her dress from slipping off her shoulder. On another relief Nero, equally muscular, supports the naked, slumping figure of Armenia, her hair spilling over her shoulders, between his wide-striding legs (Smith 1987, 115–20, with plates 14, 16).

In the late sixteenth and early seventeenth centuries America was represented, in the imperialist discourses of the European conquerors, as female. Europe is male and stands in iconography over the relaxed or naked female figure of the New Continent. America may be by turns a dangerous Amazon, an erotic seductress inviting penetration, or a maiden giving up her virginity (Hulme 1985, 17). Carr (1985, 46) quotes the song from *Eastward Ho*: 'Come, boys: Virginia longs till we share the rest of her maidenhead', and observes that 'Colonialist, racist and sexist discourse have continually reinforced, naturalised, and legitimised each other during the process of European colonisation.'

The male–female hierarchy was similarly used by the Greeks to express their sense of 'natural' ascendancy over other peoples and territories. Raping a virgin and marrying a maiden are metaphors for sacking a city (Hanson 1990, 326). Colonization myths often revolve around a mythical pivot involving the sexual union, whether by enforced rape or happy marriage, of a Greek hero or male Olympian with a female (Zeitlin 1986, 124–5). The Hesiodic *Catalogue of Women*, for example, provides a mythical *aition* for Greek colonization of the eastern Mediterranean by tracing back the genealogies of numerous barbarian peoples in North Africa, Egypt, and the Levant to Io, the Argive maiden impregnated by Zeus at the mouth of the Nile. The cyclic epics provided numerous paradigms of colonization in their accounts of Greek heroes' fleeting sexual encounters with foreign women on distant shores (Rougé 1970, 309–10). In Pindar's ninth *Pythian*, Apollo's seduction of Cyrene and Alexidamos' winning of the hand of the daughter of the Libyan Antaios both symbolize the colonization of Libya. The 'penetration' and possession of new territory are thus illustrated by the metaphor of the sexual conquest of woman.

There was, therefore, a metaphorical elision of non-Greek, defeated, and female. Since woman was the ancient Athenian's primary 'other' and, with barbarian slaves, one of the primary objects of his power, he used her as an image for the ethnically

other, thus transferring the asymmetrical power-relation embedded in her difference from the patriarchal male to the sphere of
international power struggle. This has two effects on the
narratives recounting the Persian wars. First, the oppositions
man–woman and rapist–raped are transferred to the Greek–non-
Greek relationship; Greek victory over Persia is made to appear
'naturally' sanctioned. Second, the ambivalence towards woman's
otherness, as source and symbol of violence, danger, and anarchy,
is projected onto the foreign culture against which war continued
to be waged for many years. This was to be an important part of
the ideological project by which Athenian imperialism sought to
weaken Persian influence by perpetuating the notions of panhellenism and its corollary, the 'barbarian peril' (Perlman 1976;
Baslez 1986).

The feminine in orientalism

The male–female polarity may have informed most European
conceptualizations of the non-European, but of all Europe's
'others' – Africa, America, Australasia – the one most systematically and crudely feminized is the Orient. Orientalism explicitly
equates the Europe–Asia relationship with that between man and
woman. It reflects 'male gender dominance, or patriarchy', and
Asia is 'routinely described as feminine, its riches as fertile, its
main symbols the sensual woman . . . and the despotic – but
curiously attractive – ruler' (Said 1985, 23). Herodotos' Asiatic
tyrants – their feminine ways, their transgressive women, their
eunuchs, and their luxury – create an implied reader who is not
only victorious but also emphatically Greek, democratic, self-
disciplined, and masculine (Hartog 1988, 330–9).

The definitive ancient expression of the feminine in orientalism
is Ktesias' *Persika* (*FGH* 688 F 1–44), whose lurid accounts of the
harem intrigues and cruel punishments of the Persian court,
preserved in synoptic form by Photius (*Bibliotheke*, 1. 72), have
been thoroughly discredited as a source of historical facts (see
especially Sancisi-Weerdenburg 1983). There is always a logical
connection in the Greek mind between powerful or promiscuous
women and effeminate or castrated men. Hellanikos alleged that it
was Atossa herself who had introduced eunuchs to the court

(*FGH* 4 ꜰ 178 a; c). So, too, Ktesias' narratives are populated by dangerous queens such as Amestris and Amytis who show 'great fondness for the society of men' (Freese 1920, 103), while his eunuchs, especially Artoxares, are powerful intriguers.

In tragedy, Troy was assimilated to the Persian archetype and became a byword for feminized men, despotism, and luxury. The Trojans in the fragments of some of Sophocles' plays, for example, are 'persianized', by being made to use Persian linguistic forms (*TGF* 515; 634). In *Troilos* a eunuch had a speaking part (Hall 1989, ch. 3 §8); the order to castrate him had come, of course, from the oriental queen Hekabe herself (*TGF* 620). In Euripides' *Trojan Women*, defeated Asia addresses the Greek audience in the female singing voice, its characters and chorus embodying in their feminine forms the 'Laomedon' qualities that had made Troy in its grandeur offensive to the gods (Burnett 1977, 311). In Euripides' *Orestes* a phrygianized Helen and an effeminate Menelaos come back from Troy with a whole train of Phrygian eunuchs, one of whom actually sings a wild, exotic, emotional aria in the high-pitched Phrygian mode, similar to the speeches of the barbarians in Timotheos' orientalizing dithyramb, *Persae* (*PMG* 788–91).

Persians and Amazons

Underlying even the Persian stereotype are the supernatural embodiments of barbarism appearing already in epic: the Amazons, manlike women who fight and die at the hands of heroes. The close relationship between the Amazon and the Persian is demonstrated by the way in which, after the wars, Persian details creep into the traditional type of the Amazonomachy scene, thus turning the mythological conflict into an archetype, with profound patriotic significance, of the Greeks' subordination of the Persian barbarians (Bovon 1963). The myth of the defeat of the Amazons found a new function. It now not only provided aetiologies for the pervasive system of patriarchy (Kirk 1987) and for the defeat of savagery by civilization, but was seen, especially by the Athenians, as the mythical prefiguration of the Persian wars.

As such, it is frequently found in tandem with representation of

Plate 1a An *ambari* (storage chamber) in the mountains, Methana.

Plate 1b Battle scene (left-hand side), from the Alexander Sarcophagus.

Plate 2a Detail of Alexander the Great, from the Alexander Mosaic.

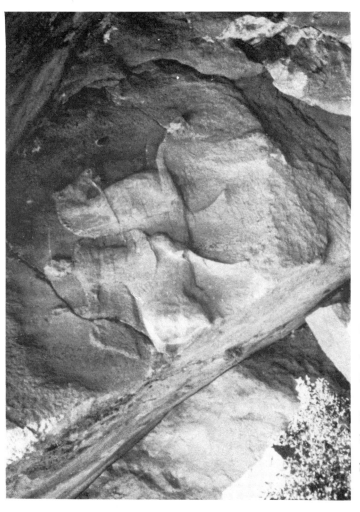

Plate 2b Alketas Tomb at Termessos, Pisidia. Sculpted relief of a mounted warrior.

Plate 3a Alketas Tomb at Termessos, Pisidia. Grave area with receptacles for offerings.

Plate 3b The Lion Monument at Amphipolis (restored).

Plate 4a The Lion Tomb at Knidos, from the sea (tomb arrowed).

Plate 4b Pyramidal tomb at Turgut in the Rhodian *peraia*.

the historical battles in the visual arts, and especially in *epitaphioi logoi* (Drews 1973, 35; Merck 1978, 103). In the Stoa Poikile the victory at Marathon was portrayed alongside the victories of Theseus and Herakles over the Amazons and Trojans (Pausanias, 1. 15. 3). The Amazons in Athenian myth start doing things the Persians had done. The Persians, for example, had besieged the Acropolis from the Areiopagos (Herodotos, 8. 52); Polygnotos' mural in the Theseion (a 'harbinger of Athenian imperialism') was the first to depict the Amazons' struggle for the Acropolis (Paus. 1. 17. 4; Tyrrell 1984, 10). In Aeschylus' *Eumenides* (685–90) we are told that the Amazons had once attempted to set up a rival state to challenge Pallas' Athens (the city of the goddess worshipped on the Acropolis), sacrificing to this end to their father Ares, the 'barbarian' of Olympos, on the rival peak of the Areiopagos.

By a dialectical process the Persians in Greek discourse began in turn to assume Amazonic features. The visual representation of the battles with the Persians in the fifth century owed much to previous representation of the Amazonomachy, borrowing postures, ethos, and details like patterned tights and wicker shields. The gender hierarchy of male over female, implicit in the old myth of the Amazons, now crept inexorably into the language and imagery of written representations of the Persian wars.

Staging the Orient

From the first drama we know to have been written concerning the victory of 480, *Phoenician Women* by Phrynichos, it is apparent that this hierarchy was crucial to the contemporary formulation of the historical conflict. The play concerned the disasters that befell the Persians on the 480 campaign. Phrynichos, who is said to have been the first to use female characters in tragedy (*TGF* 3 T 1), imagined women of Phoenicia (either widows of the Phoenician sailors or hierodules in the Persian court) singing and dancing exotic and threnodic choruses (see *TGF* 9–11). The Greek imagination constructed for itself an image of a female Asia in mourning; Asia, represented by women, addressed the Greek audience at the City Dionysia in lyrical and mournful tones. More significantly, however, the first sight that greeted the audience's eyes at the beginning of the play was a eunuch, who was arranging the cushions on the seats in the high chamber for the Persian royal council while he announced the defeat of Xerxes (*TGF* 8). In one instant, Phrynichos set the tone for his orientalizing drama. The eastern castrated male, in whose mutilation the essence of the Greeks' view of eastern effeminacy was reified, stood as a paradigm for every oriental male; the eunuch was to become a recurring figure in ancient orientalist discourse (Guyot 1980, 71–91). Athenian councillors sat on wooden benches; the seats for Phrynichos' Persian council were cushioned. The soft upholsteries of the eastern courts became a cliché in the Greeks' orientalizing texts (e.g. Xenophon, *Cyropaedia*, 8. 8. 16).

Aeschylus' version of the Salamis story retained the overall pattern of Greek masculinity and barbarian femininity. His *Persae* represents the earliest full-blown expression of orientalism in extant Greek literature. Asia, like Woman, is lush and fertile, ripe for control and government, passive, open, and vulnerable. But she is also dangerous, threatening, fickle, and emotional. Asia is the ancient night against which the new daylight of Greek civilization is to be defined; the victories of the Persian wars, and the continuing expansion of Athenian power into the eastern Aegean, are as inevitable and natural, and as divinely sanctioned, as Athenian patriarchy.

In order to appreciate how this schematization works, we must explore the byways of the play, often neglected by interpreters: the choral odes, the semantic complexes, the vocabulary, imagery, and metaphorical structures generated by Aeschylus' mythopoetic unconscious in the attempt to create a new 'grammar' for organizing his audience's perceptions of historical experience. The positivistically minded may object to some of what follows on the ground that 'too much' is being made of 'trivial' and 'obvious' aspects of the play. But imagery, though working on a subtle psychological level, is often a clue to underlying ideological currents; for, like myth, it 'transforms history into nature' (Barthes 1973, 129; cf. MacDonald 1987, 3).

The present study is confined to examining the ideas and imagery that relate Persia to femininity. Elsewhere I have shown that Aeschylus' *Persae* is pervaded by differentiative techniques that not only make the Persians speak in an elaborate and archaic manner, sing in the eastern 'Ionic *a minore*' metre, and use Persian words and strange linguistic forms, but also characterize the

defeated barbarians as despotic, slavish, emotional, cruel, cowardly, and disorderly – in short, the exact antitype of the idealized
Athenian male, distinguished by such virtues as respect for
equality before the law, freedom, self-restraint, and courage. This
fictive evocation of the barbarian personality is supported by
numerous details about the workings of the Persian imperial
administration (Hall 1989, 76–100).

The play, however, is also powerfully suggestive of the essential
femininity of Persia. This is achieved by two means. First, the
dramatis personae selected present a tableau, as in many Athenian
tragedies (except those set at Athens), in which the court is
portrayed as lacking a firm, adult male hand on the rudder of
government. Second, the text uses an imagistic and metaphorical
substratum combining numerous implications of the bereft, the
erotic, the soft, and the threnodic, which work cumulatively and
on an almost subliminal psychological level to create the
impression of a 'female' continent, vulnerable as never before to
Greek 'male' domination.

Aeschylus' Persia lacks a strong adult male in control. Darius
was once such a ruler, but he is dead, and his ghost must be raised
to predict still further disasters which will afflict the Persians at
Plataea (816–17). The chorus are too old, Xerxes too young. The
character on stage the longest is the Persian queen.[1] And, in
accordance with this vision of the court, the language and imagery
present to the Greek audience a false picture of an Asia emptied of
men (Anderson 1972, 169). Before the queen even appears, the
chorus (117–19) fear lest a Greek victory will mean that cries of
mourning are to be heard by the mighty city of Susa, 'empty of
men' (*kenandron*). The queen has been thinking that 'wealth in the
absence of men' (*chrematōn anandrōn*, 166) cannot win respect.
The chorus remember that the Athenians once before, at Marathon, rendered the beds of many Persian wives 'manless' (*anan-
drous*, 289). The queen asks which of the Persian officers were
killed, leaving the fleet 'unmanned' (298). Zeus has wiped out the
proud Persian army, which once consisted of many men (*poluan-
drōn*, 533). In Persia many a household now mourns, deprived of
its men (579–80). Wild Xerxes 'emptied' the whole continent

[1] Atossa is not named in the play, and therefore her name in the list of
characters is probably a later import from Herodotos or the scholia.

(*kenōsas*, 718); the destruction is such that the whole city of Susa weeps for its 'emptiness of men' (*kenandrian*, 730; see also 920). The army was male, but the city of the Persians and the land of Asia, in defeat, are conceptualized as female.

The Greeks, on the other hand, and especially the Athenians, are represented throughout as an unindividuated and anonymous collective male presence, like the nameless heroes of the Athenian *epitaphios* (Goldhill 1988). Not a single Greek individual is named in *Persae*. But Athens has a strong defence, for, as the messenger remarks, while men remain to a city (*andron . . . onton*, 349) its bulwark is secure. The Greeks, continually referred to as 'men' (355; 362; 375; etc.), are virile warriors, killing-machines. This is reflected in the variety of words for hitting, thrashing, and killing (e.g. 251; 279; 304; 426) that are used to describe what they did to the Persians. They include the suggestive and ambiguous *damazein*, which can be used of taming a wild animal, raping a woman, or killing a man (Vermeule 1979, 101); the entire Persian force is 'tamed' (or 'raped') by the Greeks (*damastheis*, 279).

There are no Greek characters in this play; but the Greeks dominate much of the text. Whether in reminiscence, execration, interrogation, or lament, the image of the indomitable, warrior-like Greek collective is kept constantly before our eyes. With one exception, however, the real *women* of Greece are never mentioned. The exception is in the Greeks' paean sung before the battle of Salamis, which asks the 'sons of the Greeks' to 'liberate your fatherland, your sons, your wives and the temples of the gods, and the tombs of your ancestors' (402–5). The wives are sandwiched between the children (to bear whom was their primary function in classical Athens) and the gods and ancestors.

Images of Asia

Effeminate men

Hellas is distinguished by its men; Asia has no active, adult men left. Asia is populated by women and old men, represented by the chorus. Their great age, as contemporaries of the dead Darius, is repeatedly stressed. Besides the messenger, Xerxes himself is the only man of fighting age to appear in the play (although, as a barbarian despot, he had not fought himself) and, it is implied, the only one left alive. And even he is not a 'real' man. He appears as an archer, before an audience who regarded archery as the least manly mode of warfare. He belongs to the same family of tragic figures as the young tyrant Zeus in Aeschylus' *Prometheus Bound* and the adolescent Pentheus of Euripides' *Bacchae*. He is apparently as yet unmarried. His extreme youth is often emphasized (Paduano 1978, 95–6); he has erred through 'youthful boldness' (744), and as a young man (*neos*) he thinks 'young thoughts' (782). Moreover, in Greek thought there was an androgyne quality to the very young man, the ephebe, before he was fully initiated into the adult world of hoplite warfare and politics (Vidal-Naquet 1988, 179). Xerxes is accused by his own men of *anandria*, cowardice (literally 'lack of manhood'; 755), the opposite of the Greek male virtue of *andreia*. The adolescent king of Persia is not yet fully male.

Xerxes is even characterized by vocabulary normally reserved for women. The messenger gives a picture of him sitting on a high hill overlooking the scene of the battle. When he realized the depth of the horror, we are told, he tore his *peploi* and 'shrilly screamed' (468). The term denoting Xerxes' robe (see also 1030) is used in Homer only for women's raiment (Marinatos 1967, A 11); in Greek literature it is rarely used for male clothing, which usually consists of the *himation* or *chlaina*. When Plutarch describes the ritual role-reversal of the sexes during the Hybristika at Argos, he says that 'they clothe the women in men's tunics (*chitōsi*) and cloaks (*chlamusin*) and the men in women's robes (*peplois*) and veils' (Plutarch, *De virtute mulierum*, 4 = *Moralia*, 245 e–f). With the exception of the gown in which Agamemnon dies, defeated by a woman, the *peplos* or *peploma* in Aeschylus is only worn by women and/or barbarians (e.g. Aesch. *Choephori*, 29; *Suppliants*, 432; 720). Elsewhere, when men are given the *peplos*, it is usually a narrative strategy by which they are 'effeminized' (e.g. Pentheus and Dionysos in Euripides' *Bacchae*; see Loraux 1990, 33–40). The term, however, *is* used 'especially of long Persian dresses',[1] as in Xenophon's *Cyropaedia* (3. 1. 13).

The Persians are preoccupied with fine clothing, a 'female' and 'barbarian' tendency (Conacher 1974, 165 n. 36). The queen draws

[1] LSJ s.v. *peplos*, II. 3.

attention to her removal of her gorgeous apparel when she returns to make her sacrifice (607–8). The elaborate Persian regalia (slippers and tiara) worn by Darius' ghost is described by the chorus (660–2). Both the dead king and his wife are anxious to provide Xerxes with ornate robes for him to don on his return, fearing that his torn clothing will be shameful (832–6; 847–90). The Greeks' obsession with Persian clothing, obvious in many passages of the historians (such as the mention of Xerxes' long embroidered cloak at Hdt. 9. 109), was probably fed by the examples that had fallen into their hands. Xerxes' clothes in *Persae* are ruined *poikila esthemata* ('embroidered robes', 836); the fabulous spoils from Plataea included an *esthes poikile* (Hdt. 9. 80).

The words for Xerxes' scream of lamentation (*anakokuein ligu*), again, belong to the semantic register normally reserved for women; men do not *kokuein* in serious Greek literature. The word, implying a high-pitched shriek of despair, is properly used of women's lamentations over the dead (*Odyssey*, 24. 295; Aesch. *Agamemnon*, 1313). In the *Iliad* Briseis, just like Xerxes, *lig' ekokue* over Patroklos' corpse, and Thetis' laments are denoted by 'sharp screaming' (*oxu . . . kokusasa*, 18. 71), in juxtaposition to Achilles' deep groaning (18. 70). Elsewhere in Aeschylus the only utterances described by the adjective *ligus* are delivered by women (*Suppl.* 112), or by the nightingale, whose song was explained by the mythical *aition* of the female Prokne's unceasing laments for her dead son Itys (*Ag.* 1146; see further Loraux 1986).

In *Persae* Xerxes' effeminacy is shared by other barbarian men. His chorus are also arrayed in *peploi* (1060). *Kokuma* is used of the laments of both Persian men and women (332; 427). Indeed, the play's *threnos*, the longest and most extravagant in extant Greek tragedy, is performed exclusively by males, and thereby gains much of its orientalizing force. Funerary lamentation was always associated with women. At Athens, if excessive, it was considered dangerous and subversive, and it is said to have been outlawed by Solon, 'for he made the Athenians decorous and careful in their religious services, and milder in their rites of mourning . . . by taking away the harsh and barbaric practices in which their women had usually indulged up to that time' (Plut. *Solon*, 12; Hall 1989, ch. 1. 5 c).

Various other terms used in *Persae* to evoke the luxury of the

Persian court come from the semantic register associated with women, especially the concepts of *chlidē* and of *habrosunē*; the latter combines the senses of 'softness', 'delicacy', and 'abandonment'. The epithet *habros* is used in the archaic period of lovely women and goddesses, and of Adonis, the young eastern god (Hesiod, fr. 339; Sappho, *PLF* 44. 7; 128; 140. 1). In reference to adult mortal men, however, its suggestions of effeminacy are pejorative. In *Persae* a remarkable number of compound adjectives with the 'feminizing' prefix *habro-* can be seen at work in the evocation of the Asiatic milieu. The play may have been an important factor in the welding of the concepts of easternness and *habrosunē* (see especially Hdt. 1. 71. 4). The Persian women are 'soft' in their laments, but the Lydian *men* were 'soft' in their lifestyle, and even the chorus of old Persian men are *habrobatai*, 'most delicate' of gait (135; 41; 541; 1073).

Ancient queen

The first character to appear, and the one involved in more of the play than any of the others, is not, however, the effeminate young Xerxes but the ageing queen of Persia, the 'highest queen of the deep-girdled Persian women, old mother of Xerxes, and wife of Darius' (150–8).

Why did Aeschylus choose the queen of Persia as the primary representative of the ageing Persian empire? According to Herodotos, at least, Xerxes left Artabanus in charge of governing the empire in 480 BC (7. 52). But the poet's choice allows defeated, distant Asia to speak in the female voice. The conquered as female is a tenacious metaphorical elision, running through all cultures where the oppression of women is institutionalized. Carthage, destined to fall to the might of Rome founded by Aeneas, speaks through the tragic queen Dido. Augustan propaganda used Cleopatra as a 'symbol of an effeminate, conquered East' (Wyke 1992). In Shakespeare's *Henry V* France's defeat is articulated in the submission of the French princess Katharine to marriage with the English king (Fiedler 1974, 43–5), and in the effeminacy of the French nobles. The rape and enslavement of the Trojan women, foreseen in the *Iliad*, legitimize at some mediated mythopoetic level Hellas' colonization of the western seaboard of

Asia Minor. And in Aeschylus' *Persae* the defeated continent is made to speak through the aged oriental queen; her persona combines each of the separate facets of the femininity of Asia.

Asia was seen by the Greeks as the primeval home of civilization. They admitted freely that the Asiatic cultures were considerably older than their own. So the queen, whose great age is stressed (156; 704),[1] is the paradigm of her antique continent. She is the aged, proud, despotic land whose power has been superseded (the play implies) by the young, democratic, masculine race of Attica. She is also Asia the fecund Mother, surrounded by images of lush fertility and regeneration (see below). But there was a time when she was herself, like the nubile Persian women in the choral odes, a young wife and sexual partner; on her first arrival she announces that she has come from the royal bedchamber which she used to share with Darius (160), and Darius returns to the theme of their sexual relationship of long ago (704).

Mourning mother

A dominant image of Asia is that of a woman in mourning. The citadel of Kissia resounds with ritual blows as the horde of females utter laments, tearing their linen robes as Xerxes, like a woman, had torn his *peploi* at Salamis (122–5). The Asiatic land is itself presented by metaphorical language as a mother who has nurtured the men who have gone off on the campaign and died. This is the image of the continent that first strikes the audience's imagination, as early as the opening anapaests: 'such was the flower of men put forth by the Persian land, the men whom the entire Asiatic earth (*chthōn Asiatis*) nurtured and laments in soft longing' (59–62). Asia is a mother who has nurtured men as the earth brings forth flowers.

Such images re-emerge at significant points throughout the play. The messenger's first words on arrival address 'the citadel of all the land of Asia, the Persian earth', whose 'flower of Persians' has fallen (249–52). As he moves to depart he returns to the same theme (511–12). That the term *anthos* (flower) and compounds of

[1]   In reality Atossa, as a daughter of Cyrus I, would have been at least seventy years old in 480 BC.

habro- (which, as we saw above, are so common in the play) became canonized in the semantic register of early Greek orientalism is demonstrated by the 'invented' names of two of Xerxes' brothers in Herodotos, Habrokomes and Hyperanthes (7. 224).

The city of the Persians must lament, yearning for the beloved young men put forth by the earth (512-13). The chorus respond to the messenger's news with a great threnodic ode at the heart of the play, in which the very earth of Asia is said to be mourning, 'emptied out' of its men (848-9). The image of Asia as mother resurfaces in the closing dirge, as the symbol stamped forever on the mind of the audience. The earth itself laments its 'indigenous young men' who have been taken by Hades (922-3). The Asian continent is a woman on her knees, fallen in prostration (929-30); Xerxes' own city is envisaged as a mourning mother (946).

Fruitful earth

Another view of the fertility of Asia is presented in the medical treatise entitled *On Airs, Waters, Places*, which is attributed to Hippocrates and is generally believed to be an authentic fifth-century work. The theory expounded in it connects the diverse physiology and medical conditions in different human communities with the climatic and environmental conditions to which they are subject. From chapter 12 onwards the writer embarks upon a systematic comparison of Asiatics and Europeans. In Asia, it is said, everything grows to greater beauty and size, and the character of Asia's inhabitants is gentle. The cause of these characteristics is the temperate climate (12. 7-16). As Asia is neither parched with heat and drought nor excessively cold, it has plentiful harvests from both wild vegetation and cultivated crops, and its cattle are the sturdiest one could find (12. 24-35). Such a fine natural development is also to be found in the human beings there; they are of fine physique and uniform size (12. 35-8). But there is an intrinsic disadvantage in this wealth of natural blessings. It is impossible (the writer asserts) for a temperate climate and environment to engender courage, endurance, industry, and high spirits, which are the defining characteristics of the European, bred and tested in a harsh and changeable climate.

Indeed, the ruling principle of the cowardly and slothful Asiatics can never be anything other than pleasure (12. 40–4).

It is argued that Asiatics lack spirit and courage because of the *uniformity* of their seasons. There are none of the physical changes that harden humans and steel them to passion and action (16. 3–12). The political constitutions (*nomoi*) of Asiatics are a contributory factor, for people have no motivation to self-aggrandizement when they are subjected to the rule of monarchical masters (16. 16–33). At this point it seems that the writer is applying two independent reasons for the Asiatic temperament's inherent passivity: one from *phusis* (the physical environment), one from *nomos* (their constitutions). But taken as a whole, the treatise implies that these two factors are interconnected, for the Asiatic temperament gives rise to such forms of government, which would not be tolerated by the rugged individualists of Europe. In explaining the lack of uniformity in the size of Europeans, even within a single city, the writer refers to the speed at which the foetus forms in the womb. He sees its formation as a process of coagulation; changes of seasons disturb the speed of this process, leading to variations in the size of individuals. In Asia, where the temperature remains stable, people are all the same size. More significantly, however, the changes of season while the foetus is in the womb also affect character, for shocks to the mind caused by the alteration of environmental conditions engender wildness, independence, and so on, whereas uniformity imparts slackness and cowardice (23. 9–30).

The polarized entities in this treatise are 'Europe' and 'Asia', the equivalents of 'Greeks' and 'barbarians'. The theories developed represent the earliest known attempt to base the superiority of the Greek character and Greek culture on arguments from natural science (Backhaus 1976; Jouanna 1981, 11–15).

If we return now to the text of *Persae*, we can see that similar premises inform the poet's explanation of the victory of his Greeks over his barbarians. The barbarian army, as we have seen, is repeatedly characterized by language and imagery from the natural world; it is the 'flower of the Persian land . . . nurtured by Asia' (59–62; 252; etc.). Many of the soldiers came from Egypt, the 'rich and fertilizing land of the Nile' (33–4; 311). Xerxes' troops were like a great swarm of bees (127–8), and the Greeks destroyed them as fishermen net and kill a shoal of tuna-fish (424–6). In this simile the technological inventiveness and naval prowess[1] of the Greeks annihilate the barbarians, conceived as the defenceless creatures of nature.

Some passages even prefigure the arguments of the Hippocratic treatise. The ghost of Darius, for example, enjoins the chorus never to invade Greece again, 'for their land itself fights as an ally with them' (792); he explains that it kills any excessive population through starvation (794). The very barrenness of the land of the Hellenes thus contributed to the Persian defeat. In the messenger's scene the harsh climatic changes of Greece and Thrace, which create independent and spirited Europeans, are presented as disastrous to the Persians. The remnants of the retreating army are afflicted by thirst, breathlessness, exhaustion, and hunger (483–4; 491). Heaven sent an 'unseasonable storm' (496) which made the Thracian river Strymon freeze over; sudden and unpredictable sunshine then melted it as the barbarians were walking over the ice, causing many of them to die (502–11).

The treatise *On Airs, Waters, Places* says Asiatics are handsome; the play stresses the fine physique of the barbarian forces (441; 733), and includes some unusual references to their good looks; Tharybis the Lyrnaean, we are told, was *eueidēs* (324). The Hippocratic treatise argues that these handsome Asiatics enjoy a fertile environment, so that the problems of physical survival present no challenge to their intelligence and contribute to their lack of initiative. The Hippocratic schematization also remarks on the excellence of the Asiatic livestock; by interaction with all the other imagery from nature in the context of *Persae*, even a traditional adjective like 'sheep-nurturing', applied to Asia (763), seems to take on a fresh significance. The Asiatics in 'Hippocrates' also enjoy abundant crops, both from wild plants and cultivated land; in the light of this theory, the language in the queen's speech as she prepares to make her libation is particularly striking. Her account of the various ingredients she has selected involves imagery designed both to underline her own role as mother and to create an impression of

[1] 'The barbarians are inferior to the Greeks on the sea as women are to men'; so says Artemisia at Hdt. 8. 68. 1. For a discussion of her role in the Herodotean narrative, as a Greek female fighting on the Persian side, see Munson 1988.

the luxuriant vegetation and fertility of Asia, in contrast with the emphasized barrenness of Attica. These are not just solemn periphrases; by interaction with all the other 'female' imagery, they inscribe the femaleness and fecundity of Asia in the text. The ingredients include the 'white potable milk from an *unyoked heifer*'; gleaming honey, 'liquid made from flowers'; and lustral water drawn from 'a *virgin* spring' (611–13). Wine is described as 'a pure draught taken from its *wild mother*, the delightful juice of an ancient vine' (614–15); oil is the 'fragrant fruit of a pale olive, which thrives in fruit perpetually', and garlands of flowers become 'the *children of fruitful earth*' (616–18).

Seductress

The other dominant image of the feminine is that of the young wife, newly married, filled with sexual longing for her bridegroom. The slaughtered Persians are mourned by their parents but also by their wives, who pass the days 'in long-drawn-out grief' (63–4). The marriage beds of Persia are filled with tears brought on by yearning (*pothos*) for husbands (133–4); the 'softly grieving' young Persian widows, who have sent forth their bed-partners, are left alone to think 'man-desiring' thoughts (*pothōi philanori*, 134–9). The chorus recall how once before, after Marathon, the beds of the Persian wives were left empty of men (288–9). But the longest development of the *topos* of the sexual deprivation of the Persian women is left until after the terrible news of Salamis has been brought by the messenger. In the great central *thrēnos* the audience hears an account, delivered in the singing voice of Persia, of how the 'softly wailing' Persian women long to see again their recent bridegrooms, to enjoy the 'pleasures of luxuriant youth' on 'soft-sheeted' nuptial couches; instead, however, they must mourn in insatiable lamentation (541–5). Here are the recurrent orientalizing themes of desire, yearning, softness, and insatiability; similarly in the Hippocratean treatise, 'pleasure' (*hēdonē*) was the guiding principle of Asiatics. Darius' last words enjoin the Persians to give every day of their lives over to *hēdonē* (841). Unbridled passions – physical desire and lust for power – are hallmarks of the tyrants and powerful queens in most Greek evocations of the east. In Herodotos, cognates of *erōs* are found only in reference to despots; and Xerxes, in Aeschylus' version, is 'in love with' wealth (*erastheis*, 826).

The masculine Olympians

Aeschylus' Persians often speak of indefinite 'gods' or a 'god', and attribute the disasters they have suffered to unidentified *daimones* of malevolent intent. In the course of the invocation of Darius' ghost they call upon various chthonic deities, especially Mother Earth and Aidoneus (629; 640; 649–50), as well as Hermes, the only Olympian who can pass the boundary between the Olympian and chthonic spheres (629). But there are several specific allusions, especially in the battle narratives, to certain gods of the Greek pantheon. All of them symbolize, sanction, or contribute to the Greek victory at Salamis.

The gods arrayed on the Greek side are male, and Olympian rather than chthonic. The first to consider is Apollo. The queen has seen an omen in which a falcon (representing Hellas) attacked an eagle (representing Persia) at the hearth of Apollo (205–9). Apollo in the fifth century BC was, of course, the quintessentially 'Hellenic' god of reason and order who opposes the 'barbarian' Dionysos, oversees the victory of the Lapiths over the barbarous centaurs on the pediment at Olympia, and stands in opposition to the Persians on the 'Darius vase', which may itself have been inspired by Phrynichos' *Phoenician Women* (Anti 1952). The account of the queen's omen in *Persae*, therefore, authorizes the defeat of the Persians by prefiguring it with a sign from Apollo. This must have had special significance for an Athenian audience, for one of the most important of the buildings in their agora that were destroyed by the Persians in 480 was the temple of Apollo Patroös (Travlos 1971, 3 and 96; H. A. Thompson 1981, 344).

Attic heroes and an Attic divinity are also mentioned. Ajax' presence is strong (306–7; 368; 596), as we might expect of the local hero of Salamis, to whom the Athenians had prayed before the commencement of hostilities (Herodotos, 8. 64); but the mythical Salaminian king Kychreus, supposed to have appeared to the Athenians during the battle (Paus. 1. 36. 10), is not forgotten (570). Neither is Pan, the god who dances on the islet of Psyttaleia where so many barbarians were massacred (449); a shrine of Pan in a cave among the cliffs of the Acropolis was consecrated directly after the Persian wars in thanks for his help at Marathon.[1]

But it is Zeus who is ultimately responsible for the destruction of the barbarian army (532). Darius sees the defeat of his son as the working out of the unavoidable justice of Zeus (740; 827). Like the temple of Apollo Patroös, the important shrine of Zeus Eleutherios in the agora had been demolished by the Persian invaders (Travlos 1971, 3); in *Persae* he is seen as gaining his revenge. The shrine and statue of Poseidon at Poteidaia had also been desecrated by the Persians (Hdt. 8. 129), and, as Aeschylus' play stresses, Xerxes' *hubris* was expressed in his bridging of the Hellespont, when he thought he could conquer even Poseidon (750); now it is the element sacred to Poseidon, the god of seas who was worshipped beside Athena on the Acropolis, in which the Persians are depicted struggling and drowning.

One more male Olympian comes to help in the destruction of the Persian army: Ares, that most 'macho' of all the Greek divinities. It was the war-god who killed and annihilated the Persian aggressors, treading them down on the ill-starred seashore (950-4). Ares figured large in the list of deities to whom the youths of Athens swore their ephebic oath. He had a temple at Acharnai, and is particularly beloved by Aristophanes' militant Marathonomach chorus in *Acharnians*. He was prayed to before battle. It was he who, according to an oracle of Bakis received by the Greeks before Salamis, would 'incarnadine the sea with blood' (Hdt. 8. 77). But, paradoxically, Greek representations of wars with barbarians nearly always portray him as the divine supporter of the non-Greek side. He favours Troy in the *Iliad*, and myth traditionally makes him the divine antagonist of Athena. He is ubiquitously to be found in association with those strange projections of barbarism, the Amazons; Penthesilea, the Amazon queen, was a daughter of his. In Herodotos he is the god allegedly worshipped by the barbarous Thracians and Scythians. In *Rhesos* he represents unthinking barbarian violence, and is the divine

---

[1]   Hdt. 6. 105; Eur. *Ion*, 938; Ar. *Lys*. 911; Travlos 1971, 417. Pan is said by Herodotos to have appeared in Tegea to the Athenian herald Pheidippides, enjoining him to rebuke the Athenians for their previous neglect of him. See further Borgeaud 1979, 195-7.

equivalent of the Thracian Rhesos, who is brought to heel by Athena's clever favourites, Odysseus and Diomedes. But in *Persae* he is the friend and ally of the Greeks against the barbarous Persians. One possible answer to this problem is that he can fight for the Greeks because the figure of Athena, astonishingly, has been almost completely suppressed.

The play aims to exaggerate and eulogize the Athenians' contribution to the Persian wars, and elevate it over that of other Greek states (Lattimore 1943). Yet the Athenians' own tutelary deity is mentioned only once, and then obliquely, in a metonymy for her sphere of influence, 'the city of the goddess Pallas' (347). What makes this even more surprising is that one of Athena's emanations is Nike, the goddess who brings victory. The cult of Athena Nike was installed on the Acropolis by the middle of the sixth century, but her shrine underwent repairs immediately after the Persians destroyed the monuments (Boersma 1970, 132; 42), suggesting that she was considered to have been instrumental in the victory at Salamis and was accorded due gratitude as a result. Under the Periklean building programme, Athena Nike was later to receive her famous little temple on the Acropolis which may honour the battle of Plataea. But Athena was already to be seen in the mural of the Stoa Poikile, painted at approximately the same time as the first production of Aeschylus' *Persae*, assisting her Athenian protégés at the battle of Marathon (Paus. 1. 15. 4). According to Plutarch's life of Themistokles (12. 1), an owl (Athena's bird) was seen before the battle of Salamis, a good omen for the Athenians. The near-absence of Athena from Aeschylus' celebration of victory over the Persians (which has not, to my knowledge, been previously noticed) therefore poses a problem.

The organization of the polarity of Greek versus barbarian around the notion of gender difference may help to illuminate even this unexpected theological framework. It may have helped determine the nature of the super-humans named as co-operating in the Hellenic military success. They are all males, either Olympians or heroes. All of them are famous for their virility and martial valour. Asia, the fruitful earth, the ageing mother, the nubile seductress, is being defeated, tamed, bludgeoned, disarmed, and unmanned by the men of Athens and the rest of Hellas, and by their warlike, manly gods. If, in this drama, Greek is to barbarian as male is to female, there may be little room for Athena. That the Athenians were at least conscious of the anomaly of their patriarchal polis having a woman as its tutelary deity is implied by a passage in Aristophanes' *Birds*. Euelpides suggests that Athena should rule Cloudcuckooland, and Peisthetairos scornfully responds, 'And how can that be a well-organized city, where a goddess, although born a woman, stands in full armour?' (828–31). In *Persae* the Greek soldiers are represented in the cosmic scheme of things not by Athena but by the most valorous and virile of the comely male Olympians, the Persians by the darker gods of earth and death, especially Aidoneus, the dead Darius' counterpart, and Gaia, the earth-mother and Mother Earth, the Persian queen's divine double.

Conclusion

The Orient cannot represent itself; it must be represented. Aeschylus' *Persae* presents a fictive version of the Persian court posed in tableau. The play was famous for imbuing its audiences with a 'longing for victory over their enemies' (Aristophanes, *Frogs*, 1026–7). One of the means by which this is achieved is by suggesting to the spectator an analogy between his relationship with Persia and his relationship with women. In the metaphorical register Asia is a paradigm of femininity; many of its female delineations are amalgamated in the allegorical figure representing Persia in the queen's dream, a beautiful woman 'decked in Persian *peploi*' (contrasted with her Hellenic counterpart in plain Doric raiment), proudly submitting to the harness of Xerxes' chariot (181–93). The figure of the queen, the effeminacy of the Persian men, and the numerous female figures and images presented to the audience's imagination, structure the gender orientation of the play, its semantic field, and its psychological impact. Asia's feminine configurations – fertile, maternal, seductive, raped, possessed sexually, alone, defenceless, submissive, bridled, passive, *unmanned* – were thus fundamental to the Athenians' conceptualization of their historic enemy.

Bibliography

Anderson, M. (1972), 'The imagery of the Persians', *G&R* 19: 166–74.

Anti, C. (1952), 'Il vaso Dario e i Persiani di Frinico', *Archaeologia classica*, 4: 23–45.

Backhaus, W. (1976), 'Der Hellenen-Barbaren-Gegensatz und die hippokratische Schrift *peri aeron hydaton topon*', *Historia*, 25: 170–85.

Barker, F. (ed. 1985), *Europe and its Other: Proceedings of the Essex Conference on the Sociology of Literature* (Colchester).

Barthes, R. (1973), *Mythologies* (English trans., London).

Baslez, M.-F. (1986), 'Le péril barbare, une invention des Grecs?', in C. Mossé (ed.), *La Grèce ancienne* (Paris), pp. 284–99.

Boersma, J. S. (1970), *Athenian Building Policy from 461/0 to 405/4 BC* (Groningen).

Borgeaud, P. (1979), *Recherches sur le dieu Pan* (Rome).

Bovon, A. (1963), 'La représentation des guerres perses et la notion de barbare dans la Ière moitié du Ve siècle', *BCH* 87: 579–602.

Brownmiller, S. (1973), *Against Our Will: Men, Women, and Rape* (New York).

Burnett, A. (1977), ' "Trojan Women" and the Ganymede ode', *Yale Classical Studies*, 25: 291–316.

Carr, H. (1985), 'Woman/Indian: the American and his others', in Barker (ed. 1985), ii. 46–60.

Conacher, D. J. (1974), 'Aeschylus' *Persae*: a literary commentary', in *Serta Turyniana: Studies in Honor of Alexander Turyn* (Urbana/Chicago/London), pp. 141–68.

Dover, K. J. (1978), *Greek Homosexuality* (London).

Drews, R. (1973), *The Greek Accounts of Near Eastern History* (Cambridge, Mass.).

Fiedler, L. A. (1974), *The Stranger in Shakespeare* (St Albans).

Freese, J. H. (trans.) (1920), *The Library of Photius*, i (London, etc.).

Gilman, C. P. (1911), *The Man-made World: or Our Androcentric Culture* (New York).

Goldhill, S. (1988), 'Battle narrative and politics in Aeschylus' *Persae*', *JHS* 108: 189–93.

Guyot, P. (1980), *Eunuchen als Sklaven und Freigelassene in der griechisch-römischen Antike* (Stuttgart).

Hall, E. (1989), *Inventing the Barbarian: Greek Self-definition through Tragedy* (Oxford).

Halperin, D. M. (1990), 'Why is Diotima a woman?', in Halperin *et al.* (eds 1990), pp. 257–308.

——, Winkler, J. J., and Zeitlin, F. I. (eds 1990), *Before Sexuality: The Construction of Erotic Experience in the Ancient World* (Princeton).

Hanson, A. E. (1990), 'The medical writers' woman', in Halperin *et al.* (eds 1990), pp. 309–38.

Hartog, F. (1988), *The Mirror of Herodotus: The Representation of the Other in the Writing of History* (Berkeley, etc.).

Heaney, S. (1975), *North* (London).

Hulme, P. (1985), 'Polytropic man: tropes of sexuality and mobility in early colonial discourse', in Barker (ed. 1985), ii. 17–32.

Jouanna, P. (1981), 'Les causes de la défaite des barbares chez Eschyle, Hérodote, et Hippocrate', *Ktema*, 6: 3–15.

Kabbani, R. (1986), *Europe's Myths of Orient: Devise and Rule* (Basingstoke, etc.).

Kirk, I. (1987), 'Images of Amazons: marriage and matriarchy', in MacDonald (ed. 1987), pp. 27–39.

Kolodny, A. (1973), 'The land as woman: literary convention and latent psychological content', *Women's Studies*, 1: 167–82.

Lattimore, R. (1943), 'Aeschylus on the defeat of Xerxes', in *Classical Studies in Honor of William Abbott Oldfather*, 82–93 (Urbana).

Lloyd, G. E. R. (1966), *Polarity and Analogy: Two Types of Argumentation in Early Greek Thought* (Cambridge).

Loraux, N. (1986), 'Le deuil du rossignol', *Nouvelle Revue de psychoanalyse*, 34: 253–7.

—— (1990), 'Herakles: the super-male and the female', in Halperin *et al.* (eds 1990), pp. 21–52.

MacDonald, S. (ed. 1987), *Images of Women in Peace and War: Cross-cultural and Historical Perspectives* (Basingstoke, etc.).

Marinatos, S. (1967), *Kleidung Haar- und Barttracht* (Archaeologia Homerica, 1; Göttingen).

Merck, M. (1978), 'The city's achievements: the patriotic Amazonomachy and ancient Athens', in S. Lipshitz (ed.), *Tearing the Veil: Essays on Femininity* (London), pp. 95–115.

Munson, R. V. (1988), 'Artemisia in Herodotus', *Classical Antiquity*, 7(1): 91–106.

Ogden, C. K., and Florence, M. S. (1915), *Militarism versus Feminism* (London); reprinted in C. Marshall (ed. 1987), *Militarism versus Feminism: Writings on Women and War* (London), pp. 53–154.

Paduano, G. (1978), *Sui Persiani di Eschilo: problemi di focalizzazione drammatica* (Rome).

Perlman, S. (1976), 'Panhellenism, the polis and imperialism', *Historia*, 25: 1–30.

Porter, R. (1986), 'Rape – does it have a historical meaning?', in Tomaselli and Porter (eds 1986), pp. 216–36.

Rougé, J. (1970), 'La colonisation grecque et les femmes', *Cahiers d'histoire*, 15: 307–17.

Said, E. (1978), *Orientalism* (London).

—— (1985), 'Orientalism reconsidered', in Barker (ed. 1985), i. 14–27.

Sancisi-Weerdenburg, H. (1983), 'Exit Atossa: images of women in Greek historiography on Persia', in A. Cameron and A. Kuhrt (eds), *Images of Women in Antiquity* (London, etc.), pp. 20–33.

Schauenburg, K. (1975), '*Eurymedon eimi*', *AM* 90: 97–121.

Smith, R. R. R. (1987), 'The imperial reliefs from the Sebasteion at Aphrodisias', *JRS* 77: 88–138.

Thompson, D. B. (1956), 'The Persian spoils in Athens', in *The Aegean and the Near East (Studies in Honor of Hester Goldman)* (New York), pp. 281–91.

Thompson, H. A. (1981), 'Athens faces adversity', *Hesperia*, 50: 343–55.

Tomaselli, S., and Porter, R. (eds 1986), *Rape: An Historical and Social Enquiry* (Oxford, etc.).

Travlos, J. (1971), *Pictorial Dictionary of Ancient Athens* (London).

Tyrrell, W. B. (1984), *Amazons: A Study in Athenian Mythmaking* (Baltimore, etc.).

Vermeule, E. (1979), *Aspects of Death in Early Greek Art and Poetry* (Berkeley, etc.).

Vidal-Naquet, P. (1988), 'Sophocles' *Philoctetes* and the ephebeia', in J.-P. Vernant and P. Vidal-Naquet, *Myth and Tragedy in Ancient Greece* (New York), pp. 161–79.

Wiltsher, A. (1985), *Most Dangerous Women: Feminist Peace Campaigners of the Great War* (London, etc.).

Wyke, M. (1992), 'Augustan/poetic Cleopatras: female power and authority', in A. Powell (ed.), *Roman Poetry and Propaganda in the Age of Augustus* (London), pp. 98–139.

Zeitlin, F. (1984), 'The dynamics of misogyny in the Oresteia', in J. Peradotto and J. P. Sullivan (eds), *Women in the Ancient World: The Arethusa Papers* (Albany), pp. 159–94.

—— (1986), 'Configurations of rape in Greek myth', in Tomaselli and Porter (eds 1986), pp. 122–51.

7

Farming and fighting in ancient Greece

Lin Foxhall

The effects of warfare on the rural landscape, especially on agricultural crops and practices, emerged as an issue in the work of V. D. Hanson (*Warfare and Agriculture in Classical Greece*, 1983) and J. Ober (*Fortress Attica*, 1985). This research was at least partially inspired by the 'discovery' of ancient peasants in the 1970s through the work of Jameson (1977) and others (Burford-Cooper 1977; Andreyev 1974; Garnsey 1979). But paradoxically, in the most recent writing on both agriculture (Sallares 1991; Gallant 1991) and warfare (Hanson 1989; (ed.) 1991), the two subjects have become divorced and have gone off in separate directions. This is a pity, since men in ancient Greece probably spent more time fighting and farming than in any other activities. In this paper I shall intertwine them again, arguing that they do indeed belong together, although not perhaps for the reasons that Hanson and Ober originally identified.

There are three general aspects of the interplay between war and farming. All are interconnected, and all are linked to changes in Greek warfare from the Peloponnesian war into the fourth century and the hellenistic period. (1) Battles in the countryside and the presence of invading armies represented environmental hazards for farmers (interestingly, this is not noted by either Sallares 1991 or Gallant 1991). So, too, did the perceived threat of invasion. In times of endemic warfare, then, it is logical to assume that farmers will have taken what measures they could to prevent or mitigate damage. (2) The food produced by a city locally (in its own territory) was essential in most cases to its survival in case of invasion. This has been thoroughly documented by Garnsey (1985; 1988). It was necessary in all cases for a city's strategic security; that is, as regards its confidence in making plans to resist attack. (3) The destruction of crops and other agricultural resources was an important offensive tactic in ancient warfare, despite the fact that it often seems to have been ineffective in practical terms (Hanson 1983; 1989, 33–5).

It is on this last aspect that I shall concentrate, since it is central to the arguments of both Hanson and Ober. Hanson (1983) discusses the evidence for crop destruction during the Peloponnesian war. His main conclusion is that the amount of damage to Attic farming has been considerably overestimated. Farming continued throughout the war, and recovery was rapid afterwards. The same theme is taken up more generally in his later work, with the similar conclusion that wounded honour, rather than rational practicality, provided the main motivation for wasting military resources in fending off comparatively ineffectual attacks on crops (Hanson 1989, 34–9).

Ober (1985) is primarily concerned with fourth-century warfare. He suggests that in reaction to the economically and psychologically disastrous Periklean strategy, the Athenians adopted a defensive strategy based on a system of forts guarding the borders of Attica, with the aim of preventing enemy invasions of their territory. He argues that crop destruction was an effective economic weapon, and that it was used more efficiently from the fourth century on than previously. He views traditional hoplite warfare as a kind of semi-formalized agonistic challenge, in which besieged citizen hoplites attacked invading hoplite raiders largely because they would lose prestige by not so doing. The Periklean strategy broke the 'rules', and the consequence was the development of full-scale economic warfare based on *epiteichismos* (the occupation of one or more fortified bases on the frontier of the enemy's territory) and concomitantly more effective crop destruction. He considers that Attic farming was badly damaged during the Dekeleian war, and that recovery was slow.

Both Hanson and Ober have produced thought-provoking studies. One of the major aims of this paper, however, is to refine some of their suggestions in light of agrarian practicalities. I generally agree with Hanson that attacks on farming, as practised during the Peloponnesian war, did not do a great deal of economic damage. But I think the strategy of Perikles had another harmful effect which Hanson and others have missed, namely to encourage households to put their own perceived security before the defence of the city.

Rather than citing my disagreements with Ober and Hanson by chapter and verse, I shall give a brief overview of the potential for crop destruction within the context of Greek farming and Greek warfare, with particular reference to the Peloponnesian war, since it is well documented in this regard and extensively treated by Hanson and Ober.

The agrarian landscape

Thanks to Osborne (1985a; 1987) and Garnsey (1985, 1988), most agricultural *aficionados* among ancient historians now realize that fragmented holdings were the norm for Athenian, and probably most Greek, farmers (Gallant 1991, 41–5); Hanson and Ober did *not* realize this. Moreover, particularly for peasant subsistence farmers, many of the plots would have been very small indeed. To illustrate the viability of small plots, a modern example is useful, for though modern farming in Greece differs in many respects from farming in other times, it can none the less provide useful controlled comparisons.

The peninsula of Methana presents a fairly extreme example of plot fragmentation. Plots of under 1 *stremma* (0.1 ha; 0.25 acres) are not uncommon. For the village of Kosona, landholdings presently average around 3.5 hectares, divided (on average) into eighteen different plots (Forbes 1976; cf. id. 1982, 148–54). In terms of the effects of war on the human landscape, such a degree of fragmentation would have profound consequences. This can be illustrated by the results of a fire on Methana in 1985 which destroyed *c.*30–50 ha of land in the centre of the peninsula. A total of 104 families from six different villages lost property. Many lost a little; none lost a large amount.

The effects of an ancient army trying to ravage the countryside would have been much patchier than this fire. There would certainly have been many areas that *psiloi* (light-armed soldiers), let alone hoplites, could not have reached easily, especially on steeper slopes. Cavalry seem to have been particularly used during the Peloponnesian war to defend crops and harass the invaders on the plains of Attica (Spence 1990 makes the case best, but the phenomenon is also noted by Ober 1985 and Hanson 1983). If anything, it is likely that the wealthy farmers with bigger plots, which were perhaps more likely to be located on easily ravaged flat land, will have sustained the most damage. This is suggested by the writer of the *Constitution of the Athenians* attributed to Xenophon (2. 14–16), who highlights the different attitudes of rich and poor to invasions of Attica. On the other hand, land closest to the city, especially easily accessible and valuable plain land, may well have been the most fragmented area and the area owned in the smallest plots, even by wealthy farmers.

It is possible that the *eschatiai*, marginal agricultural and forest land (mentioned in fourth-century sources but not earlier, as far as I know), came under more intensive cultivation during the Peloponnesian war. Some was coastal land, but much seems to have been in mountainous areas (Lewis 1973; Foxhall, in press) which enemy raiders could not reach. At a time when every food source was important, there may have been a great incentive to cultivate areas that had previously been exploited less intensively (for example as grazing or for forest products).

Another agricultural resource of Athens that is rarely, if ever, mentioned was cultivable land within the city walls. Intensively worked gardens and vineyards may have covered a sizeable area there, and such small-scale production could have been important in wartime. This must be the kind of cultivation referred to in Aristophanes' *Ekklesiazousai* (817), where a town-dweller sells his grapes to buy barley-meal.

The dispersion of rural settlement has also been much debated, and is crucial to the question of the effects of enemy activity on the countryside. That certain types of settlement and activity were quite widely spread around the landscape in much of Greece in the classical period is clear from the evidence provided by documents and archaeological survey. That there is less extensive rural settlement in the hellenistic period also seems to be a trend emerging from several archaeological surveys (Runnels and van Andel 1987; van Andel and Runnels 1987; Mee *et al.* 1991; Bintliff and Snodgrass 1985; 1988). The proper interpretation of this evidence, however, and of the apparent changes, is more debatable. That much residential settlement was in villages I think cannot be doubted. Osborne (1985b) has pointed out that the *oikiai* mentioned in leases and other similar documents were often probably agricultural buildings, not dwelling-houses. And the houses documented archaeologically, of which the most famous examples are the Hymettos (or Vari) house and the Dema house, were surely holiday homes for the better-off at least as often as they were (or may have been) working farms. They certainly cannot be considered as representative of peasant residences.

What *were* probably scattered throughout the countryside were agricultural installations, which Hanson, Ober, and others do not discuss. Particularly common would have been wine-treading floors (the equivalent of modern Greek *patitiria*); threshing-floors, perhaps with associated store buildings; and olive presses, most of which would have been located out in the fields, as suggested by the group of inscriptions called the Attic Stelae (Foxhall 1990, 133–40) and by survey data. All these could have been damaged, at considerable cost to Attic farmers, by enemy attacks.

The destruction of crops

In considering the vulnerability of crops and the techniques of ravaging, Hanson and Ober only consider wheat, barley, vines, and olives. Other things, especially figs, deserve mention, and I shall come back to them; the role of livestock, though it was also important, cannot be considered in detail here.

Hanson and Ober both discuss the feasibility of destroying the four crops mentioned. Hanson definitively shows that destroying olives on a large scale would have been very difficult and unprofitably slow. The case becomes even stronger if, as I suspect, many fruit trees (olive, almond, fig, pear, apple, plum) were located in areas not easily reached by invaders, even from a base like Dekeleia. Spence (1990) argues that the cavalry kept raiders from Dekeleia pretty well at bay, which further strengthens the argument. Presses and *patitiria* may in fact have been damaged more often than olive trees.

Vines, however, probably sustained a considerable amount of damage, at least those growing on the plains and accessible slopes (though this is, in fact, minimized by Hanson 1989, 33). Hoplites' great fat feet were sufficient to wreak havoc (*Acharnians*, 229–31);

indeed, in Aristophanes damage to vines, often by cutting, receives more attention than other acts of Peloponnesian vandalism. Thus the Acharnians complain to Amphitrieus, 'Why do you make treaties when our vines have been hacked about?' (182–3; cf. 512). And it cannot be accidental that the main character of *Peace* is a vineyard keeper, not a 'general purpose' small farmer like Dikaiopolis in *Acharnians*. Although vines damaged by trampling and cutting might recover eventually, the year's crop would be lost at least. Once vines were damaged, even a severe dry spell in conjunction with neglect could certainly kill them off.

Young fruit trees probably suffered similarly. Like vines, newly planted trees are easily trampled, cut, and broken. In summer, just the time when the countryside might be full of Peloponnesians, young trees need watering and weeding. The point of *Acharnians* 971–99 is that young trees only flourish in peacetime. War is an unwelcome guest; he puts the vine-props on the fire and spills the wine out by force (985–6). But if Aphrodite comes, and love and peace win out (994–8), young trees can be planted.

Cereals, however, are a more complex issue. Wheat and barley were the main staples, and the security of their supply in wartime was any city's most fundamental strategic concern. Ober takes more or less the traditional view that the Athenians abandoned Attica, intending to subsist entirely on imports. This seems to me far too risky. The Athenians must have realized that grain supplies would be threatened by revolts and disruptions if things went badly for them. Long-distance grain imports are chancy at the best of times. Garnsey (1985; 1988) has convincingly shown that, in peacetime at least, Attica could supply a considerable proportion of Athens' grain needs. I cannot believe that Perikles or the Athenians undertook their strategy of withdrawal on the assumption that Attic farming would stop, and clearly it did not.

To return to ravaging: damaging grain growing in nice flat fields should not be as difficult as ripping up olive trees. During the Archidamian war the Spartans aimed to do just that, probably arriving in Attica in mid- to late May in most years. It is generally agreed that the invaders brought some food with them, but intended to live partly off the countryside. One year they arrived too early and had to go home again (Thucydides 4. 2. 1, 6; cf. 2. 23. 3). But, as with other crops, grain located on higher slopes would have been out of the Peloponnesians' reach. And the fact that the invaders never stayed longer than forty days highlights a further problem, missed by Hanson and Ober. The cereal harvest in Greece covers a long period depending on the cultigen or cultivar, the exposure of the plot, and the altitude. For example, on Methana there is a two-month difference in the growing season for wheat between the lower altitude fields (0–50 m above sea level) and the higher altitude fields (500 m and above). That is, at the top sowing takes place a month earlier and harvesting a month later than at the bottom. And barley is earlier than wheat in any case. So an invading force staying only a few weeks could have missed a considerable portion of the cereal harvest. Furthermore, since local weather conditions which determine ripening can vary considerably from year to year, precisely when the grain harvest will start is not very predictable. Farmers, cognizant of the increased hazards of wartime farming, could have emphasized this trend by the strategic use of different varieties, species, and locations (remember the fragmented plots). Three-month wheat or barley, later-sown varieties, could also be planted as an emergency measure if crops were destroyed in the autumn or winter.

The tactic of establishing a fortified base, *epiteichismos*, might have had most impact when it came to circumventing the problem of arriving at the right moment to do maximum damage to the cereal crop. This point goes unnoticed by Ober and Hanson. Once *epiteichismos* was established as a technique in the fourth century BC, the fear that an enemy settled at such a base might be able to destroy more grain, even if they never actually did so, could have been important in fostering the 'defensivism' for which Ober argues.

Destroying grain is not as easy as it might seem at first sight. Simply trampling the grain would not stop the harvest, though it would slow it down and seriously reduce yields. Burning grain is not so easy on a large scale, if the crop is not planted in contiguous plots and if it is not quite dry. The evidence (Hanson 1983; 1989, 33–4) suggests that burning was not much practised during the Peloponnesian war. Cutting seems to have been common, and has the advantage that the enemy can use the spoils; but it is slow.

There is much evidence to suggest that farmers always stored grain when they could (Gallant 1991, 94–8), and during wartime they must have tried even harder to build up reserves. There was little or no state granary provision in most cities; this was a role explicitly taken on by individual households. Where was there safe storage in an invaded Attica? Although there is no concrete evidence for this practice in classical or hellenistic times, it is interesting to compare crisis-period food storage on modern Methana. A number of hiding-places (*ambaria*) exist up in the mountains. The one illustrated in *Plate 1a* has a corbelled roof, and Late Roman pottery was found nearby. They were used for the storage of food and supplies during the Turkish period, in order to keep essential provisions out of enemy hands. Similar underground storage chambers have also been excavated in the classical Greek city of Olynthos (Robinson and Graham 1938, 259).

Like most Greek poleis, Attica cultivated a wide range of other crops besides grain, olives, and vines. Given the varying conditions for growth that were necessary, and the spread of harvest periods, this in itself will have provided a measure of security against enemy attack. Indeed, many foods that would not normally be considered palatable might be eaten during wartime shortages (Garnsey 1988; Gallant 1991, ch. 5). But the most important wartime food was the fig. I have demonstrated the high food energy value of figs elsewhere (Foxhall 1990, ch. 3, fig. 6). Figs may have provided about 15 million kilocalories per hectare, as compared with 1.3 to 2 million for wheat, or wheat polycropped with olives. Like olives, mature figs rarely seem to have been an object of attack. Though fresh figs may have been in short supply, dried figs (*ischades*) seem to have been a major staple during the Peloponnesian war. Generally they seem to have been considered a low-status food. In *Peace* (634; 636) the country folk who poured into Athens are described as 'lovers of dried figs (*ischades*), but out of barley meal (*alphita*)'. The starving Megarian and his daughters in *Acharnians* (799–810) gratefully wolf down dried figs. Again, in *Peace* (1215–23) Trygaios offers to buy a now useless crest for three *choinikes* (!) of dried figs. The redundant crest-maker accepts gratefully, replying 'Oh well, that's better than nothing.'

One major conclusion, with many ramifications, arises from this enquiry into crop ravaging. The balance of the evidence suggests that attacks on crops would almost never actually threaten a city's food supply. To really imperil a city's subsistence would take large, intensive, and repeated attacks on crops and agricultural resources, most usually in combination with other measures like treachery, naval blockade, and so forth. Under the less professionalized methods of fighting in vogue in the fifth century and earlier, techniques of attacking agricultural crops would have been pretty ineffective in direct terms. Thus the evidence does not hold up Osborne's statement (1987, 140) about hoplite warfare that it was 'an alternative to farming, a way of making up deficiencies in one's own supplies'.

Conclusions: crop damage and the threat of social disunity

So why did the strategy persist? Ober (1985, 31–4) suggests it was part of an agonistic mentality. Hanson (1983, 150–1) attributes it to innate conservatism, and is openly puzzled by the problem: 'we hear constantly of ravaging, rarely of damage inflicted' (p. 150). In his more recent work Hanson argues that farmers' pride was hurt more than their crops (1989, 34). I think Osborne comes closest to the truth (1987, 154):

> Long invasions . . . also posed a great threat to the unity of the citizen body. Long invasions created internal pressures, partly because they did not affect all alike (farmers were hit harder than those without land, and some farmers were hit harder than others), and partly because in a city under siege there was considerable scope for treacherous action and suspicion of treachery.

The sort of behaviour Osborne mentions is one aspect of a larger phenomenon. The problem results from the use of agricultural strategies, not the use of military strategies, and it is with the former that a solution must be sought.

In a Greek city, farming was not planned by the polis. Agrarian strategies as they appear at community level were the aggregate result of household decisions. The risk of Periklean strategy was that it depended on loyalty to the polis taking precedence over household and family loyalties. The failure of that strategy was not that it left Athens exposed to economic damage, but that it left Athens exposed to envy, suspicion, and social disunity. When it came to the bottom line, it was not the city's *chora* (land) that was being ravaged, but individual households' *choriai* (fields). The private wars and private peace settlements in Aristophanes' comedies may have been uncomfortably true to life. Many must have felt that others were suffering less badly than themselves, and this would lead to a breakdown in social and political unity.

Thucydides (2. 13. 1) discusses Perikles' motives in facing the first Spartan invasion, on the basis of what must have been a current rumour: that Archidamos was going to pass by Perikles' property (though how he would have known exactly where it was is problematic). The general discontent with Periklean strategy early in the war is well known. Spence (1990) suggests it was a major reason for regular cavalry attacks on the enemy. I suggest it was the main reason for the persistence of the Peloponnesians' technique of crop ravaging as an offensive tactic; the aim was to crack the city's unity. The threat *perceived* by individual households to their own subsistence was the enemy's most powerful weapon.

The other side of the coin is the policy of border defence adopted in the fourth century. If the enemy could not reach the fields, they posed no threat to social unity; whereas, if invaders established themselves on a fortified base, then the very bonds which *were* the polis were under attack, and the social fabric of the city might be torn. As a final point, I think this examination suggests that the fundamental interplay between war and farming did not change, although the terms on which it was operated did. The fully integrated triad of civic roles – citizen, farmer, soldier – was fragmented during the course of the fourth century, as Osborne (1987) points out. For poleis to retain a sense of security, especially in periods of disruption and uncertainty, the integration of the roles of citizen and farmer continued to be crucial, even when that of soldier had become detached.

Bibliography

Andreyev, V. N. (1974), 'Some aspects of agrarian conditions in Attica in the fifth to third centuries BC', *Eirene*, 12: 5–46.

Bintliff, J., and Snodgrass, A. (1985), 'The Cambridge/Bradford Boeotian Expedition: the first four years', *Journal of Field Archaeology*, 12: 123–61.

—— and —— (1988), 'Mediterranean survey and the city', *Antiquity*, 234 (n.s. 62): 57–71.

Burford-Cooper, A. (1977), 'The family farm in Greece', *Classical Journal*, 73: 162–75.

Forbes, H. A. (1976), ' "We have a little of everything": the ecological basis of some agricultural practices in Methana, Trizinia', in M. Dimen and E. Friedl (eds), *Regional Variation in Modern Greece and Cyprus: Toward a Perspective on the Ethnography of Greece* (Annals of the New York Academy of Sciences, 268), pp. 236–50.

—— (1982), *Strategies and Soils: Technology, Production and Environment in the Peninsula of Methana, Greece* (University Microfilms, Ann Arbor).

Foxhall, L. (1990), *Olive Cultivation within Greek and Roman Farming: the Ancient Economy Revisited* (unpublished Ph.D. thesis; Liverpool).

—— (in press), 'The control of the Attic landscape', in B. Wells and J.-E. Skydsgaard (eds), *Ancient Greek Agriculture: Proceedings of the 7th International Symposium, Swedish School at Athens* (Athens).

Gallant, T. W. (1991), *Risk and Survival in Ancient Greece: Reconstructing the Rural Domestic Economy* (Cambridge).

Garnsey, P. (1979), 'Where did Italian peasants live?', *PCPS* 205 (n.s. 25): 1–25.

—— (1985), 'Grain for Athens', in P. A. Cartledge and F. D. Harvey (eds), *Crux: Essays in Greek History Presented to G. E. M. de Ste. Croix on his 75th Birthday* (London; = *History of Political Thought*, 6 (1–2)), pp. 62–75.

—— (1988), *Famine and Food Supply in the Graeco-Roman World: Responses to Risk and Crisis* (Cambridge).

Hanson, V. D. (1983), *Warfare and Agriculture in Classical Greece* (Pisa).

—— (1989), *The Western Way of War: Infantry Battle in Classical Greece* (London, etc.).

—— (ed. 1991), *Hoplites* (Stanford, Calif.).

Jameson, M. H. (1977), 'Agriculture and slavery in classical Athens', *Classical Journal*, 73 (2): 122–45.

Lewis, D. M. (1973), 'The Athenian *rationes centesimarum*', in M. I. Finley (ed.), *Problèmes de la terre en Grèce ancienne* (Paris), pp. 187–212.

Mee, C. B., Gill, D., Forbes, H. A., and Foxhall, L. (1991), 'Rural settlement change in the Methana peninsula, Greece', in G. Barker and J. Lloyd (eds), *Roman Landscapes: Archaeological Survey in the Mediterranean Region* (Archaeological Monographs of the British School at Rome, 2; London), pp. 223–32.

Ober, J. (1985), *Fortress Attica: Defense of the Athenian Land Frontier 404–322 BC* (Leiden).

Osborne, R. (1985a), *Demos: The Discovery of Classical Attika* (Cambridge).

—— (1985b), 'Buildings and residence on the land in classical and hellenistic Greece: the contribution of epigraphy', *BSA* 80: 119–28.

—— (1987), *Classical Landscape with Figures: The Ancient Greek City and its Countryside* (London).

Robinson, D. M., and Graham, J. W. (1938), *Excavations at Olynthos*, viii: *The Hellenic House* (Baltimore).

Runnels, C. N., and van Andel, T. H. (1987), 'The evolution of settlement in the southern Argolid, Greece: an economic explanation', *Hesperia*, 56: 303–34.

Sallares, R. (1991), *The Ecology of the Ancient Greek World* (London).

Spence, I. G. (1990), 'Pericles and the defence of Attika during the Peloponnesian war', *JHS* 110: 91–109.

van Andel, T. H., and Runnels, C. N. (1987), *Beyond the Acropolis* (Stanford).

∞ 8 ∞

Warfare, wealth, and the crisis of Spartiate society[1]

Stephen Hodkinson

The outbreak of war with Athens in 431 BC marked, for Sparta, the beginning of an extended period of warfare outside its traditional sphere of influence within the Peloponnese which was to last, with only temporary interruptions, for a period of sixty years. This prolonged external engagement was a new factor in Spartan history. Sparta's earlier campaigns outside the Peloponnese had been spasmodic and brief; but in this period Spartiate *commanders* (a term I shall use to embrace men with various kinds of military responsibilities outside the regular citizen army) were involved in continual military activity abroad. In the central years of the period (412–386) Sparta created an unprecedented foreign empire. The effects of this prolonged foreign engagement are worthy of investigation, especially because the end of the period witnessed Sparta's rapid decline to the status of a second-rate power with its defeat at the battle of

[1] Since it was originally delivered at a 'War and Society' seminar at Leicester, this paper has been materially improved by the comments of Paul Cartledge and John Rich. It has also been transformed by the experience of recasting its argument for presentation to the mixed academic, military, and professional audience of the Clausewitz seminar at the Norwegian Institute of International Relations. I am grateful to Jon Bingen and Bjørn Qviller for their invitation to speak to that seminar; to the Norwegian Ministry of Defence for funding my stay in Oslo; and to Graham Burton and Peter Lowe for comparative advice about Roman and Japanese imperialism.

Leuktra in 371, the subsequent secession of many of its Peloponnesian allies, and finally, in the winter of 370/69, the liberation by enemy invasion of its subject hclot populations in Messenia, the most fertile region of its core territory.

The particular concern of this essay is with the impact of war and empire upon the Spartiate citizen body, whose social system had by the end of the 370s reached a dual state of crisis. Not only had the number of citizens become so few that they were unable to prevent the 'single blow' – as Aristotle put it (*Politics*, 1270 a) – of defeat at Leuktra from leading on to more permanent catastrophes; but also, at the very height of enemy invasion, when Sparta itself was under attack, a significant number of those citizens were secretly plotting revolution (Plutarch, *Agesilaos*, 32; David 1980). For a citizen body which had long maintained a remarkable and genuine political cohesion, this latter crisis was a real setback, which limited Sparta's ability to defend its core territory. These twin crises of Spartiate society lay at the heart of its international decline; how much did they owe to the impact of prolonged foreign warfare and empire?

The limits of modern discussion

Surprisingly, there has been no sustained discussion of this question in most specialist books on Sparta. The most informed comment is to be found in the works of Finley (1986) and Cartledge (1987). It is worth quoting the relevant parts of Finley's seminal article (1986, 168 and 177):

> Presumably a sufficient equilibrium could be maintained despite the pressures so long as the Spartans remained safely cocooned within their own world. But not when they were drawn abroad. . . .

> Sparta's tragedy thereafter stemmed from a familiar cause: she did not live in a vacuum. . . . Sparta was drawn into extensive military activity, genuinely military. That entailed . . . unprecedented opportunities for ambitious individuals, extensive travel abroad and a breach in the traditional xenophobia, the impossibility of holding the line against the seductions of wealth. The system could not and did not long survive. And so the final paradox is that her greatest military success destroyed the model military state.

These are two typically trenchant Finleyesque passages which, however, beg some important questions. First, in the picture they paint of a society which, despite its tensions, remained in balance until its transformation proceeded only through the intervention of external factors; second, in their failure to indicate the precise linkage between foreign involvement and social collapse, the exact constituents of which are left unspecified.

Whilst endorsing Finley's 'final paradox', Cartledge takes the argument a stage further (1987, 34–54). He surveys several areas of change associated with war and empire which, he suggests, precipitated the Spartan crisis: manpower shortage and changes in army organization, changes in strategy and tactics, finance, individual Spartiates' involvement abroad, and increased domestic conflicts. Locating these changes within the broader context of the problems of shortage of citizens (*oliganthropia*) and of increasing concentration of property which, he argues, were the underlying components of Sparta's crisis, he contends (1987, 168) that

> the Athenian War registered a watershed. By bringing significant numbers of elite Spartans into sustained and intimate contact with hitherto unimagined amounts of coined silver and gold, this war accelerated and gave a new twist to a process that had been underway since at least the mid-fifth century.

This account has the merit that it connects the impact of the war with longer-term internal developments, but the precise causal links between access to coinage and the concentration of property still remain unclear.

Sparta's internal crisis

One reason for the elusive quality of even the best modern accounts is the lack of an explicit statement of the precise constituents of Sparta's internal crisis. Cartledge has correctly identified the twin developments of property concentration and *oliganthropia* as the central long-term phenomena. Many poorer Spartiates lost citizen status as their landholdings declined, because they became unable to provide the monthly contributions of food to their mess group, membership of which was a requirement of citizenship. Hence citizen numbers declined dramatically from 8,000 in 480 BC to less than 1,500 by the end of the 370s (de Ste. Croix 1972, 331-2; Cartledge 1979, 307-18). What processes, however, lay behind the developments of property concentration and *oliganthropia*? It seems to me that there were at least four factors involved (see Hodkinson 1986, and especially 1989, for a more detailed elaboration).

(1) There was a slow but steady trend towards inequality of land ownership among citizens, which was embedded in the combination of differential reproduction and a system of partible inheritance among both sons and daughters. By means of computer simulation, it has been possible to demonstrate how this intrinsic trend was produced regardless of conscious human intention. (2) Inequalities were increased by the actions of richer Spartiates. As early as the mid-sixth century, wealthy families can be seen conserving and extending their property through advantageous marriage practices. Aristotle's comments (*Pol.* 1307 a) on the way the notables grasped at wealth also hint at the pressurized acquisition of property. (3) Sparta's leaders failed to counteract these dangerous property and population trends. The symptoms of manpower shortage were tackled, for example, through efforts to stimulate the birth rate and by drafting non-Spartiates into the armed forces; but the roots of the malaise – the economic difficulties of poorer citizens – were left untouched. (4) Finally, underlying these developments was a fundamental breakdown in the solidarity of the citizen body, especially in the longstanding compact between rich and poor upon which Sparta's successful social system had been based.

The first factor, which operated in a manner independent of external events, must obviously be set apart. Although it had severe effects in Sparta in the context of a closed citizen body with a concealed property qualification, these effects might have been counteracted but for the operation of the other three factors; in other words, had there been less individual property accumulation, more strong-minded action by Sparta's leaders, and greater solidarity between rich and poor. It is upon these three factors that we must concentrate.

What role, then, did foreign warfare and empire play in these developments? The following discussion will be divided into four

main parts. First, I shall look at the answer to my question given
by some of the ancient sources. I shall then examine the methods
and personnel through which Sparta organized and conducted its
foreign campaigns. In the third part I shall consider the impact of
these upon Spartan politics and society. Finally, I shall briefly
compare Sparta's experience of warfare and empire with that of
the Roman republic, as a control for assessing its significance in
the development of the Spartiate crisis.

The influx of wealth

Several ancient writers claim that the Spartan social order was
ruined by the influx of foreign wealth, especially the gold and
silver coinage sent home by Lysander after the defeat of the
Athenian empire in 404 (references in David 1979–80, 38 n. 24).
The clearest statement is in Plutarch's life of Lysander (ch. 17),
which, drawing upon Ephoros and Theopompos, reports the
debate about how to deal with this wealth. According to this
account, there was considerable opposition to allowing the coinage into Sparta; but it was finally agreed to permit its introduction
for public use, though not for private possession. Plutarch
criticizes this compromise on the ground that it stimulated private
greed.[1]

Plutarch's account implies that the acceptance of foreign coinage for public use was something new. This seems to have been the
view of at least one of his sources, Ephoros, as reflected in the
comments of Diodoros (7. 12): 'as they little by little began to
relax each one of their institutions and to turn to luxury and
indifference and as they grew so corrupted as to use coined
money, they lost their leadership.' Ephoros' view, however, can
hardly be correct (see Cawkwell 1983, 396; Cartledge 1987, 88).

---

[1] At *Agis*, 5, Plutarch further claims that this greed impelled the
Spartiates to pass the so-called 'law of Epitadeus', which supposedly
ended a previous system of inheritance by unigeniture and led to the
concentration of land. Despite the attempts of David (1979–80, 44–5;
1981, 71–3) to treat this as authentic history, it is merely a house of cards,
since, as has recently been demonstrated by Hodkinson (1986, 379–91)
and Schütrumpf (1987), the supposed system of inheritance by unigeniture and the law of Epitadeus are both pure fiction.

Although it did not mint coinage of its own, the polis will long have needed foreign coinage, for instance for the use of its ambassadors and for hiring mercenaries (whose employment goes back at least to 424; Thucydides, 4. 55). Indeed, Noethlichs (1987) has recently argued that until 404 *private* possession of gold and silver had also been permitted, even in coined form. On his view the innovation introduced in 404 was that it was now banned *for the first time* because of fears about the sheer quantity of wealth being brought into Sparta – in total, some 1,500 to 2,000 talents, plus a sizeable quantity of non-coined movable wealth, according to the estimate of David (1979–80, 38–40).

So, at most, the compromise of 404 was simply a reaffirmation of existing law, and may even have marked a tightening up of previous practice. Moreover, Plato provides a corrective to Plutarch's moralizing about the corrupting effects of public use of coinage because in his *Laws* (742 a) he positively recommends the same compromise for his Cretan state. Neither was private greed for wealth anything new. The susceptibility of leading Spartiates to bribery, for example, had long been known; Noethlichs (1987, 136–45, nos 9–19) has catalogued no fewer than eleven instances recorded in the sources concerning the period before 431. In his *Republic* (548 a–b) Plato treats the avid private possession of gold and silver as an essential characteristic of his Spartan-based timocratic state. The same picture appears in the possibly pseudo-Platonic dialogue, *Alkibiades I* (122 e–123 a), in which Sokrates comments that there was more gold and silver privately held in Sparta than in the rest of Greece, since it had been passing in to them over many generations. If it is true that after 404 the greatly increased amounts of public wealth did seep into private hands, we should view its impact in terms not of its novelty but of its scale.

Of course, coinage brought back to Sparta was not the only means by which Spartiates could acquire new riches. Commanders abroad had greater than normal opportunities for self-enrichment during prolonged foreign campaigns. Agesilaos' manipulation of booty during his Asian campaign to make profits for his friends (Xenophon, *Agesilaos*, 1. 17–19) is suggestive of what other commanders could do for their own benefit. If we ask, however, why Spartiate commanders engaged in private profiteering, part of the answer must surely be their perception of the advantage to be gained at home, which implies that wealth was already important as a determinant of status and influence. Otherwise, how do we explain, for example, the suicidal self-enrichment of Thorax (Plut. *Lycurgus*, 19) so soon after the introduction of the death penalty for private possession of gold and silver?

That the significance of wealth, as against other criteria of ranking, had already developed markedly during the course of the fifth century is a proposition I have argued in an earlier study (1989, 95–100). Once again, we should view the impact of newly acquired imperial wealth as exacerbating current trends rather than initiating something new. To uncover its real role in the Spartan crisis, we need first to explore the socio-political context in which the acquisition of wealth became even more important for leading citizens, and to examine the impact of foreign warfare and empire upon that scenario.

The organization of foreign commands

In the second part of this essay I shall examine the organization and personnel through which Sparta conducted its foreign campaigning. Let me first briefly outline the main facts (cf. Parke 1930; Böckisch 1965; Sealey 1976). During the central years of empire (412–386) Sparta fought its overseas wars by means of a dual system of forces, the beginnings of which can be seen during the Archidamian war in the 420s. The first element was the Peloponnesian fleet under the admiral (*nauarchos*) and his staff of supporting officers, often with subordinate commanders in charge of subsidiary naval contingents in regions distant from the main force. The second element was a variable number of harmosts (*harmostai*), who operated usually on land, but sometimes with a few ships, and whose sphere of action might vary from the territory of a single Greek polis to an 'area command' over a large region. The essential point is that this dual command allowed Sparta to conduct simultaneous campaigns in different regions while committing abroad only a small minority of Spartiates, almost all of whom acted as commanders.

The vast majority of citizens were retained at home to ensure security against the subject helot population. The rowers in

Lakonian ships within the fleet were either helots or mercenaries (Xen. *Hellenica*, 7. 1. 12; Myron, *FGH* 106 F 1), and the harmosts' land forces contained varying combinations of freed helots (*neodamodeis*), allies, and mercenaries (see e.g. Thuc. 8. 5; Xen. *Hell.* 3. 1. 4–6; 3. 4. 2, 15). After the end of *overseas* campaigning in 386, harmosts continued in use on a reduced scale for mainland campaigns outside the Peloponnese, although during the 370s they were largely restricted to out-of-season garrison duties, while later in the decade their forces were replaced by regiments of the regular citizen army led by their traditional commanders, the polemarchs.

Scholars have often pointed to the obvious contrast between the position of the Spartiate citizen at home, living under the austere and strictly regimented, state-controlled system, and the same Spartiate as an independent commander abroad, separated from the 'Big Brother' of the home authorities. But to evaluate the significance of this contrast, we need to ask some specific questions, such as how many men were involved? For how long, typically, were they abroad? Of what social status were Spartiate commanders? How were they chosen? How much was there contact with, and supervision by, other commanders or the home authorities? And how much scope was there for the exercise of personal ambition?

The number of Spartiate commanders abroad

There is no easy answer to the question of how many Spartiates were employed abroad. One can set a baseline through the number of commanders mentioned by name in the sources (Table 1). These figures have some value, in indicating that foreign commands were already developing apace in the 420s and confirming that their peak came in the 400s and 390s when Sparta's campaigning in the Aegean, the Hellespont, and Asia Minor was at its greatest extent. But in those central decades, in particular, they are a very poor guide to global numbers; not only because they omit cases where we know of the presence of commanders but not their names, but more fundamentally because the sources fail to cover all the theatres of war, and to give full details of the personnel involved even in those theatres they do cover. For

Table 1 Numbers of named Spartiate commanders active outside the Peloponnese, 429–370 BC (by decade)

420s	410s	400s	390s	380s	370s
21	18	33	30	17	13

example, during the Ionian war the sources' heavy focus on the eastern Aegean means that it is only through a passing mention in Xenophon (*Hell.* 1. 4. 22) of a Lakonian garrison on Andros, presumably under a harmost, that we glimpse the possibility that there were otherwise totally unmentioned harmosts stationed throughout the Aegean during the 400s (Parke 1930, 49–50).[1] Similarly, only in a few semi-retrospective, general references does Xenophon reveal the presence of numerous harmosts on both the Asian and European mainlands, whose existence he otherwise completely ignores in his account of Sparta's campaigns between 400 and 389 (*Hell.* 4. 8. 1, 5, 39; cf. Diod. 14. 84). Likewise, a single reference in a speech set in the year 369 (*Hell.* 7. 1. 12) provides the invaluable information that the trierarchs of ships from Lakonia were normally Spartiates,[2] and possibly some of the marines too.[3]

---

[1]   Cf. Dunant 1978, 47–8, no. 124, for a Lakedaimonian grave-stele at Eretria (Poralla, revised by Bradford 1985, 200a, henceforth abbreviated as PB), possibly evidence for a garrison on Euboia.

[2]   Even here there is some ambiguity. The word used, *Lakedaimonios*, can include *perioikoi*; but the context suggests that it is Spartiates that the speaker is concerned with. Note that Brasidas appears as a trierarch already in 425 (Thuc. 4. 11), and that in 388 the eight Spartiates who 'happened to be with' the harmost Gorgopas on Aigina probably represent most of the trierarchs from the twelve ships under his command (Xen. *Hell.* 5. 1. 6, 11). Spartan practice was not always consistent. Perioikic naval commanders are attested during the Ionian war (ML 95 *k*). Thucydides' specification (8. 22. 1) that Deiniadas, the commander of the thirteen ships that attacked Lesbos in 412, was a *perioikos* may, however, indicate a departure from the norm; and the fleet he commanded was Chian rather than Lakonian.

[3]   The marines (*epibatai*) referred to here are not to be confused with the individual *epibatēs* who appears in Thuc. 8. 61. 2; Xen. *Hell.* 1. 3. 17; and *Hell. Oxy.* 22 (17). 4. The latter appears to be a technical Spartan term for a detachable subordinate officer of a *nauarchos*: Gomme *et al.* 1981, 150. I am grateful to the late Professor A. Andrewes for his advice on the substance of this footnote.

These considerations do not advance the cause of accuracy very much, because to estimate throughout our period the likely number of poleis under a Spartiate harmost, or the number of Lakonian ships in Peloponnesian fleets, are both problematic tasks; but I should not be surprised if we had to triple the number of named Spartiates to get the right order of magnitude for the total numbers abroad during the 400s and 390s. Possibly there were up to a hundred separate individuals in each decade. This, however, would still be a very small proportion out of a total citizen population of perhaps some 2,000–4,000.

The frequency and duration of posts abroad

To determine the significance of these figures we need to ask how often, and for how long, Spartiates were normally abroad. Of 59 named non-royal Spartiate commanders active during the peak years of empire whose careers are not known to have been terminated prematurely by death or exile, 38 (64 per cent) are attested in only a single command, while at least 21 (36 per cent) were given a second command. The latter is a minimum figure, since several men are likely to have held additional commands unrecorded in the evidence. The careers of the 21 men attested as holding at least two commands are itemized in Table 2.[1] At least 5 of them had their careers prematurely terminated by death or exile after their second command; but 10 of the remaining 16 men (62.5 per cent) were given a third command. Of these three-times commanders, at least 2 died prematurely; but 6 out of the remaining 8 received a fourth command.

The evidence suggests that among the limited number of men chosen for foreign service, a relatively high proportion were given multiple terms abroad. Sparta had, indeed, long pursued a similar policy of iteration of posts in the case of diplomatic personnel, by often selecting the same men or their descendants as envoys to particular states (Mosley 1973, 50–4).

---

[1] The ancient evidence for these men's careers may be consulted via the Lakedaimonian prosopography of Poralla, revised by Bradford (PB). My reconstruction of the military career of Pharax (PB 717–18) follows that of Mosley (1963).

Table 2 Spartiate commanders active in 412–386 BC and attested as holding two or more military commands (PB nos in brackets)

Name	Years of separate commands	Fate
Gylippos (196)	414–412, 405	exile
Philippos (725)	412, 411	
Eteonikos (283)	412, 409, 406, 405, 400, pre-390, 390/89, 389/8	
Hippokrates (391)	412/11, 411–410, 410–408	death
Klearchos (425)	412–410, 410–408, 406, 403	exile
Agesandridas (5)	411/10, 409/8	
Derkylidas (228)	411–407, 399–397, 396/5, 394–389	
Lysander (504)	407/6, 405/4, 403, 396/5, 395	death
Thorax (380)	406, 405, 404/3	execution
Pharax (717–18)	405, 398/7, 396/5	
Panthoidas (585)	403/2, 377	death
Anaxibios (86)	401/0, 389/8	
Thibron (374–5)	400/399, 390	death
Herippidas (349)	399, 396–394, 393/2, 379	execution
Pollis (621)	396/5, 393/2, 377/6	
Euxenos (310)	395/4, 394/3	
Peisandros (601)	395/4, 394	death
Teleutias (689)	392/1, 391–389, 387/6, 382/1	death
Gorgopas (193)	389/8, 388	death
Antalkidas (97)	388/7, 387	
Nikolochos (564)	388/7, 376/5	

Note The chronology of these years is often uncertain, and some of the dates given above are subject to minor variations according to different modern schemes.

For how long were commanders committed to service abroad? As Table 2 indicates, a commander's foreign posts were sometimes separated by a significant intervening period, when he will have returned to Sparta. In at least fifteen of the twenty-one cases, however, the close temporal juxtaposition of certain commands suggests that commanders often served continuous (or near-continuous) spells abroad, moving from one post to another. The most extreme case is that of Eteonikos, who seems to have served as a kind of all-purpose, often subordinate, commander, loyally performing a variety of tasks. In addition, tenure of a particular post could sometimes last for a number of years, as in the cases of Gylippos, Hippokrates, Klearchos, Derkylidas, Herippidas, and Teleutias. As a consequence, several commanders spent significant periods abroad in relation to their time in Sparta;

Eteonikos, for example, was away for at least 8 years out of 24, Hippokrates seemingly continuously for the 4 years preceding his death, Klearchos for 6 years out of 10 before his exile, Teleutias for 5 out of 11 years, and – above all – Derkylidas for at least 14 years out of 22 between 411 and 389 BC.

The social background of commanders

The comparison made above between the patterns of employment of military personnel and that of diplomatic personnel raises the question whether, like its ambassadors, Sparta's commanders typically came from the leading families. What can we say of the social backgrounds of commanders?

A major obstacle to answering this question is the paucity of prosopographical information about individual Spartiates, especially the frequent failure of the sources to provide patronymics. Consequently, several of the more prominent commanders (for example, thirteen of the twenty-one men listed in Table 2) are to us just names whose family affiliations are unknown. In Tables 3 and 4, however, I have collected some suggestive evidence which can, I would argue, stand proxy for the large number of cases in which evidence is lacking. Table 3 shows that of the eight men listed in Table 2 whose family affiliations *are* known, all have indications of high social status. Table 4 provides evidence (based largely upon those few passages in which Thucydides provides patronymics) concerning several men prominent in the late 430s and 420s whose sons later appear as military commanders. (There are a few overlaps with Table 3.)

The final case in Table 4, the family of Leon (also referred to in Table 3), is of particular interest (see Whitehead 1979; Cartledge 1987, 145–6). This lineage was clearly of the highest status. Leon's Olympic chariot victory is evidence of considerable wealth; the victory was won with Enetic horses acquired from the region of the upper Adriatic (Anderson 1961, 37). One of his sons, Antalkidas, became noted for his diplomatic negotiations with Persia, where he was a guest-friend of the noble family of Ariobarzanes. Leon's other son, Pedaritos, is described by Theopompos as a man of good birth. The name of Pedaritos' mother, Teleutia, suggests a connection by marriage with

Table 3 High-status indicators of Spartiate commanders named in Table 2 (PB nos in brackets)

Name	Family affiliations and status indicators
Gylippos (196)	son of Kleandridas (420), adviser to King Pleistoanax
Klearchos (425)	son of Ramphias (654), ambassador and commander (K. himself is proxenos of Byzantion)
Agesandridas (5)	son of Agesandros (6), ambassador
Lysander (504)	son of Aristokritos (129) and brother of Libys (490); family claims descent from Herakles and is linked to Libyan king of Ammonians (Malkin 1990)
Pharax (717–18)	grandson of Pharax (717), adviser to King Agis II (the younger P. is proxenos of Thebes)
Peisandros (601)	son of Aristomenidas (134), judge at Plataia and ambassador; brother-in-law of King Agesilaos II
Teleutias (689)	half-brother of King Agesilaos II; cousin of Antalkidas (see next entry)
Antalkidas (97)	son of Leon (481), colony founder, ephor, and Olympic victor

Table 4 Father–son roles among Spartiate commanders, late fifth and early fourth centuries BC (PB nos in brackets)

Father	Son(s)
Sthenelaidas (664), ephor	Alkamenes (56), harmost
	Sthenelaos (665), harmost
Agesandros (6), ambassador	Pasitelidas (592), harmost
	Agesandridas (85), vice-admiral and naval commander
Ramphias (654), ambassador and commander	Klearchos (425), harmost
Leon (481), colony founder, ephor, and Olympic victor	Pedaritos (599), harmost
	Antalkidas (97), admiral, ambassador, and ephor

Note For fuller discussion of these cases see Hodkinson 1983, 262.

Teleutias, the prominent commander of the late 390s and 380s (see Table 2), who was in turn linked to the Eurypontid royal house through his mother's remarriage to King Archidamos II, which made him the half-brother of King Agesilaos II. (For the resulting stemma see Cartledge 1987, 146.) The military careers of Pedaritos, Antalkidas, and Teleutias are an excellent example of two interlinked, highly-placed lineages providing commanders for Sparta's foreign campaigns.

The kinds of prominent family affiliations indicated in these tables can be documented in several other cases outside the central period selected for detailed scrutiny. For example, although Brasidas (PB 177), the most prominent commander of the 420s, rose in position through merit, he also hailed from a background which gave him connections at Pharsalos in Thessaly (Thuc. 4. 78), and which put his father Tellis (PB 690) on the board of Spartiates who concluded the peace and alliance with Athens in 421. In the period after 386, the brothers and fellow-commanders Eudamidas (PB 295) and Phoibidas (PB 734) appear to have been connected by patronage, and later by marriage, to the Eurypontid royal house (Cartledge 1987, 147-8). Similarly, Sphodrias (PB 680), harmost of Thespiai in 378, was a close associate of King Kleombrotos I.

The names of several commanders also provide clues to their high status, even when their family affiliations are unknown. Names derived from foreign places, such as Chalkideus ('the Chalkidian'; PB 743), Samios ('the Samian'; PB 659), and Skythes ('the Skythian'; PB 686), indicate ties with leading families in other states. Names formed from *hippos* ('horse') suggest a wealthy, horse-breeding background: for example, Gylippos, Philippos, Hippokrates, and Herippidas (all four of whom appear in Table 2), not to mention Kratesippidas (PB 456), Lysippos (PB 506), Mnasippos (PB 538), Orsippos (PB 582), and Pasippidas (PB 591), as well as Polos, 'the foal' (PB 653).

Limits of space prevent discussion of several other cases of commanders for whom there are indicators (of varying degrees of certainty) of high social status. Solely on the basis of the evidence considered above, however, the conclusion that foreign commands were generally dominated by men from the leading families seems inescapable.

Methods and criteria of appointment

How were these commanders chosen? Appointments to foreign commands are normally likely to have been ratified by an official body; but the significance of that procedure is another matter. Only occasionally are we able to glimpse the *formal* appointment procedures, and those few glimpses are suggestive. One occasion on which the procedure for the choice of a *nauarchos* is described is when King Agesilaos, on campaign in Asia Minor, is given the power to select an admiral of his choice (Xen. *Hell.* 3. 4. 27–9). The situation was unusual, but it does indicate the absence of a principle of popular election. Already in 403 Lysander, seemingly speaking at an official meeting in support of the ambassadors from Eleusis and Athens, had managed to arrange a harmostship for himself and the appointment of his brother Libys as *nauarchos* (*Hell.* 2. 4. 28).

Evidence for the selection of harmosts, indeed, parallels that concerning *nauarchoi*. King Agis II's proposal in *c*.410 to send a force to Chalkedon and Byzantion under the command of Klearchos seems (to judge from the tenor of Xenophon's account: *Hell.* 1. 1. 35–6) to have been made in an official meeting. The reference to the fact that Klearchos was proxenos of Byzantion sounds like a reason given by Agis for suggesting his appointment, which implies that his name was advanced as part and parcel of the overall plan. So, despite the formal opportunity for genuine choice of personnel, in practice the available options were circumscribed by the influence of the king who proposed the expedition.

An even more blatant example of the manipulation of an appointment is that worked in 389 by Anaxibios, who 'owing to the fact that the ephors had become friends of his, succeeded in getting himself sent out to Abydos as harmost' (*Hell.* 4. 8. 32). Similarly, in 382 the commander Eudamidas persuaded the ephors to give an auxiliary command to his brother Phoibidas (*Hell.* 5. 2. 24). Diodoros (15. 19–20) gives a different account, but it is at the very least indicative that Xenophon should believe in such family influence.

In these instances the decisions were taken in Sparta; but on many occasions harmosts were selected by commanders in the field, from among their own associates or staff officers. For example, at Dekeleia in the winter of 413/12 Agis II summoned Alkamenes and Melanthos from Sparta on his own initiative (Thuc. 8. 5). A few months later, however, the commanders of the Peloponnesian fleet appointed Philippos, one of their own number, harmost at Miletos (8. 28). After the victory at Aigospotamoi in 405 Lysander had a free hand to appoint his aides as harmosts of several important cities. Sthenelaos became harmost of Byzantion and Chalkedon; Eteonikos of an area command in Thrace; and Thorax, later, of Samos (*Hell.* 2. 2. 2, 5; Diod. 13. 106; 14. 3). In the early fourth century the kings Agesilaos and Kleombrotos both took advantage of their foreign campaigning to leave favoured supporters behind as harmosts when they themselves returned to Sparta.[1]

In spite of the formality of public ratification, the dominant principles of selection were not election but appointment and co-optation (cf. Finley 1986, 166). Royal patronage, for example, might influence entire careers (Cartledge 1987, 139–59). The rise of Lysander, up to his appointment to the nauarchy, was due to the support of the Eurypontid royal family, with whom he had been associated since the time (no later than the early 420s) when, as a young man, he had become the *erastēs* (lover) of Agesilaos (Plut. *Lysander*, 22; *Ages.* 2; Cartledge 1987, 28–9). Lysander was a suitable candidate for the exercise of patronage, owing to the reputed poverty of his family (Plut. *Lys.* 2) and his possible *mothax* status when young (Phylarchos, *FGH* 81 F 43). A similar case is that of Agesilaos' half-brother Teleutias (PB 689). The poverty of Teleutias' family led the king to give them half the estates he had inherited from his elder brother, King Agis (Xen. *Ages.* 4; Plut. *Ages.* 4). Owing to the influence of Agesilaos, Teleutias rose to be *nauarchos* and held several subsequent commands (Plut. *Ages.* 21; Cartledge 1987, 145–6).

Some men, of course, were sufficiently influential in their own right to attain commands without the help of patronage and regardless of merit. Anaxibios' cultivation of the ephors' friendship shows one means by which it could be done. The well-born Pedaritos achieved his harmostship at Chios despite failing, in his twenties, to gain selection on merit to the élite corps of 300 *hippeis*. The roles of patronage and of inherited social status will have been an important reason for the tendencies, observed above, towards the limitation of access to foreign commands and the iteration of posts for those few men who were selected.

---

[1] E.g. Euxenos in Asia Minor (394); Sphodrias and Phoibidas at Thespiai (378 and 377 respectively): *Hell.* 4. 2. 5; 5. 4. 15 and 41.

Competing sub-imperialisms and personal ambitions

The pattern observed above, according to which commanders from prominent backgrounds often spent several years abroad, provided the optimum conditions for the exercise of personal ambitions. There were some restrictions, to be sure, since the home authorities were evidently alert to the dangers of over-independence. On receipt of the first complaint about the actions of Astyochos, the *nauarchos* of 412/11, a high-powered commission was sent with powers to replace him; the fact that the complainant was the well-born Pedaritos is no doubt relevant (Thuc. 8. 38–9). So, too, in the early 390s the authorities intervened at least three times to redirect, or check up on, the activities of the area harmosts in Asia Minor, Thibron and Derkylidas (Xen. *Hell.* 3. 1. 7; 3. 2. 6, 12). In addition, by no means all Spartiates abroad operated independently. Fellow commanders often had to co-ordinate their activities; trierarchs, staff officers, and sometimes even harmosts had to work under the command of admirals or other superior officers. We should not overdraw the picture of the autonomous Spartiate abroad.

These restrictions did not, however, prevent commanders from initiating their own 'sub-imperialisms' (a phenomenon whose importance is well attested in the history of modern imperialism),[1] attempting to exert their own stamp upon the direction of military strategy and policy in the pursuit of personal ambitions. The most notable example is of course that of Lysander, who exploited his naval commands to create a personal following among his fellow Spartiate officers and partisans in the Greek states of the eastern Aegean. Following his decisive defeat of Athens at Aigospotamoi he was able, albeit temporarily, to impose his personal settlement upon Athens' former allies, and he

---

[1] Fieldhouse 1973, esp. 80–1, 98–9; cf. the definition of 'sub-imperialism' given by a recent historian of Japan: 'initiatives taken by men in positions of responsibility overseas, confident that a successful *fait accompli* would be ratified by their government at home' (Beasley 1987, 198). The activities of Japanese commanders in the 1930s – especially the independent actions of the Kwantung Army, the rivalry between it and the Tientsin garrison (later renamed the North China Army), and the conflicts within the NCA – could provide interesting comparative material for a more extended study of Spartiate sub-imperialisms.

wielded great influence over Spartan policy-making until his death in 395 (Rahe 1977; Bommelaer 1981).

But Lysander's independent exploitation of his military commands was exceptional only in its scale and degree of success. Many more petty sub-imperialisms can be observed throughout Sparta's period of foreign engagement. Despite the interventions from Sparta, Derkylidas in Asia Minor was able to pursue his personal revenge against the Persian satrap Pharnabazos, and even used information gained from a supervisory commission to pre-empt the home government's intended expedition to the Thracian Chersonese by mounting his own privately planned campaign.[1] Similar independent action is evident in the notorious cases of Phoibidas' unauthorized seizure of the Theban Kadmeia in 382, and Sphodrias' disastrous attack upon the Peiraieus in 378.[2]

Furthermore, precisely because commanders were not always autonomous, there was frequently a clash of ambitions. For the degree of insight it provides into the endemic conflict between commanders, even over relatively minor issues, the most illuminating episode concerns the varying reactions to the return of the independent mercenary army of the 'Ten Thousand' to north-west Asia Minor after their expedition into the Persian interior (Xen. *Anabasis*, 6. 6–7. 2). Kleandros, the harmost at Byzantion, would but for unfavourable sacrifices have taken them into his service. But the *nauarchos* Anaxibios adopted an antagonistic attitude. Acting in collusion with the Persian satrap Pharnabazos, in return for the promise of personal favours, he compelled the Ten Thousand to depart from Asia into Thrace. He also ordered that any mercenaries remaining in Byzantion be sold as slaves; Kleandros ignored this order, but it was later carried out by his successor as harmost, Aristarchos. Then Anaxibios altered his policy, after being snubbed by Pharnabazos on the expiry of his term of office. Despite his lack of authority, he ordered the people of Perinthos to transport the Ten Thousand back into Asia; but then Aristarchos, who had himself now entered into collusion with Pharnabazos, came in person to prevent this manoeuvre.

[1] Xen. *Hell.* 3. 1. 9–27; 3. 2. 8–11; Diod. 14. 38.
[2] See discussion and refs in de Ste. Croix 1972, 134–6; Cartledge 1987, 156–8.

Finally, however, when Thibron arrived a few months later as the new supreme regional harmost, he brought the Ten Thousand into Asia and recruited them into his forces. In this episode we see in microcosm the kind of personal ambitions and conflicts, and the consequent twists and turns in policy, that characterized much of the Spartan war effort.

Such competing sub-imperialisms became evident at the very start of the Ionian war, with the 'private empire-building' of Pedaritos on Chios (Andrewes, in Gomme *et al.* 1981, 83–4) and his challenge to the authority of the *nauarchos* Astyochos. They flared up again over much larger issues, in the clash of personalities and policy towards Persia between the retiring and succeeding admirals Lysander and Kallikratidas (Proietti 1987, 11–20; Gray 1989, 22–4; 81–3), in the conflict between Lysander and King Pausanias over the settlement of Attica in 403 (de Ste. Croix 1972, 144), and in the conflict between Lysander and King Agesilaos in Asia in 396 (Cartledge 1987, 151–3). In the late 380s and 370s this type of conflict became institutionalized, as there developed a permanent policy struggle between the kings of the two royal houses (Smith 1953–4), who used their prerogative of commanding the regular citizen army to implement their mutually contradictory sub-imperialisms. The final consequence of this conflict came in 371, when King Kleombrotos was compelled to fight the battle of Leuktra, despite unfavourable religious omens, for fear of condemnation to death.[1] The outcome was the crushing defeat which triggered Sparta's rapid decline to the status of a second-rate power.

War, empire, and socio-political crisis

In the third part of this essay I want to ask how precisely involvement in foreign warfare and empire contributed to the internal crisis which rendered Sparta unable to recover from the defeat at Leuktra and resist the subsequent dismantling of its power. Several interconnected developments can be identified.

The fighting of a new type of war, major controversies regarding policy, and the choices involved in the maintenance of empire

[1] Xen. *Hell.* 6. 4. 4–8; Cic. *div.* 1. 34. 76; 2. 32. 69.

all raised fresh issues of a significance and difficulty surpassing any that Sparta had previously had to tackle. These entailed fundamental and often new sources of strife, which raised the temperature of political conflict to an unparalleled level, as is attested by the number of 'political' trials in this period; seven out of nine known trials of non-royal citizens in the classical period fall between the years 404 and 378.[1]

Overseas campaigning also meant an unprecedented extension of influential and independent positions open to leading citizens. Although there were traditionally many officerships within the regular Lakedaimonian army, these operated within a strict chain of subordination under the king, in which independent action was effectively squashed (cf. Thuc. 5. 71–2). In contrast, some commanders abroad could take independent military and even political decisions which diverged from the reactions of home authorities. Indeed, as we have seen, for many Spartiate commanders the chance to enhance their reputations before returning to the relative anonymity of life at home was often irresistible.

The effects were especially destabilizing because commanders came from a different age group from that which had traditionally exercised the most important *collective* influence upon Spartan political life. Traditionally, political debate was heavily influenced by the powerful conservative lobby of old men, especially through the council of elders, the *gerousia*, whose members were aged 60 or over. Commanders, however, were typically younger men – usually in their 40s or 50s, but sometimes even younger (Hodkinson 1983, 251 and n. 28) – for whom there were normally few formal political roles inside Sparta. Xenophon's comment[2] that the ambition of leading Spartiates was continuous harmost-ships abroad makes perfect sense for this age group. The attitude of Derkylidas (Xen. *Hell.* 4. 3. 2), who 'always liked being abroad', is not surprising; but it is striking that he was prepared thereby to incur the disgrace deriving from his failure to marry and have children which, among other things, caused him to forfeit his right

---

[1]   See lists in de Ste. Croix 1972, 133 and appendix 26, to which add the trial of Thorax in 404 (Plut. *Lys.* 19).
[2]   *Lakedaimonion politeia* (*Polity of the Spartans*; translated by R. J. A. Talbert, in the Penguin Classics volume *Plutarch on Sparta*, as 'Spartan Society'), 14 (henceforth cited as '*Lak. pol.*').

to deference from younger men (see Plut. *Lyc.* 15). Part of the tension between commanders and home authorities was probably a more overt conflict between age groups, as the overall control of Spartan policy by a gerontocracy was threatened by the decisions of younger commanders abroad, and also by the increased influence at home of men of military prowess. The consequent partial undermining of traditional deference to the elders may also have led to an increased role for other sources of influence, such as patronage and wealth.

A related point is that the traditional political system involved a natural rotation of office-holding. There were always many leading families taking a temporary 'back seat' because they lacked males over the age of 60 to be eligible for the *gerousia*, and because the ephorate, which was available to younger men, could be held only once. Excessive competition was thereby reduced, and access to office shared more evenly. The availability of foreign commands for men in their 40s and 50s will have upset this natural regulation of competition, because leading families were considerably more likely to have males of these ages than males over 60. In a plausible model life table (Princeton Model South, mortality level 3, growth rate zero; see Coale and Demeny 1983, 449), men aged 40–59 are over two and a half times as numerous as those over 60, forming over 35 per cent of the adult male population. The importance of family influence is also likely to have increased. Family influence upon elections to the *gerousia* must always have been limited by the fact that a candidate aged 60 or over would only rarely have had elder relatives alive to provide support. Supporting senior relatives will have been available far more frequently for men in their 40s, or younger, competing for foreign commands. This may in part explain the pattern observed earlier, by which sons of prominent men are often found holding important posts.

The availability of commands for younger men thereby exacerbated two weaknesses of the political system identified by Finley (1986, 168–9): (1) the absence of a unified leadership principle, the outcome of which was permanent rivalry, now broadened by the increased numbers of individuals and families involved in competition for positions; and (2) the conflict between men of energy and ambition and the rest, now intensified by the greater opportunities available for commanders, including opportunities for extended tenure of foreign posts, which offered the possibility of monopoly in place of rotation.

In addition, the selection of commanders through appointment and personal influence stands in stark contrast to the procedure used for the *gerousia* – and probably for the ephorate also – whose members were elected in open assembly through shouting for each of the candidates.[1] The development of foreign commands was, in this respect, an oligarchic trend which worked against the cohesion of the citizen body. The traditional ambition of leading men to gain election to the *gerousia* must have restrained their behaviour towards ordinary citizens, since it was upon such men that their election depended. The ambition for foreign commands, however, made no such demands, but depended rather upon the possession of influence or a patron's goodwill. There was less need for moderate behaviour towards ordinary Spartiates; on the contrary, there was a built-in incentive for would-be commanders and patrons to increase their personal status through the acquisition of additional property, often at the expense of poorer citizens.

Solidarity within the citizen body probably also suffered from the exclusion of ordinary citizens from the forces of commanders abroad. Cartledge (1987, 40) is right to emphasize the importance of this 'serious breach in the principle of the citizen militia'. In traditional Lakedaimonian warfare, individual glory could be gained by rank-and-file soldiers as much as by commanders (Hodkinson 1983, 259–60). The absence of rank-and-file citizens from most of Sparta's overseas campaigning meant that military glory now accrued solely to a few leading men; the classic example is that of Lysander and his fellow commanders, who vaunted themselves through personal statues on the victory monument at Delphi after Aigospotamoi (Paus. 10. 9. 4; ML 95). Moreover, the fact that it was upon non-citizen troops or rowers that commanders depended for their ambitions may have contributed to the feeling that the rank-and-filers were irrelevant and dispensable in the scramble for personal position.

The developments discussed above can be linked to the three causes of property concentration and *oliganthropia* referred to above: individual property accumulation, the failure of Sparta's

---

[1] Plut. *Lyc.* 26; Arist. *Pol.* 1270 b; 1271 a.

leaders to provide remedies, and the breakdown in solidarity between rich and poor. The traditional political system had, through its varied checks and balances, acted as a powerful restraining force upon the destabilizing potential of growing wealth inequalities. But the developments mentioned above transformed the socio-political context, in which pressures towards the acquisition of status-defining wealth, and its deployment through patronage, are likely to have increased in significance.

Existing trends towards the concentration of landed property in a few hands are likely to have been intensified by the heightened level of competition for foreign commands. Aristotle's comment (*Pol.* 1307 a) on how the Spartan notables grasped after wealth is perfectly intelligible in this context. As he implies elsewhere (1270 a), leading men could acquire land by manipulating ordinary citizens' rights of gift and bequest and the freedom of guardians to choose any husband for an heiress. The acquisition of foreign wealth may also have had a direct impact upon the concentration of land. Xenophon's remark (*Lak. pol.* 14) that in his time some men even boasted about their gold and silver – the context suggests that he is referring to coinage – indicates that the prohibition of private possession of money in 404 had become a dead letter.

The availability of large quantities of coinage in the hands of leading men is likely to have stimulated and facilitated a higher volume of transactions in landed property. Purchase and sale of most land, although traditionally deemed dishonourable, was not illegal.[1] Gold and silver coinage could also be employed in transactions which were nominally ones of gift, bequest, or the betrothal of an heiress. We must be cautious about the danger of over-speculation; but even on a minimal interpretation, there are sufficient reasons to conclude that the combined impact of competition for foreign commands and the availability of new sources of wealth will have accelerated the process of property concentration and hastened the decline in citizen numbers.[2]

[1] Herakleides Lembos, fr. 373. 12 Dilts = Arist. (?), *Lakedaimonion politeia* (*Polity of the Lakedaimonians*), fr. 611. 12 Rose; cf. Hodkinson 1986, 388.
[2] By this I mean that the decline in citizen manpower after 431 was faster than it would have been without the impact of war and empire, not necessarily that it was now more rapid than before. Computation of the

Furthermore, the transformation of political life discussed above helps to explain the breakdown in the solidarity of the Spartiate citizen body and the consequent lack of intervention by Sparta's leaders, who were themselves the beneficiaries of the new developments.

Agesilaos and the crisis of Spartiate society

The momentum of these developments was maintained, or even intensified, during the 380s and 370s by the personal dominance of King Agesilaos II, which was itself a product of Sparta's crisis. He represented a conservative backlash against the independence of foreign commanders. Indeed, he did much to resolve tensions between commanders abroad and the home authorities, especially between harmosts and *gerousia*, by bringing both under his control. Most of the harmosts after 386 were his personal associates: Eudamidas (PB 295), Phoibidas (PB 734), Teleutias (PB 689), and Herippidas (PB 349) – and his mediation between harmosts and *gerousia* is demonstrated, appropriately enough, by his successful interventions at the trials of two errant harmosts, Phoibidas and Sphodrias (PB 680), both of whom would otherwise probably have been condemned to death (de Ste. Croix 1972, 134–6; Cartledge 1987, 156–9). His austere personal life (illustrated at many points in Xenophon's life of the king) and his deferential attitude to officials (Xen. *Ages.* 6–7; Plut. *Ages.* 4) seemed to restore traditional Spartan values. Unlike other commanders, he identified his career interests with those of the state, cushioned by the fact that once back in Sparta he could rely upon

---

rate of decline in different periods is impossible, since it depends upon calculations of the size of the citizen body at certain dates which are based upon extrapolations from controversial evidence as to the size of Lakedaimonian armies. Even if it were possible, it would not be very informative about the rate of concentration of property; partly because of extraneous factors (e.g. the earthquake of *c*.465, or differential mortality in war), partly because the fact that more Spartiates became 'inferiors' through poverty in one period than in another would not necessarily indicate a more rapid concentration of land; that would depend on another unknown factor, how close those men were initially to the 'poverty line'.

the traditional power base of his kingship. In this way his power increased, and he was supported by those Spartiates who yearned for a return to old ways after the upheavals of recent years.

The problem was that, although his values were traditional, Agesilaos' political methods followed the new circumstances of power. As Cartledge has reminded us (1987, 140–1), social scientists have often observed that at times of change and crisis, networks of patron–client relationships tend to coalesce into more solid factions. Without accepting a rather mechanistic view of Spartan political life as permanently dominated by a conflict between three enduring factions (Hamilton 1971; 1979), the emergence of more solid groupings can be identified as a genuine development during this period. The emergence of the faction around Lysander (e.g. Xen. *Hell.* 1. 6. 4–6) is of particular importance. The influence of Lysander's faction and its persistence even after his death (Plut. *Ages.* 20) meant that Agesilaos' rise to dominance was by no means unopposed. He achieved it only through his own faction-building, which relied upon the deployment of large amounts of wealth.[1]

Agesilaos was also affected by his own experience as a mercenary commander in Asia Minor. In Sparta he cemented and increased his personal following through gift-giving, just as in Asia he had built up his army through abundant supplies, incentives, prizes, pay and plunder.[2] The episode in Asia (Xen. *Ages.* 1. 17–19) in which he made huge profits for his friends through the manipulation of booty stands as a model for his wealth-based patronal politics at home. One might say without too much exaggeration that he applied the politics of commanding a mercenary army to the politics of leading his fellow citizens.

Despite his claim to be a loyal servant of the polis, Agesilaos' politics were fundamentally divisive of the solidarity between rich and poor that had traditionally underpinned the polis's survival and success. Relying, as it did, upon the deployment of significant economic resources, his mode of politics intensified the growing pressures towards individual acquisition of property, and deflected still further the attention of the authorities from the plight of poor citizens. In addition, the magnitude of his personal

[1]   Xen. *Ages.* 4; 11. 8; Plut. *Ages.* 4; Cartledge 1987, 132–59.
[2]   Xen. *Ages.* 1. 18–20, 25, 33; *Hell.* 3. 4. 16; 4. 2. 5–8.

power led to a sharper polarization than ever before among
leading men, with a clustering of opposition around the kings of
the other royal house, especially Kleombrotos, whose partial
success in frustrating Agesilaos' anti-Theban policies during the
370s (Smith 1953–4) led to the threat of judicial condemnation
which forced him into fighting the fatal battle of Leuktra. The
revolutionary plotting of Spartiates during the Theban attack on
Sparta in winter 370/69 is intriguing.[1] Were they poor
Spartiates, desperate to escape from the threat of losing citizen
status? Were they leading men, former associates of Kleombrotos,
frustrated after the death of the one leader who had challenged the
dominance of Agesilaos? Or a potent combination of the two? The
alienation of a significant proportion of its own citizen body –
which was less than one thousand in number after Leuktra,
according to Aristotle (*Pol.* 1270 a) – must have exacerbated
Sparta's inability to defend its territories and resist the dismantling of its power.

Comparison and conclusions

This essay has attempted to define, more precisely than has been
hitherto been attempted, the ways in which prolonged foreign
warfare and the experience of empire precipitated the crisis of
Spartiate society in the early fourth century, leading to its decline
to the status of a second-rate power. But how important were the
factors of war and empire in relation to the longer-term, underlying developments that already threatened the social order?

Comparative analysis is often helpful, not only in highlighting
trends shared by societies undergoing comparable experiences,
but also in isolating distinctive features which are of critical
significance. Comparison with the Roman republic, another
society in which prolonged foreign warfare and imperial
expansion – in this case over several centuries – culminated in
socio-political crisis, may illuminate important aspects of the

---

[1] Plut. *Ages.* 32. 6; cf. David 1980, 304–7. Plutarch refers to this
conspiracy as being 'greater' (*meidzōn*) than an earlier conspiracy of non-
citizens involving 200 persons. It is unclear whether he means greater in
numbers or in the magnitude of the danger it posed.

Spartan crisis.[1] Similarities with Sparta abound: the resort to iteration of office at times of emergency; the creation of new positions (chiefly the promagistracy) for the maintenance of empire; the emergence of talented individuals who gained unusual terms of command and extraordinary fame during periods of exceptional warfare; the tensions between senior senators and younger generals; the endemic political prosecutions; the destabilizing impact of new foreign wealth; and the concentration of land in the hands of the rich.

The contrasts between the internal impacts of Spartan and Roman imperialism are, however, equally significant if not more so. As their empire expanded over the long period from the fourth to the first centuries BC, the Romans adapted their social structures in important ways, especially by extending citizenship; Rome did not have a problem of manpower shortage. The Spartiates proved less adaptable, attempting to preserve unchanged their long-standing social system with its ever-diminishing citizen body. Furthermore, whereas at Rome there was a high degree of mobility into and out of the office-holding élite, partly in response to the weight of military and administrative responsibilities incurred during imperial expansion, at Sparta the evidence suggests a greater limitation of military posts to men from the highest backgrounds. An important reason for this was the allocation of such posts to appointees rather than, as at Rome, to men who had to achieve their positions through continuing success in competitive popular elections.

Other structural differences had equally powerful effects. In the more tightly controlled Spartan society, in which prohibitions against ostentatious living and display could be more effectively enforced, a larger proportion of foreign wealth may have been channelled into the acquisition of land. Since Spartan territory was also more modest in extent than that of Rome, and all private land was citizen-owned, such acquisition was even more directly at the expense of poorer citizens, especially given the existence of a concealed property qualification in the form of compulsory mess

---

[1]   For the Roman *comparandum* I have drawn esp. on Hopkins 1978, 1–98; Harris 1979, 9–130; Hopkins and Burton 1983; Rich 1983; Astin 1989; Cornell 1989; and Staveley 1989.

contributions. Again in contrast with Rome, no compensatory material benefits of empire were passed on to ordinary Spartiates. Moreover, in spite of the resulting hardships and loss of rights, there is no evidence that in the classical period the concentration of land and impoverishment of the poor ever became a live political issue, as it did at Rome owing to the role of the tribunes and the popular influence upon elections and (to a lesser extent) legislation.

Although overshadowed by the dominance of the senatorial oligarchy, the significant level of popular influence in Roman politics is an important point of differentiation from the character of Spartiate political life. This is signalled by the fact that none of Sparta's foreign commanders displayed any tendency towards espousing populist causes against the established leadership, as did several Roman generals in the late second and early first centuries. Nor did the Lakedaimonian army become a political force in the hands of independent military leaders, because rank-and-file citizen troops were excluded from most foreign campaigns; this was a result of the position enjoyed by the Spartiate citizen body, that of an élite dominating a much larger servile population.

Another point of differentiation is that Roman society was not divided along age–class lines. Roman commanders had a permanent political position, as members of the leading official body, the senate. This meant that susceptibility to adaptation and change, in response to the experience of foreign warfare and empire, was embedded in Roman political life to a far greater extent than at Sparta, where returning commanders had no political roles and formal authority lay, until the time of Agesilaos, with men who had no direct imperial experience. The power of the hereditary dual kingship, another factor alien to the Roman republic, was also crucial in the hands of Agesilaos, as a source of authority in inhibiting tendencies towards change and in imposing collective cohesion.

For all these reasons the outcomes of Roman and Spartan imperialism were divergent. Rome's empire expanded, and Roman society adapted and survived, at the expense of a fundamental change in its political system; Sparta lost its empire and its territorial integrity, while its social institutions (the upbringing, common meals, and austere way of life) went into

174 *Stephen Hodkinson*

decay, even though its formal political structures survived for another century and a half.

This comparison suggests two complementary points: first, that Sparta's response to involvement in foreign warfare and empire diverged from that of Rome because of fundamental differences in their social and political structures; but, second, that the particular nature of its response itself had important implications for the future development of Spartan society.

Involvement in war and empire should not be seen as the root cause of Sparta's crisis; there are several indications that that crisis was developing strongly before the start of our period. Note, for example, the significant decline in Spartiate numbers attested by the time of the battle of Mantineia in 418;[1] the high levels of spending on chariot-racing from the 440s onwards (Hodkinson 1989, 96–100), indicating that wealth was already becoming important as a determinant of status; the long-standing operation by leading families of marriage practices that isolated them from poorer citizens (ibid. 90–3); and the fact that by the 420s, at the latest, the government had resorted to the cosmetic solution of solving army manpower problems by increased reliance on non-citizen troops (cf. Thuc. 4. 38, 80; 5. 34). The fact that these prior developments helped condition the character of Spartan warfare and imperialism makes Finley's claim (1986, 177) that 'her greatest military success destroyed the model military state' altogether too simple.

On the other hand, we should not fall prey to the determinist view that these prior developments would have 'destroyed the model military state' regardless of the experience of war and empire. This would be counterfactual history at its most pointless, since (owing to the heavy concentration of sources in the late fifth and early fourth centuries) the only Sparta we can know evidentially in any detail is the one which was undergoing that experience.

As we have seen, involvement abroad introduced important socio-political changes, with significant implications for Spartiate landownership and manpower. Sparta's sixty years of foreign warfare and empire were a major factor, which accelerated the onset of the internal crisis and conditioned the particular way in

[1] Compare Hdt. 7. 234 with Thuc. 5. 68; cf. Cartledge 1979, 254–7.

which it evolved. Without that prolonged external engagement and its consequences, the timing, circumstances, and international repercussions of the Spartiate crisis would surely have been very different.

Bibliography

Anderson, J. K. (1961), *Ancient Greek Horsemanship* (Berkeley, etc.).

Astin, A. E. (1989), 'Roman government and politics, 200–134 BC', in *CAH* viii (2nd edn), 163–96.

Beasley, W. G. (1987), *Japanese Imperialism, 1894–1945* (Oxford).

Böckisch, G. (1965), *'Harmostai* (431–387)', *Klio*, 46: 129–239.

Bommelaer, J.-F. (1981), *Lysandre de Sparte: histoire et traditions* (Paris).

Cartledge, P. (1979), *Sparta and Lakonia: A Regional History, 1300–362 BC* (London).

—— (1987), *Agesilaos and the Crisis of Sparta* (London).

Cawkwell, G. L. (1983), 'The decline of Sparta', *CQ* 77 (n.s. 33): 385–400.

Coale, A. J., and Demeny, P. (1983), *Regional Model Life Tables and Stable Populations* (2nd edn, New York).

Cornell, T. J. (1989), 'The recovery of Rome' and 'The conquest of Italy', in *CAH* vii. 2 (2nd edn), 309–412.

David, E. (1979–80), 'The influx of money into Sparta at the end of the fifth century BC', *Scripta classica israelica*, 5: 30–45.

—— (1980), 'Revolutionary agitation in Sparta after Leuctra', *Athenaeum*, n.s. 58: 299–308.

—— (1981), *Sparta between Empire and Revolution, 404–243 BC* (New York).

de Ste. Croix, G. E. M. (1972), *The Origins of the Peloponnesian War* (London).

Dunant, C. (1978), 'Stèles funéraires', in *Eretria*, vi. 21–62 (Berne).

Fieldhouse, D. K. (1973), *Economics and Empire, 1830–1914* (London, etc.).

Finley, M. I. (1986), 'Sparta', in *The Use and Abuse of History* (2nd edn, London), ch. 10 (pp. 161–78); = 'Sparta and Spartan society', in *Economy and Society in Ancient Greece* (eds B. D. Shaw and R. P. Saller, London, 1981), ch. 2 (pp. 24–40); = 'Sparta', in J.-P. Vernant (ed.), *Problèmes de la guerre en Grèce ancienne* (Paris, 1968), pp. 143–60.

Gomme, A. W., Andrewes, A., and Dover, K. J. (1981), *A Historical Commentary on Thucydides V* (Oxford).

Gray, V. (1989), *The Character of Xenophon's Hellenica* (London).

Hamilton, C. D. (1971), 'Spartan politics and policy 405–401 BC', *AJP* 91: 294–314.

—— (1979), *Sparta's Bitter Victories: Politics and Diplomacy in the Corinthian War* (Ithaca, etc.).

Harris, W. V. (1979), *War and Imperialism in Republican Rome, 327–70 BC* (Oxford).

Hodkinson, S. (1983), 'Social order and the conflict of values in classical Sparta', *Chiron*, 13: 239–81.

—— (1986), 'Land tenure and inheritance in classical Sparta', *CQ* 80 (n.s. 36): 378–406.

—— (1989), 'Inheritance, marriage and demography: perspectives upon the success and decline of classical Sparta', in A. Powell (ed.), *Classical Sparta: Techniques behind her Success* (London), pp. 79–112.

Hopkins, K. (1978), *Conquerors and Slaves* (Cambridge).

—— and Burton, G. P. (1983), 'Political succession in the late republic (249–50 BC)', in K. Hopkins (ed.), *Death and Renewal* (Cambridge), pp. 31–119.

Malkin, I. (1990), 'Lysander and Libys', *CQ* 84 (n.s. 40): 541–5.

Meiggs, R., and Lewis, D. M. (1989), *A Selection of Greek Historical Inscriptions* (2nd edn, Oxford).

Mosley, D. J. (1963), 'Pharax and the Spartan embassy to Athens in 370/69', *Historia*, 12: 247–50.

—— (1971), 'Spartan kings and proxeny', *Athenaeum*, n.s. 49: 433–5.

—— (1973), *Envoys and Diplomacy in Ancient Greece* (Historia Einzelschriften, 22; Wiesbaden).

Noethlichs, K. L. (1987), 'Bestechung, Bestechlichkeit und die Rolle des Geldes in der spartanischen Aussen- und Innenpolitik vom 7. bis 2. Jh. v. Chr.', *Historia*, 36: 129–70.

Parke, H. W. (1930), 'The development of the second Spartan empire (405–371 BC)', *JHS* 50: 37–79.

Poralla, P. (rev. by A. S. Bradford) (1985), *A Prosopography of Lacedaemonians: From the Earliest Times to the Death of Alexander the Great (X–323 BC)* (2nd edn, Chicago).

Proietti, G. P. (1987), *Xenophon's Sparta* (Mnemosyne supp. vol. 98; Leiden).

Rahe, P. (1977), *Lysander and the Spartan Settlement, 407–403 BC* (Ph.D. diss., Yale).

Rich, J. W. (1983), 'The supposed Roman manpower shortage of the later second century BC', *Historia*, 32: 287–331.

Schütrumpf, E. (1987), 'The rhetra of Epitadeus: a Platonist's fiction', *Greek, Roman and Byzantine Studies*, 28: 441–57.

Sealey, R. (1976), 'Die spartanische Nauarchie', *Klio*, 58: 335–58.

Smith, R. E. (1953–4), 'The opposition to Agesilaus' foreign policy, 394–371 BC', *Historia*, 2: 274–88.

Staveley, E. S. (1989), 'Rome and Italy in the early third century', in *CAH* vii. 2 (2nd edn), 420–55.

Whitehead, D. (1979), 'Ant[i]alkidas, or the case of the intrusive iota', *LCM* 4: 191–3.

Warfare, economy, and democracy in classical Athens[1]

Paul Millett

Classical Athenian warfare: 'grandeur, crisis, and decline'?

How do Greek historians go about packaging and presenting the history of classical Athens? What I have in mind is the overall conception or 'shape' of Athenian history, used as the basis of further elaboration. From a Greek vantage-point, our Roman colleagues seem fortunate in having for their 'core' period (roughly from the middle republic to the early principate) what might be termed the 'Beard–Crawford–Hopkins' model.[2] Without going into detail, this formulation suggests a whole framework of relationships, linking together factors that include internal politics, the role of the élite, acquisition of empire, accumulation of wealth, and of course warfare. The waging of war is central to the whole process; as documented by W. V. Harris in his *War and Imperialism in Republican Rome 327–70 BC*, war is the dynamic element in the model, serving to set everything else in

---

[1] The paper is here presented more or less as it was delivered at the Leicester–Nottingham seminar, with minor modifications and the addition of necessary documentation. I am grateful to the editors for their patience in awaiting its revision.
[2] The works in question are Beard and Crawford 1985 and Hopkins 1978. Other authors could be cited, and it will be appreciated that I write from a Cambridge perspective.

motion. No doubt there is plenty of scope for disagreement with the approach to Roman history I have outlined (some of it telling); but it does at least provide a possible and plausible basis for understanding the development of the Roman state through two or three centuries.

If we turn to Greek history, there are difficulties in conceiving a properly integrated account of Athens through the fifth and fourth centuries BC. Perhaps the favoured approaches are a set of variations on the theme of what might be called 'grandeur and decline'. In its simplest and crudest form, this presentation has three stages. First, there is the rise of Athens, after the defeat of the Persian invaders, to the climax of the 'Golden Age' under the guiding hand of Perikles, its greatness exemplified by the wealth and power of the empire. Then there is the climacteric of the Peloponnesian war, culminating in the defeat of Athens and loss of empire. After that, the third stage is downhill all the way, via the confused decadence and decline of the 'fourth-century crisis', to Macedonian domination, the destruction of the democracy, and the end of Athens as an independent state.

My picture is admittedly overdrawn; few historians continue to subscribe to the full-blown theory of 'grandeur and decline'. Yet fourth-century Athens (like fourth-century Greece) continues to be presented in terms that are muted in comparison with the positive achievements of the fifth century. I have tried elsewhere to show how Athens in the fourth century has its own accomplishments in the ordering of social relations (Millett 1991).[1] But what is relevant for this paper is another legacy of the 'fifth century good, fourth century bad' approach, which encourages an attitude to warfare and its consequences that can be misleading.

From the rapid sketch of Athenian 'grandeur and decline' given above, it is clear that war plays an important part in the process; but not along the same lines as in the Roman model, where the

---

[1] Mention might be made of the standard textbook by Ehrenberg (1973), who closes his account of Greek history in 400, which he regards as the end of the true 'classical age' (p. 384). The century or so that followed is damned with faint praise ('On the positive side the decline of the *polis* showed remarkable retardments'). The recent synoptic study of the democracy by Bleicken has a chapter on 'Symptome des Niedergangs der Demokratie im 4. Jahrhundert' (1985, 289–94).

concern is with warfare – war as an institution. What matters on the Athenian side is one war – the Peloponnesian war. No doubt the Peloponnesian war was, to quote Sally Humphreys (1978, 143), 'a period of shattering social change and consequently of changes in attitudes', and possible theoretical and practical reactions to the war have been assessed by Gilbert Murray (1944). But we are helped towards that conception of the war as something cataclysmic by two factors. From the ancient world there is the eloquence of Thucydides, who has effectively created the Peloponnesian war for us.[1] Helping us to believe his claims about the paramountcy of 'his' war are our own awareness, and even experience, of twentieth-century analogues to the Peloponnesian war. Thucydides called the war 'the greatest upheaval (*kinesis*) in the history of the Greeks' (1. 2); for Winston Churchill (1923–9) the Great War was *The World Crisis*. More recently, Arthur Marwick has summed up the impact of the first world war on society in the title of his book *The Deluge* (1968). Much the same could be, and has been, written about the second world war.[2] Parallels between the ancient and modern conflicts were perceived at the time. In 1915, placards on London buses displayed excerpts from Perikles' funeral speech, intended to remind the heirs of Athenian culture of the values for which they were fighting (Turner 1981, 187). In 1940, the future head of Scientific Intelligence in Britain quoted from the same speech in an official report, to illustrate the dangers for a state at war of the Athenian quality of openness: 'Athens lost the war' (Jones 1978, 109–10).[3]

[1] Not only the conception of the Peloponnesian war as a unity (in spite of an interim period of relative peace), but also its name, is owed to Thucydides. Cartledge's attempt (1987, *passim*) to redress the balance by referring to 'the Athenian war' makes the point, but is unlikely to win many converts.
[2] From the mass of material, I would single out Gilbert 1989 (esp. 720–48) – annalistic in arrangement, but more than Thucydidean in its humanity and breadth of treatment.
[3] 'Parallels have frequently been drawn between the Peloponnesian War and that between England and Germany' is how Jones prefaces his quotation (1978, 109). It was, however, against enemies in domestic politics that Beaverbrook sought to stiffen Churchill by sending him a quotation from Thucydides (the end of Perikles' funeral speech, ii. 64. 6; quoted in Churchill 1951, 81).

However striking the similarities between the Peloponnesian war and the second world war may have appeared to contemporaries of the latter, historians have to be more cautious about assimilating the effects of ancient warfare to those of modern warfare (cf. Foxhall, this volume). The dangers of a modernizing approach to Greek warfare are presumably as serious as the more familiar anachronism of treating the ancient economy as if it were capitalist. Both types of modernism are found fused together in theories of the 'fourth-century crisis'.[1]

By way of brief illustration, mention may be made of the influential theory of Michael Rostovtzeff, conceived in the 1930s (Rostovtzeff 1941, i. 104–25). In essence, he interprets the consequences of the Peloponnesian war in terms of the economic aftermath of the Great War. He sees the extended conflict as resulting in the decline of the industrial competitiveness of the states of mainland Greece, leading to an inability to afford imports of raw materials, including food. This in turn resulted in mass unemployment, pauperization, starvation, and acute class war. As evidence for the deterioration, Rostovtzeff points to the growing numbers of citizens who were ready to sell their services as mercenaries. Although Rostovtzeff's overall theory has been discredited as hopelessly anachronistic (there were no ancient Greek equivalents of the Lancashire cotton industry), it continues to resurface. In his study of 'The practical and economic background to the Greek mercenary explosion', H. F. Miller (1984, 153–4) cites as one of the factors 'a diminishing export trade coupled with food shortages and inflation'. Miller goes on to point to the devastations wrought by the Peloponnesian armies in Attica as a major cause of fourth-century impoverishment. The theory is expressed in its fullest form by Claude Mossé (1962, 35–66), as part of her general theory of a fourth-century crisis. This view of war-related destruction has convincingly been shown to depend on an anachronistic understanding of the relationship between warfare and agriculture in the ancient world (Hanson 1983); but it continues to find favour with those who persist in the idea that fourth-century 'decline' somehow had its origins in the Peloponnesian war (Fuks 1974; David 1984).

---

[1] For a succinct survey of 'crisis' literature see Pecirka 1976 and, at inordinate length, Weiskopf 1974.

In what follows, an attempt is made to break away from crisis-dominated views of the fourth century, and from the baleful influence of the Peloponnesian war. As an alternative, warfare may be presented as having been conceived by fourth-century Athenians as having the more positive, paradoxical function of stabilizing and preserving the democratic polis. In short, I want to try to emulate (however inadequately) colleagues in Roman history by constructing a model in which warfare feeds back into internal economic and political structures.[1]

Fourth-century democracy: control of the élite?

The problem with theories of grandeur, crisis, and decline is their dependence on the choice of criteria. The difficulty applies as much to the modern as to the ancient world. The purpose of Correlli Barnett's *The Audit of War* is, as the author says in his preface, 'to uncover the causes of Britain's protracted decline as an industrial country since the Second World War' (Barnett 1989, xi). As a whole, the book is a relentless indictment of Britain's failure to preserve the basis needed in order to maintain its status as a world power (classicists, it may be noted, do not escape without blame). As an antidote to the pessimism of Barnett may be cited the closing paragraph of A. J. P. Taylor's study *English History 1914-1945*, on the aftermath of the second world war:

> Traditional values lost much of their force. Other values took their place. Imperial greatness was on the way out; the welfare state was on the way in. The British empire declined; the condition of the people improved. Few now sang 'Land of Hope and Glory'. Few even sang 'England Arise'. England had risen all the same.
>
> (Taylor 1965, 600)

---

[1] Acceptance of the idea of crisis mars the treatment of fourth-century warfare in the otherwise thoughtful studies by Garlan, who sees the mercenary system as growing 'out of the crisis accompanying the birth, and later death, of the city-state' (1975, 103). My own interest in the interrelationship between warfare, the economy, and democracy overlaps only marginally with the papers (re)printed in Garlan 1989, despite that volume's title. For contrasting responses to his brand of the 'sociology of warfare', see reviews by Cartledge (1990) and Lazenby (1991).

That, shorn of Taylorian rhetoric, is a perspective that might be applied to Athens after the Peloponnesian war. If the criteria of success are deemed to be military power and control over resources, then it cannot be denied that Athens in the fourth century, without an empire, was in decline. But other criteria are possible: mention might be made of social and political stability, and the strength of democratic institutions. A persuasive case can be made out for seeing the fourth-century *politeia* down to the Macedonian takeover as the extended climax of Athenian democracy. Such is the view of Josiah Ober in his path-breaking book *Mass and Elite in Democratic Athens* (1989). The fourth-century democracy is there interpreted as the end of a long process of adjustment by trial and error, in the course of which many lessons were learned – not least those taught by the political upheavals of the Peloponnesian war. Ober argues in detail how the political process was structured so as to reinforce the popular, democratic element and control the Athenian élite. By way of illustration, the political trials of the fourth century, so easily read as signs of weakness and factionalism, are reinterpreted by Ober as a necessary way of checking the political élite, restraining their influence. So effective was this control that it is scarcely possible to think of an Athenian politician who was never fined, exiled, or executed (Knox 1985).

Ober has not told the whole story about fourth-century success. I have noted elsewhere (Millett 1989a) how his insistence on the primacy of political structures and ideology masks the economic dimension: the redistribution of income down the social scale that the demos needed if they were to preserve their independence from the élite (Millett 1989b). An additional factor, complementing Ober's political analysis of democratic stability, might be the contribution of warfare.[1]

That said, it would be foolish to argue that buttressing democracy was the only, or even the most important, function of Athenian warfare in the fourth century. We are told by

---

[1] If anything, Ober views warfare in the fourth century as an overall impediment to the establishing of democratic stability (1989, 98–9). Against war as an 'intrusive, irrational force', see the important paper by Austin (1986), with specific reference to the presentation of war by Rostovtzeff.

anthropologists that 'primitive warfare' is multi-functional (Vayda 1966); and that was surely the case with Athens. Hanson (1989) and Connor (1988) have recently asserted the ritual and symbolic functions of hoplite warfare. What made feasible the socio-political function claimed for warfare was the nature of much of the fighting in the first half of the fourth century. One thing making the traditional history of fourth-century Greece so complicated, and even repellent, is the confusing frequency with which states make and break alliances so as to switch sides. In particular, there existed what has been called an 'eternal tri-wrangle' between Athens, Sparta, and Thebes (Cartledge 1987, 247–313). These divisions and redivisions are typically represented as signs of Greek weakness; the poleis fritter away their strength in fighting each other, rather than uniting against the common enemy, Macedon. A hint of a different interpretation is suggested by a study of warfare between tribes and villages in modern North Africa by the anthropologists Bazin and Terray (1982). They show how the complex juggling of alliances and coalitions is so contrived that no single group can acquire sufficient power to dominate the rest. In this way, warfare is able to preserve its various ritual functions. The parallel with fourth-century Greece, which was not a primitive tribal society, should not be pressed too far; yet the apparent confusion of warfare and diplomacy, with its constant readjustments, may have been a more effective (and safer) means of maintaining a balance of power than the massive, opposing power blocks of the later fifth century.

   The remainder of this paper focuses on the internal effects of warfare on Athenian economics and politics; specifically, how the process of waging war, with its financial implications, served to consolidate the power of the demos. Hitherto, the usual approach to war and finance has been the 'balance sheet' technique. The costs of a campaign are calculated, and an estimation is made of whether they were outweighed by the likely profits from plunder, indemnities, and the like (see Pritchett 1991, 485–504). Apart from the absence of accurate figures in what would be an impossibly complex calculation (a cost–benefit analysis in reverse), the whole process involves imposing the principles of neo-classical economics onto a world with a different rationality. All we can do is to think in terms of contemporary perceptions, where the evidence seems clear. As far as the Greeks themselves were concerned, warfare was conceived of as potentially profitable. 'War is a kind of acquisition', says Aristotle in his *Politics* (1256 b; cf. *Oikonomika*, 1343 a); and the sentiment is borne out by other texts (Pritchett 1991, 439–45). Plutarch preserves a report that Alexander, on the eve of his Asian campaign, was in debt to the tune of 200 talents (*Alexander*, 15), which sum he presumably expected to make good from the profits of war.

As an alternative to aggregate profits and losses, there is the scope that warfare brings for the redistribution of resources within the polis. The message from the Roman model is unambiguous; while benefits were reaped by the élite, the burdens borne by the peasant-soldiers were such that a substantial proportion were dispossessed of their land (Hopkins 1978, 56–74). In Athens, if anything, the reverse seems to have been the case, with wealthier citizens bearing the cost of campaigns while the mass of the people enjoyed any benefits. To demonstrate this proposition in detail is not easy, given the perspective from which Athenian public finances have typically been examined. The relatively recent study of military finance by Brun is traditional in its approach and conclusions (Brun 1983, 183–5). 'Il y a bien crise', he writes of the later fourth century, 'dans le sens d'une détérioration des conditions de vie économique'; he follows this up with a quotation from Rostovtzeff (1941, i. 94). Finally, Brun points to the financial insufficiency of Athens as the explanation of its eventual failure: 'C'est cette incapacité à organiser, à planifier dirions-nous aujourd'hui, qui est la raison directe de la mort de la cité en tant qu'Etat indépendant.' As he notes, this is hardly a new idea; in fact, it marks a return to the view expressed some fifty years earlier by Andreades in his classic study *Greek Public Finance* (1933). In support of the crucial part played by an inadequate financial system, Andreades (207) cites no less an authority than Mr Gladstone to the effect that 'Athens perished because of its poor public finance'.

A variation on this theme, and a step closer to the argument of this paper, is the view that the burden of financing Athens' military operations fell increasingly on the wealthy, who either dodged their responsibilities or opted for the inexpensive policy of inaction. Such is the conclusion reached by Thomsen (1977) in his study entitled 'War taxes in classical Athens': 'the *eisphora* contributed largely to the pacifism of the upper classes, and this in the long run led to the loss of Athenian independence' (ibid. 144), and endorsed by Mossé in her 'intervention' that follows (ibid. 145). This also echoes the opinion of de Ste. Croix, in his standard study of the Athenian *eisphora* (1953, 69–70), that the Athenian élite undermined democracy through their evasion and avoidance of the taxation needed to pursue an active external policy.

The plausibility of these views is examined in the final sections of this paper, which try, however impressionistically, to assess the redistributive effect of warfare in the fourth-century polis.

The costs of waging war

On whom, in Athens in the fourth century, did the burden of waging war fall? In the ancient no less than in the modern world, the waging of wars was an expensive and potentially ruinous activity, not usually catered for in the budgets of poleis. Athens, in the earlier stages of the Peloponnesian war, was exceptional in having a large reserve of cash, the product of empire, stored on the Acropolis (Thuc. 2. 13). Isokrates, some eighty years later, recalled with nostalgia the occasion when the Acropolis had been 'filled with silver and gold' (15. 307).

Something of the hand-to-mouth methods by which more typical poleis funded their campaigns emerges from the evidence of public credit. In the catalogue of more than a hundred public loans from the Greek world drawn up by Migeotte (ed. 1984), the great majority are sought (where any reason is given) in connection with warfare. To the examples cited by Migeotte (ibid. 361) may be added two instances not included in his register. In 370 the Eleians are reported by Xenophon to have lent the Thebans thirty talents to support their invasion of Lakonia (*Hellenica*, 6. 5. 19); and what Aeschines (3. 103–4) interprets as interest on a bribe owed to Demosthenes by the city of Oreus ('exhausted by war and completely without means') might more plausibly be interpreted as interest payments on a loan. Pointing in the same direction are many of the anecdotes in the second book of the Aristotelian *Oikonomika*, which consists of a series of tricks whereby states in tight financial corners contrived to raise extra cash. Most of the dodges involve some species of forced loan, and in a majority of cases the funds are needed in time of war. For example, the author records how the city of Mende, 'being at war with Olynthos and needing funds, decreed that all the slaves they possessed, with the exception of one male and one female apiece, should be sold on behalf of the state, which was thus enabled to raise a loan from private citizens' (1305 a).[1]

In Athens, during and particularly after the Peloponnesian war, a substantial proportion of the cost of waging war seems to have fallen directly on the élite, without even the use of loans. There were three main sources of direct revenue, which may be set out schematically. The simplest were straightforward donations (*epidoseis*), the importance of which has been emphasized by Migeotte (1983; cf. Pritchett 1991, 473-8). These offerings were apparently solicited in the assembly (Theophrastos' 'mean man' gets up and quietly slips out when the matter is raised: *Characters*, 22), and seem to have had about them an air of competitive gift-giving. Plutarch records how Alcibiades was enticed into the assembly by hearing a burst of applause consequent on the promise of a donation, which he was moved to emulate with an offer of his own; this resulted in an even louder outbreak of clapping and cheering (*Alcibiades*, 10). These public offerings tend to occur in time of war (Isaeus, 5. 37-8, from the Corinthian war), and, in the literary sources at least, are associated with prominent individuals: Demosthenes, Hypereides, Lykourgos, Demades, and Phokion (Migeotte 1983, 147-8). A second source of élite expenditure on warfare was the trierarchy, too well known to need a detailed account, whereby a wealthy citizen (and, from the Peloponnesian war onwards, increasingly large groups of citizens) paid anything up to a talent for crewing and equipping a trireme. Finally, there was the *eisphora* or 'emergency tax', levied on the property of wealthier citizens when funds ran short for the waging of war. By way of refinement, the system was revised in the fourth century so that citizens who were identified as exceptionally rich were held responsible for paying *eisphora* in advance (*proeisphora*) on behalf of a designated group of payers, from whom they subsequently collected what they were owed. In this

---

[1] The translation (in Armstrong 1935) reflects the obscurity of the original Greek. For fuller details of war-related borrowing and repayment, see Millett 1991, 275 n. 43.

way, the state not only saved on the trouble and cost of collection, but also had immediate access to the necessary funds.[1]

Although *epidoseis*, trierarchies, and *eisphorai* were not the only financial responsibilities imposed on the Athenian élite, they were probably the most burdensome. At least, this is the message contained in the words addressed to the wealthy Kritoboulos by Sokrates, as conceived by Xenophon (*Oikonomikos*, 2. 5–6):

> I also observe that the polis is already laying on you heavy expenses, in keeping horses, acting as *choregos*, gymnasiarch, or *prostatēs*. If a war should break out, I know they will impose on you the trierarchy, and *eisphora* payments so great that you will not find it easy to bear them. And if ever you are thought to have fallen short in your performance of these duties, I know that the Athenians will punish you just as much as if they had caught you stealing their property.

Is this, as de Ste. Croix and others would have us believe, the predictable reaction of a disaffected élite, uncommitted to supporting the democratic polis? Or were wealthy Athenians pressurized into expending, in Athens' military interest, a greater part of their resources than their fortunes could bear? In support of over-expenditure there are those occasions, well documented in the fourth-century sources, on which apparently well-to-do Athenians were forced to borrow in order to discharge their obligations as trierarchs and *eisphora* payers. 'Because of my liturgies and *eisphorai* and ambition (*philotimia*) towards you, some of my furniture has been pledged as security and some has been sold.' With these words the speaker tries to win over the jury in the Demosthenic speech *Against Euergos and Mnesiboulos* (47. 54); and the circumstances described by Demosthenes in his *Second Speech against Aphobos* are even more heart-rending (28. 17–18; cf. 21. 78–80). He recounts how he was forced by his opponents to assume the trierarchy at such short notice that the obligation could only be discharged by offering as security all

---

[1] There are brief accounts of the liturgy system and some of its implications in Hands 1968, 26–48; Finley 1985, 150–4; Veyne 1976, 185–200. Successive changes in the *eisphora* system are discussed by Rhodes 1982; MacDowell 1986; Gabrielsen 1989.

his property, including the family home (the sum involved was 20 minas).[1]

The motif is not uncommon that only those with the largest fortunes can perform their liturgies from income, without selling or hypothecating real property (Isae. 6. 38; Dem. 36. 41; cf. Isae. fr. 34, in Forster 1927). But one case of a debt-inducing liturgy deserves a more detailed citation. The trierarch in question was one Apollodoros; no ordinary citizen, but son of the banker Pasion, who had enjoyed a remarkable (and utterly exceptional) transformation from rags to riches, rising from the position of banker's slave to that of full Athenian citizen. Apollodoros evidently felt that he had something to prove. Although the son of a former slave, he had to show himself to be as good as any other citizen; and the way he chose was by massively over-performing his liturgy obligation. In the Demosthenic speech *Against Polykles* (50), Apollodoros describes in detail the five loans he raised (two secured on real property) in order to finance his admittedly de luxe trierarchy. The figures given for three of the five loans add up to almost a talent (5,700 drachmas). To make matters worse, at the same time as being appointed trierarch (362 BC) Apollodoros was also designated *proeisphora* payer. He claims never to have recovered the cash he had to advance on others' behalf, 'because at the time I was abroad in your service as trierarch; and afterwards, when I returned, I found that the money from those who had resources had already been gathered in by others, and that those who were left had nothing' (50. 8–9). As if to support Apollodoros' sob story, Demosthenes describes how, a few years later, defaulting *eisphora* payers escaped the official collector by climbing over roofs and hiding under beds (21. 53).

To be sure, Apollodoros was hardly a typical member of the Athenian élite. But his behaviour shows how liturgies were caught up in the creation of prestige; and also how the timing of obligations could prove financially embarrassing, even to one of the wealthiest Athenians.[2]

---

[1]   What follows is based on the more detailed treatment in Millett 1991, 67–71.

[2]   A detailed account of the career of Apollodoros son of Pasion, potentially one of the most illuminating characters of this period, is being prepared by Jeremy Trevett.

More problematical than the burden of paying for warfare in classical Athens is the distribution of material benefits. A hint is provided by Thucydides' account of the motives of the demos for supporting the expedition to Sicily in the middle of the Peloponnesian war (6. 24): 'The great mass of the people and the soldiers thought that they would get money (*argurion*) at the present, and also make an addition to their power (*dunamis*) that would be an inexhaustible source of pay (*misthophoros*).' The practice of pay for public employment, including rowing in the fleet, continued through the fourth century, long after the empire was lost. The relationship between imperialism, public pay, and democracy has already been documented (Millett 1989b, 37–43; Finley 1978, 121–4; Schuller 1984). But a contrasting aspect of resource distribution also arises out of Thucydides' account of the Sicilian expedition, via the motivation attributed to Alcibiades (6. 16). He explains how Alcibiades strongly supported the proposed expedition because he had been indulging in conspicuous expenditure far beyond his means, and looked on the campaign in Sicily as a way of restoring his fortune. Was this imputed motive just another illustration of Alcibiades' outrageous behaviour, or were there recognized (if informal) opportunities for members of the fifth-century élite to make personal gain from holding commands? Perhaps the fringe benefits associated with winning, controlling, and administering the empire should be added to the acquisition of land in subject areas as significant material benefits enjoyed by wealthier and more powerful Athenians.[1]

Whatever the picture for the fifth century, that for the fourth is clear. According to the terms of the foundation charter of the Second Athenian League, Athenian citizens were explicitly forbidden from acquiring land in allied states (*SIG*[3] 123. 35–46; Cargill 1981, 146–50). Attitudes towards those waging war on Athens' behalf were similarly uncompromising, as may be

---

[1] The existence of substantial but hidden financial advantages open to the Athenian élite would go some way towards explaining the upper-class support for the empire that so puzzled Finley (1978, 123–4). A full discussion of possible economic benefits from the fifth-century empire for Athenian citizens – rich and poor – is now available in Schmitz 1988 (cf. Millett 1990).

illustrated by the procedures relating to plunder.[1] Virtually all the booty from Athenian campaigns was destined for public rather than private consumption; in theory, that meant the treasury. Victorious commanders could be granted a share of the plunder only by a vote of the demos; and *strategoi* returning from campaigns had to render a formal account of expenditures and gains. To assist (and control) them, they were accompanied on their travels by *tamiai* or treasurers. The contrast with Roman commanders and their attitude towards plunder could hardly be more striking (Harris 1979, 74–93); and much the same could be said of the administrative and judicial control that the Athenians exercised over their *strategoi*. All known occasions (more than twenty) on which Athenian commanders were brought to trial between 404 and 322 are catalogued by Pritchett (1985, 4–33). The penalties were not mild; in approximately half the recorded cases, the death penalty was awarded, and usually it was carried out. To give a single example, the twenty-eighth speech of Lysias is delivered against one Ergokles, who stands accused of misappropriating thirty talents while commanding an expedition in Asia Minor. The accusation was successful; Ergokles was condemned and executed, and his property was confiscated (cf. Lys. 29).

The evidence so carefully collected by Pritchett provides a valuable corrective to the once prevailing view that, as the fourth century wore on, the Athenians exercised diminishing control over their commanders. Rather less persuasive is the interpretation placed on this material. Pritchett's expressed aim is to try to determine how much justice or otherwise there might be behind the charges brought against Athenian commanders, and whether the fear of being brought into court had any adverse effect on these commanders' discharge of their duties. Although it is impossible to assess the likelihood of innocence or guilt from the evidence at our disposal, Pritchett concludes by making the sensible suggestion that it seems unlikely that all the accused were guilty. He gives as his explanation for the large number of trials the increasing pauperization of Athens through the fourth century; the demos wanted to ensure that all possible proceeds from military campaigns found their way into the treasury. And

---

[1] In what follows, I have to acknowledge a heavy debt to the detailed researches of Pritchett 1971, 53–101; 1991, 363–542.

so we arrive back at the idea of crisis and decline as characteristic of the fourth century.[1]

An alternative approach might be to interpret the trials of commanders as equivalent to the trials of politicians catalogued by Ober, and to see the demos as exercising collective control over members of the military élite. To support this hypothesis in detail would require a lengthy and complex study. By way of a substitute, the following and final section examines some aspects of the career of the *strategos* Timotheos, whose experiences pull together several of the strands of thought offered in this paper.

The career of Timotheos

Timotheos was an aristocrat, son of the outstanding naval commander Konon.[2] He was also a pupil of Isokrates, who writes about him in glowing terms in a pamphlet entitled *Antidosis* (15. 101–39). Warm support from Isokrates might by itself seem to arouse suspicion about Timotheos' democratic credentials; all the more so since Isokrates thinks it necessary to refute the charge that Timotheos was 'hostile to the people' (*misodemos*, 15. 131). Isokrates alludes to Timotheos' chequered career as a naval commander who was twice brought to trial. We are concerned with the circumstances of the first trial and acquittal in *c*.362.

In the later 370s Timotheos had been campaigning around northern Greece, where he suffered from serious shortages of funds. Something of this is reflected in his appearance as the subject of several anecdotes in the Aristotelian *Oikonomika* (1350 a–b), where he is shown as introducing a fiduciary copper coinage and tricking his men into believing that pay was on its way. But Timotheos also resorted to raising cash through borrowing, and

---

[1] The concept of fourth-century crisis recurs in the context of Pritchett's magisterial treatment of booty (1991, 458–9), where he unfortunately accepts at face value the uncritical reference-gathering of Fuks relating to the impoverishment of citizens.

[2] The most convenient, connected account of Timotheos' career still seems to be the general history of Athens' fourth-century external relations in Cloché 1934, 55–242.

among his creditors was the banker Pasion. We hear about this in some detail because years later, after Pasion's death, his son Apollodoros prosecuted Timotheos on the grounds that he had failed to repay the monies owed. Apollodoros' accusations are preserved as the Demosthenic speech *Against Timotheos* (59). Here is how he addresses the jury (§6):

> Timotheos was about to set sail on his second expedition and was already in the Piraeus on the point of putting to sea when, being short of money, he came to my father in the port and urged him to lend him 1,351 drachmas 2 obols, declaring that he needed the additional sum.

The odd sum involved suggests that the loan was needed to cover some specific payment. Timotheos got his money and set off for Corcyra, but was soon in difficulties again. While stationed at Kalaureia, an island off the Peloponnese, some of the Boiotian trierarchs serving under him became restless. In order to retain their services, we are told, Timotheos was forced to borrow 1,000 drachmas from Philippos the shipowner (*naukleros*) and his treasurer (*tamias*) Antiphanes (§§14–15). It was at this point that Timotheos returned to Athens to face his first trial; the charge was apparently that of failing to take up his command at Corcyra at the earliest opportunity. Once back in Athens, Philippos and Antiphanes began to put pressure on Timotheos to repay their loan. Although he was frightened that word would get around as to his use of private funds to square the trierarchs, prior commitments made it impossible for Timotheos to discharge his 1,000-drachma loan. Here is how Apollodoros describes his predicament (§§11–13):

> he was in desperate need of money. All his property was pledged as security, *horoi* had been set up on it, and other people were in control. His farm on the plain had been taken over as security by the son of Eumelidas; the rest of his property was encumbered for seven minas each to the sixty trierarchs who set out with him, which money he as commander had forced them to distribute among the crews for maintenance. . . . he gave them his property as security. Yet now he is robbing them by digging up the *horoi*. He was hard pressed on every side, his life was in extreme danger because of the seriousness of the misfortunes which had befallen the polis.

Under these circumstances Timotheos again turned to Pasion,

seeking to borrow the money he needed to repay his creditors and keep them quiet. According to Apollodoros, Pasion felt sorry for Timotheos in his plight, and provided the cash.

At his trial Timotheos received support from Alketas, king of the Molossoi, and Jason, tyrant of Pherai, for whom he had apparently performed some favours while on campaign. The two of them turned up unexpectedly at his house one evening, and he found himself without the money and household articles needed to entertain such important guests. Apollodoros takes up the story (§§22–3):

> Being at a loss how to entertain them, he sent his personal slave Aischrion to my father and told him to ask for a loan of some bedding and cloaks and two silver bowls, and to borrow a mina of silver. My father, hearing from Aischrion . . . that they had both arrived, and of the urgent need for which the request was made, both supplied the items for which the slaves had come and lent the mina he asked to borrow.

The support of Timotheos' two distinguished witnesses may have had the right effect; he was, on this occasion, acquitted.

Why had Pasion been willing to lend these substantial items to Timotheos – to say nothing of his spare bedding and clothing? Apollodoros is explicit about his father's motives (§3):

> He thought that if Timotheos got safely out of these dangers and returned home from the service of the king of Persia, when the defendant was in better circumstances he would not only recover his money but would be in a position to obtain whatever else he might want from Timotheos.

The idea that Timotheos would pay up, and more, when again in funds is twice repeated in the speech (§§24, 64). What may be noted is the idea that it was when he was in the service of the Persians, not the demos of Athens, that Timotheos would be in a position to make money. A similar sentiment is expressed in Lysias' speech *On the Property of Aristophanes* (19. 23), where Aristophanes is said to have supplied the king of Salamis (in Cyprus) with everything in his power (including borrowed money totalling six talents) 'with a view to recovering more'. Unlike Aristophanes, Timotheos met with success in non-Athenian service, and apparently restored his fortune. Renewed service on behalf of the Athenians resulted in fresh difficulties, leading to a trial and a fine of 100 talents (Isoc. 15. 129).

Plenty more could be said about Timotheos and the financial implications of his campaigns, but the aspects here highlighted give some impression of the conditions under which Athenian *strategoi* of the fourth century were forced to operate. The chronic under-funding of campaigns seems to have had a double function. In part it reflected the straitened circumstances of a polis fighting wars without the revenues of empire; commanders were forced to raise their own resources, easing the strain on the treasury. In addition, lack of funds drove commanders into plundering activity that laid them open to prosecution and condemnation, depending on the strength of their political enemies and the mood of the demos. This was the danger that Timotheos apparently tried to avoid by deploying his own resources. Isokrates therefore feels able to stress both the strict economy of Timotheos' campaigning and his avoidance of plundering (15. 123–4). Nor was Timotheos the only *strategos* to draw on his own fortune in support of a campaign (Davies 1984, 128–9); but no one else contributed on such a lavish scale. The loan of seven talents that Timotheos took from his trierarchs, secured on his own property, is the biggest single piece of borrowing in the corpus of the Attic orators; and yet, if Apollodoros can be believed (Dem. 59. 16), Timotheos feared that even this piece of apparent generosity might be presented by his opponents as a financial irregularity, and be judged accordingly by the demos.

Bibliography

Andreades, A. M. (1933), *A History of Greek Public Finance* (Cambridge, Mass.).

Armstrong, G. C. (trans. 1935), *Aristotle, Metaphysics X–XIV, Oeconomica and Magna Moralia* (Loeb Classical Texts; London, etc.).

Austin, M. M. (1986), 'Hellenistic kings, war and the economy', *CQ* 80 (n.s. 36): 450–66.

Barnett, C. (1989), *The Audit of War* (London).

Bazin, J., and Terray, E. (1982), *Guerres le lignages d'état en Afrique* (Paris).

Beard, W. M., and Crawford, M. H. (1985), *Rome in the Late Republic* (London).

Bleicken, J. (1985), *Die athenische Demokratie* (Paderborn).

Brun, P. (1983), *Eisphora, syntaxis, stratiotika: recherches sur les finances militaires d'Athènes au IVe siècle av. J.-C.* (Paris).
Cargill, J. (1981), *The Second Athenian League: Empire or Free Alliance?* (Berkeley).
Cartledge, P. (1987), *Agesilaos and the Crisis of Sparta* (London).
—— (1990), review of Garlan 1989, *Gnomon*, 464–6.
Churchill, W. S. (1923–9), *The World Crisis* (London).
—— (1951), *The Hinge of Fate* (London).
Cloché, P. (1934), *La Politique étrangère d'Athènes de 404 à 338 avant Jésus-Christ* (Paris).
Connor, W. R. (1989), 'Early Greek land warfare as symbolic expression', *Past and Present*, 119: 3–29.
David, E. (1984), *Aristophanes and Athenian Society of the Early Fourth Century BC* (Leiden).
Davies, J. K. (1984), *Wealth and the Power of Wealth in Classical Athens* (New York).
de Ste. Croix, G. E. M. (1953), 'Demosthenes' *timēma* and the Athenian *eisphora* in the fourth century BC', *Classica et mediaevalia*, 14: 30–70.
Ehrenberg, V. (1973), *From Solon to Socrates* (2nd edn, London).
Finley, M. I. (1978), 'The fifth-century empire: a balance sheet', in P. D. A. Garnsey and C. R. Whittaker (eds), *Imperialism in the Ancient World* (Cambridge), pp. 103–26.
—— (1985), *The Ancient Economy* (2nd edn, London).
Forster, E. S. (trans. 1927), *Isaeus* (Loeb Classical Texts; London, etc.).
Fuks, A. (1974), 'Patterns and types of social–economic revolution in Greece from the fourth to the second century BC', *Ancient Society*, 5: 51–81.
Gabrielsen, V. (1989), 'The number of Athenian trierarchs after ca. 340 BC', *Classica et mediaevalia*, 40: 145–59.
Garlan, Y. (1975), *War in the Ancient World: A Social History* (London).
—— (1989), *Guerre et économie en Grèce ancienne* (Paris).
Gilbert, M. (1989), *Second World War* (London).
Hands, A. R. (1968), *Charities and Social Aid in Greece and Rome* (London).
Hanson, V. D. (1983), *Warfare and Agriculture in Classical Greece* (Pisa).
—— (1989), *The Western Way of War: Infantry Battle in Classical Greece* (London).
Harris, W. V. (1979), *War and Imperialism in Republican Rome 327–70 BC* (Oxford).
Hopkins, K. (1978), *Conquerors and Slaves* (Cambridge).
Humphreys, S. C. (1978), 'Economy and society in classical Athens', in *Anthropology and the Greeks* (London), pp. 136–58; = *Annali della scuola normale superiore di Pisa*, 39: 1–26.
Jones, R. V. (1978), *Most Secret War: British Scientific Intelligence 1939–1945* (London).
Knox, R. A. (1985), ' "So mischievous a beaste"? The Athenian *demos* and its treatment of its politicians', *G&R* 32: 132–61.

Lazenby, J. F. (1991), review of Garlan 1989, *JHS* 111: 244–5.

MacDowell, D. M. (1986), 'The law of Periandros about symmories', *CQ* 80 (n.s. 36): 438–49.

Marwick, A. (1968), *The Deluge* (London).

Migeotte, L. (1983), 'Souscriptions athéniennes de la période classique', *Historia*, 32: 129–48.

—— (ed. 1984), *L'Emprunt public dans les cités grecques* (Québec, etc.).

Miller, H. F. (1984), 'The practical and economic background to the Greek mercenary explosion', *G&R* 31: 153–60.

Millett, P. (1989a), review of Ober 1989, *Times Literary Supplement* (29 Dec.), 1449.

—— (1989b), 'Patronage and its avoidance in classical Athens', in A. Wallace-Hadrill (ed.), *Patronage in Ancient Society* (Leicester–Nottingham Studies in Ancient Society, 1), 15–48.

—— (1990), review of Schmitz 1988, *CR* 104 (n.s. 40): 137–8.

—— (1991), *Lending and Borrowing in Ancient Athens* (Cambridge).

Mossé, C. (1962), *La Fin de la démocratie athénienne* (Paris).

Murray, G. (1944), 'Reactions to the Peloponnesian war in Greek thought and practice', *JHS* 64: 1–9.

Ober, J. (1989), *Mass and Elite in Democratic Athens: Rhetoric, Ideology and the Power of the People* (Princeton).

Pecirka, J. (1976), 'The crisis of the Athenian *polis*', *Eirene*, 14: 5–30.

Pritchett, W. K. (1971), *The Greek State at War*, i (Berkeley).

—— (1985), *The Greek State at War*, iv (Berkeley).

—— (1991), *The Greek State at War*, v (Berkeley).

Rhodes, P. J. (1982), 'Problems in Athenian *eisphora* and liturgies', *American Journal of Ancient History*, 7: 1–19.

Rostovtzeff, M. (1941), *Economic and Social History of the Hellenistic World* (Oxford).

Schmitz, W. (1988), *Wirtschaftliche Prosperität, soziale Integration und die Seebundpolitik Athens* (Munich).

Schuller, W. (1984), 'Wirkungen des ersten attischen Seebunds auf die Herausbildung der athenischen Demokratie', *Xenia*, 8: 87–101.

Taylor, A. J. P. (1965), *English History 1914–1945* (Oxford History of England, 15; Oxford).

Thomsen, R. (1977), 'War taxes in classical Athens', in *Armées et fiscalité dans le monde antique* (Paris).

Turner, F. M. (1981), *The Greek Heritage in Victorian Britain* (London).

Vayda, A. P. (1966), 'Warfare', in *International Encyclopaedia of the Social Sciences* (London).

Veyne, P. (1976), *Le Pain et le cirque: sociologie historique d'un pluralisme politique* (Paris); trans. and abridged by B. Pearce as *Bread and Circuses: Historical Sociology and Political Pluralism* (Harmondsworth, 1990).

Weiskopf, E. C. (1974), *Hellenische Poleis: Krise, Wirkung, Wandlung* (Berlin).

∞ 10 ∞

Alexander and the Macedonian invasion of Asia: Aspects of the historiography of war and empire in antiquity

Michel Austin

The focus of this paper is primarily historiographical rather than historical. It seeks to relate some current views on the causes and objectives of war as presented by ancient writers to the specific case of the Macedonian invasion of Asia under Alexander.[1] I do not wish to suggest that historiographical and historical aspects can be entirely dissociated. But there are numerous questions about the invasion beyond the purely historiographical, some of which are touched on below, that deserve fuller investigation than can be given here. Perhaps I should add that the emphasis in what follows on the material motives for the invasion of Asia by the Macedonians is not meant to imply that no other motives were present (such as the search for glory, at least on the part of the kings). I simply wish to react against the tendencies in some writers to underplay this aspect (e.g. Ducrey 1968, 159; 170; 1985, 228) or to draw a distinction between 'political' and 'economic' motives for wars that is perhaps artificial (cf. Garlan 1975, 183; 1989, 33–6). This approach may derive ultimately from state-ments in some of the ancient sources, which stress Alexander's lack of interest in wealth and self-indulgence, as compared

[1] My thanks are due to the participants at seminars in St Andrews and Leicester, and to the editors of this volume; their comments and suggestions have helped to improve the original, though the responsibility for any remaining errors and omissions remains my own.

with his pursuit of glory and his generosity to others, and draw a (perhaps artificial) contrast between him and his friends and followers.[1]

Before the invasion

Preliminaries to the war

> No single topic occupies more attention in ancient history, more space in print, than the preliminaries leading to a war. . . . Yet it is neither mischievous nor perverse to suggest that there is no topic on which we are less well equipped to express any views at all.

Thus M. I. Finley in his chapter on 'War and empire'; and he then went on to suggest (1985b, 80; 81) that 'ancient wars can normally be examined concretely only after they have got under way'. Although Finley was chiefly concerned with the wars between the republican states of antiquity, in Greek and Roman history, and had little to say about royal wars of the hellenistic or other periods, these statements apply particularly well to the Macedonian invasion of Asia initiated by Philip and carried out by Alexander. It is striking how little the extant sources have to say about the preliminaries leading to the expedition, and its possible aims and motives before it was launched.

The fullest extant ancient statement appears to be the sensible, but brief remarks of Polybios in relation to his discussion of the differences between the causes, pretexts, and beginnings of wars (3. 6). According to Polybios, the 'causes' of the war were the march of the Ten Thousand (in 400–399) and the expedition of Agesilaos to Asia Minor (in 396–394), which convinced Philip of the weakness of the Persians and revealed the rich rewards to be gained. The 'pretext' was Philip's proclaimed intention to avenge the injuries inflicted by the Persians on the Greeks. The 'beginning' of the war was Alexander's crossing into Asia. Brief as Polybios' remarks are, they are far more informative than any of the principal extant sources for the Macedonian expedition.

Of those sources, Diodoros presents Philip as thinking of the

---

[1]   E.g. Arr. 7. 28. 3, cf. Bosworth 1988b, 137; 139; Plut. *Alex.* 5; 39–40.

war against the Persians already by the time of the peace of Philokrates in 346 BC (16. 60). In 336 Philip, about to launch the war, was confident of overthrowing the Persian king and making Asia a captive of the Macedonians (16. 91–2). But Diodoros gives no further analysis or explanation for the decision. Similarly, Arrian presents Alexander's wish to invade as self-evident from the start and in no need of comment.[1] So, too, Plutarch portrays Alexander as very interested in the Persian empire and anxious from an early date to get on with conquest (*Alexander*, 5), but does not feel the need to provide any further explanation. (How Quintus Curtius presented the decision to invade is unknown, since his first two books are lost.)

Nor are we much informed about the debates that led to the decision to invade Asia. No extant ancient source enables us to date precisely when and why Philip formed the plan of invading the Persian empire (see below). As for Alexander's own decision after his accession, all we have is a brief and tantalizing report in Diodoros (17. 16) of a debate involving Alexander, his officers, and his leading friends on the timing and handling of the invasion. Antipater and Parmenion urge Alexander to provide heirs to the throne before undertaking the invasion, but Alexander is anxious to make a start and argues successfully for immediate action.

Concerning the expectations of the mass of the army at the start of the invasion, we would have no direct information at all but for Justin, of all sources, who provides in a few lines (11. 5) the only concrete picture of the mood of the Macedonian rank and file, avid for rich plunder from the Persian empire and oblivious, according to him, of their families at home.

With this general dearth of information concerning the beginnings of one of the most momentous wars in the history of the ancient world, compare for example the extensive contemporary reporting by Thucydides of the debates at Athens that led to the launching of the Sicilian expedition in 415 BC (6. 8–26), and his vivid description of the contrasted hopes and fears of the various participants as they set out on their journey (6. 30–1).

Discussing the 'causes of wars' was in fact a favourite pastime of ancient authors, as may be seen from Herodotos on the Persian wars, Thucydides on the Peloponnesian war, the Oxyrhynchus

---

[1]   Brunt 1976–83, i, pp. li–lv (paras 39–42); ii. 567 (para. 30).

historian on the Corinthian war, Polybios on the second Punic war, and others (Momigliano 1966). Why, then, the apparent dearth of such discussion in the sources for the war of the Macedonians against the Persians? The short answer may be simply that we do not have a Thucydides or a Polybios for this war. The historians of Alexander, whether the original writers, starting with Kallisthenes, or the later derivative sources, had other purposes, literary or moral in character rather than historical, and were not primarily concerned with analysing the background of the invasion.

It may also be suggested that the sources felt little need to discuss the causes and aims of the war, precisely because it was so conspicuously successful and the material benefits for the victors so self-evident, at least from the time of the battle of Issos in 333, the turning-point of the invasion. Unlike all the many ancient wars that ended in failure (the Persian wars – from the point of view of the invaders – the Peloponnesian war, the Sicilian expedition, and many others), this one left no *Kriegsschuldfrage* to be debated retrospectively.

It might also be mentioned that the actual beginning of the war was less clear-cut than Polybios suggested. The plan of the war had been initiated and put into action by Philip in 336, and early campaigns had been waged by Attalos and Parmenion in advance of Philip's projected assumption of the command. His assassination in 336 delayed the campaign, and the disturbances that resulted from the death of Philip postponed the start of Alexander's own campaign until 334.[1] When Alexander did eventually take over, he was clearly anxious to make the expedition his own and to place his personal stamp on it.

The pretext for the war

What the extant sources do tell us about specifically, and in some detail, is of course the pretext put forward, first by Philip and then by Alexander. The expedition was meant to be a panhellenic war of revenge against the Persians. Philip, and then Alexander, were supposedly leaders of a united Hellenic expedition which aimed at

---

[1] Cf. Badian 1966, 39–41, on the campaigns before Alexander's takeover.

exacting retribution from the Persians for the harm they had done, and for their burning of the temples of Athens during the Persian wars.[1] Whether liberation of the Greek cities of Asia was also part of the original propaganda motive, as only Diodoros asserts (16. 91. 2 on Philip's advance invasion; 17. 24. 1 on Alexander in Asia Minor), is uncertain.[2]

On this well-known subject I shall simply list without discussion some familiar points. The propaganda posture was aimed clearly at the Greek world, and was of no direct interest to the Macedonians themselves. It was felt necessary by the Macedonian kings to make this claim, because they needed status in relation to the Greek world. Pretensions at leadership over other Greeks had to be cloaked and justified in terms of the championship of a Greek cause (Perlman 1976). The Greekness of the Macedonians, long a matter of doubt, had become a subject of renewed argument and propaganda. The Athenians in the time of Demosthenes were presenting their resistance to Macedon as a re-enactment, on behalf of the Greeks, of their resistance to the Persians in the fifth century (Habicht 1961; Thomas 1989, 84–6). Failure on the part of the Macedonian rulers to answer this with their own counter-claim, that of leadership of the Greeks, would mean that they were conceding by default the Athenian view. As for the theme of revenge, wars in the Greek world in the classical period, whatever their real motives, needed to be justified in terms of the requital of harm done by the enemy in the past.[3] Unprovoked raids had once been not merely acceptable, but a matter of glory, as in the Homeric poems (as Thucydides remarked, 1. 5); but this had long ceased to be the case (Jackson 1985).

Possible motives

The sources thus leave unanswered many questions about the

---

[1]   See Brunt 1976–83, i, p. lii (para. 40), for the sources.
[2]   Brunt 1976–83, i, p. li (para. 39); Seager 1981, 106–7. Isokrates (5. 123) had suggested to Philip the liberation of the (Greek) cities of Asia as a minimum objective.
[3]   On revenge in Greek thought and practice see Gehrke 1987, esp. 144 on Philip, Alexander, and Persia.

most fundamental aspects of the Macedonians' decision to invade Asia. Historians are still uncertain as to the point at which Philip conceived his plan to turn away eventually from the Greek world and to invade Asia. Was the plan conceived early, by the time of the peace of Philokrates in 346 or perhaps even before this, as many believe? Or was it only a late decision that did not take shape until the time of the battle of Chaironeia in 338?[1] We do not know for sure, and are reduced to arguing over a small number of allusions or statements in contemporary (Demosthenes) or later sources (Diodoros), and speculating about how far Isokrates' writings may or may not have influenced Philip's plans.

While there is no such problem in the case of Alexander, the respective war aims of Philip and Alexander at the start of the invasion remain a matter of conjecture.[2] The silence of the ancient sources on the preliminaries to the invasion has had the effect of discouraging modern discussion. It is striking how, in all the prolific modern literature on Philip and Alexander, down-to-earth questions about the initial motives for the invasion rarely receive extended treatment.[3] On the other hand, Alexander's alleged future aims for his Asiatic conquests – in terms, for example, of a 'civilizing mission', a 'policy of fusion', or the so-called 'Last Plans' – are raised explicitly in some of the ancient sources, and consequently receive much attention in modern writing.

A number of obvious suggestions can be made. The material advantages to be expected by the Macedonians from an invasion

---

[1]   See Errington 1981, esp. 77–83, who argues for the latter against other recent views; *contra*, Borza 1990, 229–30.

[2]   See e.g. Fredericksmeyer 1982 for a maximalist view of Philip's aims, with references to earlier work.

[3]   Among many, see Berve 1926, who apparently gives no systematic discussion of the question; Tarn 1948, i. 8–9; Brunt 1965, 205–8; Seibert 1972, 70–8, who has nothing on the subject in his survey of Alexander's early years down to the start of the expedition; Hamilton 1973, 38–9 (Philip); 46, 50–1 (Alexander); Lane Fox 1973, chs 3–4; Hammond and Walbank 1988, 66–7; Errington 1990, 87–9 (Philip); 103–5 (Alexander); Borza 1990, 226; 228–30. Even Bosworth (1988a, 17–19; 34; 38–9; 43; 50; 54; 179) provides no systematic treatment of the question. Rather fuller on Philip are Hammond and Griffith (1979, 458–63; 631–4) and Fredericksmeyer (1982).

of Asia can easily be conjectured. The notion that the Persian empire was a soft target, and a suitable object for profitable aggression, antedated the fourth century and all the Greek propaganda of that age (Starr 1976, 48–61). It was not Xenophon, Isokrates, and others who first argued the point; it is already found in essentials in Herodotos, whose *Histories* read like a forecast before the event of the downfall of the Persian empire over a century later (see below). This is seen in a number of passages, notably in the advice Aristagoras of Miletos reportedly gave to Kleomenes I of Sparta in 499 when trying to enlist support from the mainland Greeks for the Ionian reolt (5. 49). Aristagoras dangles before Kleomenes prospects of an easy and lucrative invasion: gold, silver, fine embroideries, beasts of burden, and slaves are all there for the taking.[1] Aristagoras' advice is evidently anachronistic, and reflects Greek experiences in their encounters with the Persians during and after the Persian wars; but that does not matter here. Subsequently, by the middle of the fifth century, the era of profitable aggression by the Greeks against the Persians in practice came to an end (see de Ste. Croix 1972, 312, for this formulation). Relations between the two began to take on new forms, which involved political, diplomatic, and financial intervention instead of military confrontation.

In the early fourth century, ideas of Greek aggression revived. The expedition and return of the Ten Thousand, as presented by Xenophon in his *Anabasis* (see esp. 3. 2. 26), were a powerful stimulus. Not long afterwards, the campaigns of Agesilaos in Asia Minor (396–394) showed what might be achieved in terms of conquest, and provided a possible model for Philip and Alexander in the early stages of their expedition.[2] All this fed the negative views of fourth-century Greek writers on the (alleged) weakness and degeneracy of the contemporary Persian empire. Modern historians of Persia have emphasized the shallowness of these

---

[1] The Persian kings' vast treasures of uncoined gold and silver were a special temptation; cf. de Callataÿ 1989, 260–4, for an attempt to quantify the amounts of precious metals captured by the Macedonians from the Persians.

[2] See Xen. *Hell.* 6. 1. 12; *Ages.* 1. 36, cf. 7. 7; Isoc. 4. 144; Plut. *Ages.* 15; cf. Cartledge 1987, 212–18.

views.[1] The point is taken, though the fact remains that this was a widely expressed Greek conception of the Persian empire at the time, which may conceivably have influenced the Macedonian rulers.

To this view of the Persian empire as a suitable target for profitable aggression should be added the evidence for contemporary Greek attitudes to wars between Greeks, and to empire exercised at the expense of other Greeks. Though Greeks continued to fight each other with undiminished zest, the idea had been growing since at least the fifth century that this was somehow disreputable and unnatural, and that Greeks ought not to enslave other Greeks.[2] Besides, wars between Greeks were not always very profitable, compared to what might be expected from a successful attack on Asia.[3] On the subject of empire, one of the by-products of the fifth-century Athenian experience was that *phoros* (tribute), a word probably initially neutral in colouring (Powell 1988, 15), came to acquire a pejorative connotation, as the history of the second Athenian naval confederacy illustrates.[4] Again, levying of tribute from barbarians was another matter (cf. Jason of Pherai's boast, Xen. *Hell.* 6. 1. 12).

All this was of particular relevance to the Macedonian rulers, since the Greekness of the Macedonians had become a matter of intense political propaganda. The expansion of Macedonian power in the earlier years of Philip, down to the peace of Philokrates in 346, involved the capture and destruction of some Greek cities, the dispersal or actual enslavement of their populations, and the redivision of their territory for the benefit of Macedonian settlers; this is true at least of Methone in 354[5] and

---

[1]   See e.g. Momigliano 1975, 132–6; Starr 1976, 1977; Cartledge 1987, 184–5; Sancisi-Weerdenburg (ed.) 1987, 33–45, on Ktesias; ibid. 117–31, on Xenophon's *Cyropaedia*; Kuhrt 1988, 60–1.
[2]   For some passages see Garlan, in Finley (ed.) 1987, at pp. 13–15 (= Garlan 1989, 83–4); Garlan 1988, 50–2; cf. also Xen. *Hell.* 3. 2. 22.
[3]   See explicitly Hdt. 5. 49, and cf. Xen. *Hell.* 3. 2. 26; cf. also Xenophon's comment on the inconclusive outcome of the battle of Mantineia (362), *Hell.* 7. 5. 27.
[4]   Tod ii. 123, line 23; Theopompos, *FGH* 115 F 98; Plut. *Sol.* 15; cf. Wilson 1970.
[5]   Diod. 16. 34, with Hammond and Griffith 1979, 361–2.

Olynthos in 348,[1] and perhaps of others as well. Though Demosthenes' rhetoric magnified the numbers and distorted the character of these 'destructions', they were nevertheless a stigma. As his career progressed, Philip came to appreciate more and more the sensitivity of Greek public opinion, as did the later hellenistic dynasties. One may compare the changing Roman attitude to the Greek world from the first to the second Macedonian war. Philip's defeat of the sacrilegious Phokians, and his consequent admission to the Amphiktyonic Council, marked a breakthrough in this respect (cf. Diod. 16. 60; Just. 8. 2. 5–9). Greeks had to be treated with some care, hence the need to redirect Macedonian energies against the Persian empire and try to enlist Greek support. This did not mean that Greek recalcitrance against the Macedonians would not still be met with violence, as Alexander showed in his sack of Thebes in 335. In the initial stages of the invasion before Alexander took over, Parmenion did sack a small Greek city in Asia Minor, Gryneion, and sold its inhabitants into slavery.[2]

While the value of a Macedonian invasion of Asia from Philip's point of view is obvious enough, the aim should not be discussed purely in terms of the ruler alone. Too much attention can be devoted to the leader, too little to the influence of his followers and their own demands (see Austin 1986, 461–5, for the general point). The approach of the ancient sources, which focus upon the kings, obscures this point. Among recent writers, Ellis (1976, esp. 6–13; 219–22; 227–34) has put particular emphasis on the need to see the development of Macedonian society and military power in the time of Philip as a process of interaction between leaders and followers. Philip brought together the Macedonians by developing the army and the Companion class, and by providing them with profitable military objectives. This created an expansionist momentum, almost independent of the ruler himself, that had to be supplied with fresh objectives. The notion of a powerful, but impersonal, 'war machine' may have a somewhat too modern ring (cf. Errington 1981, 85–6, against Ellis); it also begs questions about how much influence different sections of Macedonian

---

[1] Diod. 16. 53, with Hammond and Griffith 1979, 324–8; 365–79 (Chalkidike); see also McKechnie 1989, 48–51.
[2] Diod. 17. 7. 9; see Badian 1966, 40; 44–5; Seager 1981, 106–7.

society actually had on royal decisions under Philip. This may be impossible to assess, since evidence on this subject is so scarce for Philip's reign as compared with Alexander's. Nevertheless, this seems a fruitful line of explanation, as valid for Alexander as for Philip.

Nor is it difficult to see why Alexander should have been in such a hurry after his accession to move against the Persian empire, as soon as he had consolidated his position in Macedon, the Balkans, and Greece. Whether his ultimate conquest aims coincided with or diverged from those of Philip, Alexander, to put it crudely, needed a great war of his own. He needed it to prove his leadership inside and outside Macedon, to counteract the influence of possible rivals, to establish his personal hold over his followers and the Macedonian army by distributing to them the spoils of successful warfare, and to replenish the Macedonian finances, which were reportedly in a depleted state at the end of Philip's reign (Arr. 7. 9. 6; Plut. *Alex.* 15). There were limits to how far expansion could profitably be pursued on the European mainland. An invasion of Asia was the only viable course of action available, once control of the Balkans and of the Greek world had been enforced.

The invasion itself

Ancient sources on wars for self-enrichment

At this point it may be appropriate to quote from Momigliano's celebrated and influential paper on the causes of war in ancient historiography. He wrote (1966, 120), 'The Greeks came to accept war as a natural fact like birth and death about which nothing could be done. They were interested in the causes of wars, not in causes of war as such.' The statement has been frequently cited with commendation (e.g. Finley 1985b, 68–70; Garlan 1989, 22–3); yet it now appears to be increasingly in need of modification. Recently Garlan (1989, 21–40) has shown in detail that Plato and Aristotle had clear views about the causes of war in general, and took for granted that wars aimed at material self-enrichment at the expense of one's enemies. A few years ago, Cobet took issue with Momigliano, arguing that both Herodotos and Thucydides had implicit or explicit views about why wars were fought (Cobet 1986, 2–3; cf. also Gould 1989, 114–15). I would like to take these remarks further, and apply them specifically to the case of the extant historians of the Macedonian invasion of Asia. While, as we have seen, these historians, for the most part, say little explicitly about what were the aims and motives for launching the invasion in the first instance, they all take for granted in varying degrees that once the expedition was under way, material profit was the name of the game.

Ancient sources frequently refer to the doctrine that the persons and property of the defeated belong to the victor by right of conquest.[1] Indeed, the frequency of such references is in itself suggestive. One wonders whether they did not feel the need to keep reminding themselves that the brutality of war was simply a universally accepted convention that had to be accepted with a shrug of the shoulders – just like slavery, one of the concomitants of ancient wars.

In the extant Alexander sources there are a number of references to this doctrine of the right of appropriation through victory. In Diodoros (17. 17; cf. Just. 11. 5) Alexander, before landing in Asia, casts his spear onto the land to signify that he is taking possession of it at a stroke as 'spear-won' (*doriktetos*) territory. This was a notion with a long history behind it, as far back as Homer, which was explicitly appealed to by the successors of Alexander in their struggles for power and control of territory (cf. Schmitthenner 1968; Mehl 1980–1; Hornblower 1981, 53).[2] In Arrian (2. 14. 9) Alexander, in correspondence with Darius after Issos, tells Darius to regard him as master of all his possessions: 'if you claim the kingship (*basileia*), stand your ground and fight for it.' Later (2. 25. 3) Alexander refuses an offer of money and territory from Darius, 'for the money and the country all belonged to him'. After Gaugamela, Babylon and Susa are described as 'the prize (*athlon*) of war' (3. 16. 2). In Plutarch (*Alex.* 20. 12), after Issos and the plundering of the Persian camp, Alexander decides to go and have a wash in Darius' bath, at which one of his Companions exclaims that it is Alexander's bath; 'the

[1] For some examples see Garlan, in Finley (ed.) 1987, at p. 8; Garlan 1989, 75–6.
[2] I have not seen Instinsky 1949, 29–40.

conqueror takes over the possessions of the conquered and they should be called his'.

The same point is made in different forms in many of the sources on Alexander. Plutarch (*On the Fortune or Virtue of Alexander the Great*, 2. 336 a) quotes the view of Antisthenes: 'we should pray that our enemies be provided with all good things, except courage; for thus these good things will belong, not to their owners, but to those that conquer them'. Again, compare the fourth saying of Alexander in Plutarch's *Sayings of Kings and Commanders* (*Moralia*, 179 e–f); Alexander can offer frankincense and cassia to his tutor Leonidas, now that he is master of the land that produces these. In the fifth saying, before the battle at Granikos, Alexander urges his troops to eat without stint, since on the next day they will dine from the enemy's stores. In Polyainos (4. 3. 6) Alexander refuses a request from Parmenion, at the battle of Gaugamela, to protect the camp and baggage train, on the grounds that, 'if defeated, they would not need them, and if victorious they would have their own and that of the enemies'. A final example: on the looting of Darius' belongings after his death, Quintus Curtius comments that this was done 'as though in accordance with the laws of war' (*quasi belli iure diripitur*, 5. 12. 17).

The idea of the succession of empires

At this stage I would like to open a digression, though one related to the topic under discussion.

One of antiquity's views of ancient history was that, in political and military terms, it could be seen as a succession of empires. These were empires exercised by collective peoples, not by individual monarchical figures – even though the various imperial peoples who formed part of the scheme, until the coming of the Romans, were all peoples living under monarchies. In this scheme, a sequence of imperial peoples held sway, one at a time, over part or all of the known world, eventually to be defeated and superseded by another, stronger people. The subject has received much discussion; modern writers debate whether the notion was originally of eastern, perhaps specifically Persian, origin (Swain 1940, 7–8; 11–12; Flusser 1972, esp. 153–4, 172–4; Gruen 1984, 329

n. 53), or whether it was from the beginning yet another invention of Greek historiography, subsequently taken over by the Romans and the Jews – a view which is at present gaining ground (Mendels 1981; Momigliano 1982; Kuhrt, in Kuhrt and Sherwin-White (eds) 1987, 47–8).

The scheme was susceptible of numerous variations in detail, and could be adapted for a variety of political and propaganda purposes. It appears for the first time in Herodotos, in the sequence of the ruling peoples who held power in Asia: first the Assyrians, then the Medes, and finally the Persians (1. 95–6 and 130). In the fourth century, the fall of the Persian empire prompted contemporaries to add the Macedonians to the list, as we know from the remarks of Demetrios of Phaleron (*FGH* 228 F 39) quoted by Polybios (29. 21), as well as from references to the scheme in some of the sources for the Macedonian invasion (see below). It is also known that the Seleukids are frequently referred to as 'the Macedonians who ruled Asia' in sources of the imperial period, notably Strabo, Justin (summarized from Trogus Pompeius), and many others as well.[1] Subsequently, with the downfall of the hellenistic monarchies, the Romans were to take over from the Macedonians, and were themselves added to the scheme (Alonso-Nunez 1983; Gruen 1984, 329; 339–40).

Does this conception of a succession of empires merely register mechanically a sequence of historical events, without seeking to explain it? Or does it imply some causal mechanism for the process? I suggest the latter may be the case, though I put this forward as a tentative hypothesis which may not work systematically in every case. To reconstruct a 'model' of how the succession of empires may have worked involves speculative extrapolation, since the relevant ancient writers provide at best only implicit views, not an explicitly argued scheme. But the essentials of that scheme are already there in Herodotos, and are to be seen in at least two of the Alexander sources: Justin (from Pompeius Trogus) and Quintus Curtius. I shall now outline the main steps in the argument in a schematic form.

First, wealth. Wealth consists essentially of land, all its products, whether vegetable or mineral, and all the life that the land

[1] See Edson 1958, though the conclusions he draws about the nature of the Seleukid monarchy do not necessarily follow.

sustains, whether animal or human. The consequence of this conception is that the total wealth to be found in the world is, in practice, finite. It is already there, and new wealth cannot be created, except for the discovery and exploitation of new resources previously untapped, such as mines of precious metals, or the bringing into productive use of land not hitherto exploited.

Second, the ownership of wealth. It follows from the view just outlined that existing wealth is already, for the most part, distributed among the various peoples of the world. Some people inhabit poorer territories and so are poor, others inhabit richer lands and so are better off. Richest of all are those who control the lands of others and the peoples who live there. From these they can draw rich revenues in the form of tribute or services from dependent peoples. Hence the principal way for peoples who are not themselves rich to acquire wealth is for them to take it from those who control existing wealth. Since those who have wealth cannot be expected to give it up without a struggle, wealth will usually have to be seized by superior force. Since wealth is assumed to be intrinsically desirable, the possession of wealth therefore makes a people an automatic target for possible attack. Conversely, poor people are assumed to be protected from aggression on the grounds that it is simply not profitable for any aggressor to want to attack them. The assumption is, therefore, that successful wars ought normally to be profitable.

Third, the moral and physical characteristics attached to poor and wealthy peoples.[1] Poor peoples are by definition tough and warlike, able to defend themselves against attack and to attack others; wealthy peoples, on the other hand, are soft and unwarlike, and hence an object of contempt (cf. Austin 1986, 459, on this notion); they are unable to defend themselves adequately against poorer but tougher peoples, and this makes them an obvious target for aggression. The trouble is, on this view of things, that people may not in fact be well advised to covet the wealth of others. Poor people who attack and seize the wealth of rich people make themselves vulnerable to attack in their turn. By becoming wealthy they are in danger of losing their original national characteristics; they take on those of the people they

[1] On this section, and on 'soft' and 'hard' peoples in Hdt., see Redfield 1985, 109–18; Gould 1989, 58–60.

defeated, and so become softened and an object of contempt. Their newly acquired wealth encourages further aggression by others, who will dispossess them in their turn. Hence, perhaps, the cycle of rising and falling imperial peoples. Hence also, perhaps, the ever-recurring consciousness in ancient authors of the fragility and evanescence of empires, even at the height of their prosperity and success.

All these views are already found in essentials in Herodotos. He takes it for granted that successful wars ought to be profitable, and that there is therefore no point in attacking poorer people. At 1. 71 Croesus of Lydia is warned by a wise Lydian not to attack the (then) poor, hardy Persians, since if he is victorious there will be nothing worth taking from them, while if he is defeated the Persians will then covet the wealth of the Lydians themselves. At 1. 126 Cyrus graphically makes the point to the Persians that being ruled means a life of poverty and toil, whereas ruling others means plenty and enjoyment. Conversely, after the battle of Plataea, the Spartan Pausanias is astonished at the sumptuous lifestyle of the defeated Persian commander Mardonios, and comments on the madness for such a wealthy man of attacking the poverty-stricken Greeks (9. 82). Mardonios, in urging Xerxes to invade Greece, emphasizes its wealth, fit for a king, and minimizes the Greeks' military ability (7. 5. 3; 7. 9). Demaratos the Spartan gives the lie to this: Greece is poor and the Greeks defend their independence (7. 102). Hence the Greek view, which may have originated at this time if not earlier, that if the Greeks were sensible they would stop fighting unprofitable wars between themselves and turn instead to the far more lucrative business of attacking Asia, as is argued (in Herodotos) by Aristagoras to Kleomenes in 499 (5. 49, discussed above).

The concluding chapter of the whole work repeats the theme that if poor people acquire wealth they risk being softened and becoming liable to attack (9. 122). The Persian Artembares is there said to have advised Cyrus, now that the Persians had achieved hegemony, to move them from their barren, rocky land to better territory in order to increase their status. To this Cyrus is made to answer that if they did so, they would become ruled instead of rulers. 'Soft countries', Cyrus says, 'produce soft men; the same land cannot produce both wonderful crops and warlike men.' Hence, says Herodotos, 'the Persians preferred to inhabit poor land and rule, rather than cultivate the plain and be slaves to others.' The statement is loaded with irony, since Herodotos otherwise portrays the Persians as having fully discovered the material pleasures of life, as the aftermath of the battle of Plataea revealed to the astonished Greeks (9. 82).

The views outlined above are in fact commonplaces about war and the rise and fall of empires in ancient writings, and a large anthology could no doubt be compiled. How are they presented in the Alexander sources?

Arrian

Arrian is familiar with the notion of the 'succession of empires', which he refers to at 2. 6. 7: 'It was destined that the Persians should forfeit the sovereignty of Asia to the Macedonians, just as Medes had lost it to Persians, and Assyrians even earlier to Medes.' But for Arrian it seems to be merely a familiar cliché, mechanically applied without further reflection. He is also familiar with the idea that the possession of wealth is in itself an inducement to aggression from outsiders, while poverty normally protects against attack. At 3. 24. 2 (on 330 BC) he remarks that 'no one had invaded the country [of the Mardians] for a long time, owing to the difficulty of the terrain, and because the Mardians were not only poor, but warlike'. Similarly, at 4. 1. 1, he says of the Scythians who live in Asia 'they are independent (*autonomoi*), chiefly through their poverty and their sense of justice' (see also 6. 23. 1–3 on the poverty of Gedrosia). Conversely, at 5. 25. 1–2, 'the country beyond the Hyphasis was reported to be fertile. . . . These people also had a far greater number of elephants than the other Indians, and the best for size and courage. This report stirred Alexander to a desire for further advance.' Similarly, in relation to the projected Arabian expedition of Alexander, Arrian comments (7. 20. 2–3):

> The prosperity of the country was also an incitement, since he [Alexander] heard that cassia grew in their marshes, that the trees produced myrrh and frankincense, that cinnamon was cut from the bushes, and that spikenard grew self-sown in their meadows. Then there was also the size of their territory, since he was informed that the sea-coast of Arabia was nearly as long as that of India, and that there

were many islands off-shore and harbours everywhere in the country, enough to give anchorages for his fleet, and to permit cities to be built on them, which were likely to prosper.

In general, Arrian is perfectly aware that the invasion of Asia had resulted in massive enrichment for the invaders. This is the view given in general terms in the speeches of Alexander and Koinos at the Hyphasis in 326 BC (5. 26. 7–8 and 27. 6–8), and in Alexander's speech at Opis in 324 BC (7. 10. 3–4).

Yet beyond this there are significant differences between the presentation by Arrian of the material gains of the expedition and that put forward by the other sources, especially Justin and Quintus Curtius.

First, Arrian does not seem to reproduce the idea that the acquisition of wealth by the conquerors is likely to have a debilitating effect on them in turn. He is aware of the idea that poverty toughens while wealth softens, as is shown by his reference to the Mardians (above). Similarly, at 2. 7. 4, before Issos Alexander is made to contrast Macedonian fitness with the long habit of luxury of the Medes and Persians. What Arrian does not do, however, is to apply this notion to the future and suggest that the Macedonians in their turn may be affected by the same process. In so far as the rapid acquisition of conquered wealth had any effects on the Macedonians at all, it merely stimulated others at home in Macedon to join the expedition in order to enjoy the same benefits (note the speeches at the Hyphasis, 5. 27. 7–8, and at Opis, 7. 8. 1). All this may reflect Arrian's primary focus on Alexander and his lack of interest in the Macedonians.[1]

Second, Arrian's detailed reporting of the material gains made and distributed during the expedition appears incomplete and understated when compared with all the other extant Alexander sources. What Arrian seems to present is a rather bland, 'sanitized' version of the expedition. It hardly makes clear the essential role played in the expedition by the forcible acquisition and redistribution of wealth. It does not dwell on all the brutalities involved, and fails to convey what the presence of an invading army must have

---

[1] See notably Arrian's final evaluation of Alexander (7. 28–30), with Bosworth 1988b, ch. 6.

meant to the local populations. Several examples may illustrate this.

(1) Arrian's reporting of the sequels to the major battles against the Persians – first Issos and the capture of the Persian camp (2. 11. 9–10), then Gaugamela (3. 15. 4–6) and the captures of Babylon (3. 16. 3–5), Persepolis, and Susa (3. 16. 6–7) – is consistently sketchier than that of all the other sources, and neutral in tone. In the case of Persepolis he manages to obscure the facts that the army stayed there for four months, and that Alexander gave the city to his army to plunder (see 3. 18. 10–12; Bosworth 1980, 329–33).

(2) Arrian underplays the gift-giving by Alexander that played a major part in the expedition, and about which there is much evidence from many sources (Berve 1926, i. 195; 304–6; 311–13; cf. esp. Plut. *Alex.* 39). Alexander was one of the most prodigal rulers in antiquity, and was in a good position to be so, thanks to the captured wealth of the Persian empire. His gift-giving had obvious functions: to assert his hold over his followers, and to present himself as the supreme dispenser of wealth in competition with other possible rivals, such as Attalos at the start of his reign (Diod. 17. 2; Berve 1926, no. 182), and later Philotas (Plut. *Alex.* 48; Berve 1926, no. 802), both of them described simultaneously as generous in their gift-giving and popular with the army. There is much less evidence in Arrian on all this than in other sources. For example, we know from Plutarch (*Alex.* 15) that at the start of the expedition Alexander made lavish gifts to his friends, evidently to confirm them in their loyalty to him. There is no mention of this in Arrian, and only a belated and oblique reference (at 7. 9. 6) to the debts of Philip and Alexander at the start of the expedition, which does not make clear what had happened in 334. Again, Arrian's account (7. 5. 1–3) of the settling of the army's debts, which amounted to 10,000 talents, at Susa in 324 leaves many questions unanswered. It does not make clear how and why those debts had been contracted, nor to whom the soldiers were in debt (perhaps members of the Macedonian élite? cf. Plut. *Eumenes*, 2, for their lending of money to Alexander). Nor does it make clear that by settling the debts of his soldiers Alexander was in effect cutting the bond that tied them to their creditors and putting them under obligation to himself.

(3) Arrian virtually ignores the important, though rather

neglected, role in the expedition that was played by women. I am not referring here to the conspicuous royal figures – Alexander's mother Olympias, the Persian royal ladies captured after Issos, or Roxane – about whom the sources all have much to say. I mean the very numerous ordinary captives seized as a result of victories at major stages of the expedition, distributed to the soldiers as spoils of war, or perhaps sometimes simply snatched by them along the way in more or less irregular fashion. Something is known about them; but chiefly from sources other than Arrian (see Berve 1926, i. 172–3). No mention from him, for instance, of Thais the mistress of Ptolemy, who may have incited the burning of the palace of Persepolis (Plut. *Alex.* 38; Berve 1926, no. 359); or of Antigone, mentioned in Plutarch as one of the captives made after Issos, who fell to the share of Philotas and became his mistress (Plut. *Alex.* 48–9; Berve 1926, no. 86). In 324, in relation to the marriages of Alexander and the leading Macedonians with noble Persian women, Arrian mentions casually (7. 4. 8) that 'there proved to be over ten thousand Macedonians who had married Asian women; Alexander had them all registered, and every one of them received a wedding gift'. But he provides no explanation of how those 'marriages' were supposed to have come about.

It is clear, therefore, that Arrian's reporting of the material and acquisitive sides of the expedition is incomplete. It is interesting to compare him in this respect not only with the other Alexander sources, who all provide more detail, but also with Xenophon's *Anabasis*. Arrian explicitly refers to this as a literary model (1. 12. 3),[1] and cites the expedition of the Ten Thousand as a precedent for the Macedonian invasion (see Alexander's speech before Issos, 2. 7. 8–9). Yet the character of the two narratives, as accounts of military history, could hardly be different. Where Xenophon's account gives us a view from within the army itself, albeit from the vantage point of an officer with an itch for leadership, Arrian allows us very little insight into the mood and reactions of the army. Where Xenophon is disarmingly frank about all the raiding and snatching of captives performed by the army, and about how these captives were disposed of, Arrian is again bland and uninformative, even though the quantities of booty and captives

[1] Cf. Bosworth (1988b), 25–6; 138–9; index, s.v. Xenophon.

seized by the Macedonians vastly exceeded anything the Ten Thousand could have dreamt of.

Justin and Trogus Pompeius; Quintus Curtius

It is unfortunate that the account of Trogus can only be divined through the meagre summary of Justin; for Trogus was one of the most interesting of ancient writers on the subjects of war and empire. In Trogus, the ideas that are left implicit in Herodotos seem to have been brought out explicitly, and his debt to Herodotos is extensive, as numerous echoes show. He adopts and systematizes the scheme of the succession of empires as the framework for his view of history, from the Assyrians via (among others) the Medes, Persians, and Macedonians to the Romans (see notably Just. 1. 1, 3, 6; 6. 9 and 7. 1; 9. 15. 2; 30. 4. 1–4; 41. 1).

Of particular interest is his hostility to aggressive imperialism as such (cf. Momigliano 1982, 91–2), at least in so far as imperialism was motivated by material greed and not just glory. This idea runs through his work, and is most clearly expressed in relation to the 'Scythians', who act in Trogus as the noble savages, an object-lesson to supposedly civilized peoples who indulge in wars for profit and empire. They are introduced (at 2. 2) as a people who are just because they are poor. They despise gold and silver, which others covet, and do not grasp after what their neighbours have. Greed for the wealth of others is the cause of wars, says Trogus, and we ought to imitate the example of the Scythians, who are wiser than the Greeks and all their philosophers. They did, it is true, conceive the ambition to exercise empire over Asia on three occasions. But, for one thing, they remained themselves largely unconquered even by the Romans (2. 3), unlike so many imperial peoples who eventually fell subject to others. For another, they did not seek material profit from empire, only glory; and when they reduced Asia they only imposed a modest tribute, as a token of power rather than as a reward for victory (2. 3). Other would-be conquerors came to grief against them, starting with Darius (2. 5; cf. 37. 3; 38. 7). Later Philip of Macedon made an unprovoked plundering raid upon them (339 BC), which resulted in the capture of (reportedly) 'twenty thousand' prisoners and countless cattle. But Philip found out to his dismay that the Scythians had no gold and silver, and he himself lost some of his spoils through an attack by the Triballi (9. 1–3). The moral of the story is obvious.

It is unfortunate that Justin's summary does not make clear how Trogus presented the story of Alexander's relations with the Scythians. An indication, however, comes from the mention of the activities of Zopyrion (Berve 1926, no. 340). He was appointed governor in 'Pontus' (Thrace, rather) by Alexander, was anxious for personal exploits, and made an unprovoked invasion of the Scythians, but was defeated and paid the penalty for his rash attack on an innocent people (12. 2; cf. 37. 3; 38. 7).

For the Scythians in relation to Alexander, we have to turn to the account of Quintus Curtius (7. 8. 12–30), who makes the point explicit. The Scythian envoys, whose speech Curtius promises to report accurately (7. 8. 11), are made to rebuke Alexander at great length, and with a wealth of rhetorical flourishes, for his insatiable greed which leads to ever more wars; all the Scythians want is to be left in peace, neither slaves nor masters of anybody. The presentation is identical in spirit to that in Trogus, and Curtius may have drawn on him directly or indirectly. It is interesting to contrast this highly pointed and 'thematic' presentation of the Scythians with Arrian's brief and neutral account of Alexander's decision to attack them (4. 1. 1–2).

If the Scythians are the noble savages who disdain material wealth and wish neither to dominate others nor to be dominated by anybody, then the Macedonians are to be reckoned among the imperial culprits. They start off from humble beginnings (7. 1), but then under their kings Philip (books 7–9) and Alexander (books 11–13) they turn to aggression for material gain. They pay the penalty in becoming themselves corrupted by greed and luxury (30. 1; 36. 1; 38. 10). This results in attacks by others (24. 6; 25. 1), strife between themselves (13. 1; 14. 5–6; 15. 4; 17. 1; 27. 2–3; 39. 5), and internal dynastic conflict, a persistent theme in Trogus (14. 5–6; 15. 2; 16. 1; 24. 2–3; 26. 3; 27. 1; 30. 2; books 35 and 39–40). Hellenistic history, as presented by Trogus, is the story of the decline of the Macedonians as a direct consequence of their imperial success, and reflects Roman preoccupations with their own decline.

Quintus Curtius' presentation of the motive for the invasion, and of its effects on the Macedonians, is similar to that of Trogus, though his focus is primarily on Alexander himself and his evolution into an 'oriental despot' rather than on the Macedonians collectively (cf. e.g. 6. 6. 1–10). Although the first two books are lost, we can imagine how the Macedonians were presented as initially a hardy and poor people. 'Do not think that they are motivated by a desire for gold and silver', says the Athenian Charidemos to Darius before Issos; 'until now their discipline has been maintained by poverty's schooling'.[1] Darius believes otherwise (4. 13. 14; 5. 1. 4–6), and the narrative of the campaign gives the lie to him. Curtius draws an elaborate and colourful picture of all the material gains of the victors, for which they invade Asia, and of the debilitating effects these have on them.[2] After Alexander's death the Macedonians fall out between themselves, unable to be satisfied with what they have already gained (10. 10. 6–8).

Conclusions

To sum up. The sources for the Macedonian invasion all show, in their different ways, definite views, implicit or explicit, about the motives for war in general, as well as for the Macedonian invasion in particular. No one would claim profundity for these views; still less would one wish to suggest that 'softness' and 'luxury' are necessarily useful analytical tools for the study of the fall of ancient empires, though 'greed' may be for their rise. Nor does the schematic division between rich and poor peoples work very well in practice – certainly not in the case of the Macedonians. At the end of the reign of Philip the Macedonians could no longer be described as a poor people,[3] but had already started to enjoy the material benefits of successful military expansion, and so had both the taste for more and the means of acquiring it.[4] Successful warfare in the world of the fourth century needed

[1] 3. 2. 15: *ne auri argentique studio teneri putes, adhuc illa disciplina paupertate magistra stetit.*
[2] See esp. 3. 11. 20–2 and 3. 13. 2–11, 16–17 (Issos); 5. 1. 36–9 (at Babylon); 5. 6. 1–8 (Persepolis, Pasargadae); 6. 6. 14–17 (destruction of booty); 8. 8. 9 and 12 (before the invasion of India); 9. 1. 1–3 (after the Hydaspes); 9. 10. 12 (in Gedrosia).
[3] Cf. Arr. 7. 9. 1–5 (Alexander at Opis, on Philip).
[4] Cf. Theopompos, *FGH* 115 F 224–5, on the Companions of Philip.

financial resources, as all Greek states found out, and that was something the Macedonians did already possess at home in the shape of their mines.

But at least the sources have a view of sorts, which takes for granted that wars are fought for material gain, and that therefore wealth by itself attracts aggression. This is a view so common in many ancient writers over a long period of time that it has to be taken seriously.[1] One may repeat here the important observation of Finley, that the richest and most prosperous states in antiquity were conquest states who owed their wealth to the fruits of superior military power, whatever precise form that took (Finley 1983, 61–4; 109–16; 1985a, 204–7). It should be added that wealth in the ancient world was not a matter of invisible bank accounts and the like, but was generally highly visible and concrete. Wealth consisted of good land, agricultural stores, flocks and cattle, human beings, and precious metals stored in one form or another, all of which were there for the taking by an aggressor.

A few general points in conclusion. What of the attitudes to war and empire revealed by these sources? There seems to be no wholly favourable endorsement of the Macedonian invasion of Asia, apart from Plutarch's in his *De Alexandri Magni fortuna aut virtute*; but for all the considerable historiographical importance of this work as the starting-point of many an idealized modern view of Alexander, from Droysen onwards, it can hardly be regarded as a realistic source on Alexander. Otherwise, ambivalence seems to be the keynote, in that no source is wholly free from some note of doubt.

Diodoros, like Quintus Curtius, reproduces pathetic descriptions of the brutalities of the soldiery after Issos (17. 35–6) and at the sack of Persepolis (17. 70). This probably follows Kleitarchos, who relished the opportunity for colourful writing. Arrian carefully avoids this particular theme; but for all his avowed admiration for Alexander and the general blandness of his account, he does nevertheless introduce a note of censure against the restless conqueror who is unable to stand still, vain as his exertions will ultimately be in the face of inevitable mortality (4. 7. 5; 7. 1–2; cf. Bosworth 1988b, 72–4; 148–9). This is a common theme in ancient

[1] See e.g. Cassius Dio, 39. 56. 1–2 (Gabinius) and 40. 12. 1 (Crassus), on Roman motives for attacking the Parthians.

writers, found for example in Plutarch's portraits of Alexander (ch. 64, where the Indian gymnosophists put him in his place) and Pyrrhos (ch. 14, the confrontation between the wise Kineas and the king; on Pyrrhos compare also Just. 17. 3–18. 1; 25. 3–5). Plutarch's *Pyrrhos* also carries a sweeping condemnation of the insatiable aggressiveness of the Successors (ch. 12; so, too, Justin in books 14–17).

What of the Roman imperial writers? They provide an apparent critique of war and empire in the form of the theme of 'Alexander the brigand', a theme that appears peculiar to them. This is the view found in Quintus Curtius, but also in a number of other authors, notably Seneca, Lucan (see the splendid outburst at the beginning of book 10 of his *Pharsalia*, lines 20–45), and St Augustine (in a famous and much-quoted passage from the *City of God*, 4. 4). To this theme Plutarch's *De Alexandri Magni fortuna aut virtute* might seem to be a reply, in its explicit denial that Alexander was a brigand who devastated Asia (333 d).

Yet how far does this critique of empire really go? Cobet (1986) argues that despite all the negative presentation of war and its attendant suffering in many passages of Herodotos and Thucydides, at the end of the day there seems to be a positive acceptance of the inevitability of war and empire. The same may be largely true, in varying degrees, for the Alexander sources.

Diodoros endorses the invasion as a whole (17. 1; 17. 117), and so does Arrian (1. 12. 2–4; 7. 28–30); they both regard it as an outstanding achievement.[1] As for Plutarch in his *Parallel Lives*, his real regret is that the invasion should have been carried out not by the Greeks, but by Macedonians, whom Plutarch, espousing the Athenian democratic view of Demosthenes, does not consider to be authentic Greeks (*Alex.* 37 and 56; contrast *Kimon*, 19; and *Agesilaos*, 15). In the Roman writers the negative presentation of Alexander is inspired by republican-minded opposition against Roman incarnations of 'oriental despotism' – Caesar, Mark Antony, and some Roman emperors (see Rufus Fears 1974; Ceausescu 1974; Vidal-Naquet 1984, 333–5; 371–3) – and this opposition was directed more against a certain style of political behaviour on the part of rulers than against war and empire as

---

[1] Cf. Bosworth 1988b, 156: 'Arrian had a thoroughly conventional view of the desirability and glory of conquest.'

such. Even the condemnations of acquisitive imperialism, as voiced by Trogus Pompeius and Quintus Curtius, may not mean as much as they appear to. In practice there was no alternative. A parallel may be drawn between slavery and empire; as we saw above, attitudes to war and attitudes to slavery frequently converge. Just as ancient writers could only imagine a world without slaves by placing it in the utopian setting of a mythical golden age before civilization (Vogt 1974, 26–38; Finley 1975, 178–92; Garlan 1988, 130–8), so too the only peoples to reject imperialism motivated by greed had to be an imaginary people like the mythical Scythians, who remained outside the confines of the civilized world and so could manage to stay untainted by its corruption.

Bibliography

Alonso-Nunez, J. M. (1983), 'Die Abfolge der Weltreiche bei Polybios und Dionysios von Halikarnassos', *Historia*, 32: 411–26.

Austin, M. M. (1986), 'Hellenistic kings, war and the economy', *CQ* 80 (n.s. 36): 450–66.

Badian, E. (1966), 'Alexander the Great and the Greeks of Asia', in *Ancient Society and Institutions: Studies Presented to V. Ehrenberg* (Oxford), pp. 37–69.

Berve, H. (1926), *Das Alexanderreich auf prosopographischer Grundlage* (Munich).

Borza, E. N. (1990), *In the Shadow of Olympus: The Emergence of Macedon* (Princeton).

Bosworth, A. B. (1980), *A Historical Commentary on Arrian's History of Alexander*, i: *Commentary on Books I–III* (Oxford).

—— (1988a), *Conquest and Empire: The Reign of Alexander the Great* (Cambridge).

—— (1988b), *From Arrian to Alexander: Studies in Historical Interpretation* (Oxford).

Brunt, P. A. (1965), 'The aims of Alexander', *G&R* 12: 205–15.

—— (1976–83), *Arrian: History of Alexander and Indica* (Loeb Classical Library; Cambridge, Mass.).

Cartledge, P. (1987), *Agesilaos and the Crisis of Sparta* (London).

Ceausescu, P. (1974), 'La double image d'Alexandre le Grand à Rome: essai d'une explication politique', *Studii Clasice*, 16: 153–68.

Cobet, J. (1986), 'Herodotus and Thucydides on war', in I. S. Moxon, J. D. Smart, and A. J. Woodman (eds), *Past Perspectives: Studies in Greek and Roman Historical Writing* (London), pp. 1–18.

de Callataÿ, F. (1989), 'Les trésors achéménides et les monnayages d'Alexandre: espèces immobilisées et espèces circulantes?', *REA* 91: 259–74, with comments on pp. 274–6, 334.

de Ste. Croix, G. E. M. (1972), *The Origins of the Peloponnesian War* (London).

Ducrey, P. (1968), *Le Traitement des prisonniers de guerre dans la Grèce antique* (Paris).

—— (1985), *Guerre et guerriers dans la Grèce antique* (Fribourg, Switzerland).

Edson, C. F. (1958), '*Imperium Macedonicum*: the Seleucid empire and the literary evidence', *CP* 53: 153–70.

Ellis, J. R. (1976), *Philip II and Macedonian Imperialism* (London).

Errington, R. M. (1981), 'Review discussion: four interpretations of Philip II', *AJAH* 6: 69–88.

—— (1990), *A History of Macedonia* (Berkeley, etc.).

Finley, M. I. (1975), *The Use and Abuse of History* (London).

—— (1983), *Politics in the Ancient World* (Cambridge).

—— (1985a), *The Ancient Economy* (2nd edn, London).

—— (1985b), 'War and empire', in *Ancient History: Evidence and Models* (London), pp. 67–87.

—— (ed. 1987), *Classical Slavery* (London).

Flusser, D. (1972), 'The four empires in the fourth Sibyl and in the book of Daniel', *Israel Oriental Studies*, 2: 148–75.

Fredericksmeyer, E. A. (1982), 'On the final aims of Philip II', in W. L. Adams and E. N. Borza (eds), *Philip II, Alexander the Great and the Macedonian Heritage* (Lanham, etc.), pp. 85–98.

Garlan, Y. (1975), *War in the Ancient World: A Social History* (London).

—— (1988), *Slavery in Ancient Greece*, trans. J. Lloyd (Ithaca).

—— (1989), *Guerre et économie en Grèce ancienne* (Paris).

Gehrke, H. J. (1987), 'Die Griechen und die Rache: ein Versuch in historischer Psychologie', *Saeculum*, 38: 121–49.

Gould, J. (1989), *Herodotus* (London).

Gruen, E. (1984), *The Hellenistic World and the Coming of Rome* (Berkeley).

Habicht, C. (1961), 'Falsche Urkunden zur Geschichte Athens im Zeitalter der Perserkriegen', *Hermes*, 89: 1–35.

Hamilton, J. R. (1973), *Alexander the Great* (London).

Hammond, N. G. L., and Griffith, G. T. (1979), *A History of Macedonia*, ii: *550–336 BC* (Oxford).

—— and Walbank, F. W. (1988), *A History of Macedonia*, iii: *336–167 BC* (Oxford).

Hornblower, J. (1981), *Hieronymus of Cardia* (Oxford).

Instinsky, H. (1949), *Alexander der Grosse am Hellespont*.

Jackson, A. H. (1985), review of W. Nowag, *Raub und Beute in der archaischen Zeit der Griechen*, *Gnomon*, 57: 655–7.

Kuhrt, A. (1988), 'The Achaemenid empire: a Babylonian perspective', *PCPS* 214 (n.s. 34): 60–76.

—— and Sherwin-White, S. (eds 1987), *Hellenism in the East* (London).

Lane Fox, R. (1973), *Alexander the Great* (London).

McKechnie, P. (1989), *Outsiders in the Greek Cities in the Fourth Century BC* (London).

Mehl, A. (1980–1), '*Doriktetos chora*: kritische Bemerkungen zum "Speererwerb" im Politik und Völkerrecht der hellenistischen Epoche', *Ancient Society*, 11–12: 173–212.

Mendels, D. (1981), 'The five empires: a note on a propagandistic topos', *AJP* 102: 330–7.

Momigliano, A. (1966), 'Some observations on the causes of war in ancient historiography', in *Studies in Historiography* (London), pp. 112–26; = *Secondo contributo alla storia degli studi classici* (Rome, 1960), pp. 13–27.

—— (1975), *Alien Wisdom: The Limits of Hellenization* (Cambridge).

—— (1982), 'The origins of universal history', *Annali della Scuola Normale Superiore di Pisa, classe delle lettere e filosofia*, series 3, 12(2): 533–60; = *Settimo contributo alla storia degli studi classici e del mondo antico* (Rome, 1984), pp. 77–103.

Perlman, S. (1976), 'Panhellenism, the polis and imperialism', *Historia*, 25: 1–30.

Powell, A. (1988), *Athens and Sparta: Constructing Greek History* (London).

Redfield, J. (1985), 'Herodotus the tourist', *CP* 80: 97–118.

Rufus Fears, J. (1974), 'The Stoic view of the character and career of Alexander the Great', *Philologus*, 118: 114–30.

Sancisi-Weerdenburg, H. (ed. 1987), *Achaemenid History*, i: *Sources, Structures and Synthesis* (Leiden).

—— and Kuhrt, A. (eds 1987), *Achaemenid History*, ii: *The Greek Sources* (Leiden).

Schmitthenner, W. (1968), 'Über eine Formveränderung der Monarchie seit Alexander dem Grossen', *Saeculum*, 19: 31–46.

Seager, R. (1981), 'The freedom of the Greeks of Asia: from Alexander to Antiochus', *CQ* 31: 106–12.

Seibert, J. (1972), *Alexander der Grosse* (Erträge der Forschung, 310; Darmstadt).

Starr, C. G. (1976, 1977), 'Greeks and Persians in the fourth century BC: a study in political contacts before Alexander', *Iranica antiqua*, 11: 39–99; 12: 49–116.

Swain, J. W. (1940), 'The theory of the four monarchies: opposition history under the Roman empire', *CP* 35: 1–21.

Tarn, W. W. (1948), *Alexander the Great* (Cambridge).

Thomas, R. (1989), *Oral Tradition and Written Record in Classical Athens* (Cambridge).

Vidal-Naquet, P. (1984), 'Arrien entre deux mondes', in *Arrien: Histoire d'Alexandre* (trans. P. Savinel; Paris), pp. 311–94.

Vogt, J. (1974), *Ancient Slavery and the Ideal of Man* (Oxford).

Wilson, C. H. (1970), 'Athenian military finances, 378/7 to the peace of 375', *Athenaeum*, 48: 302–26.

The glorious dead: Commemoration of the fallen and portrayal of victory in the late classical and hellenistic world

Ellen Rice

This brief consideration of war memorials and victory monuments is, of necessity, selective. I do not consider the *tropaion*, the victory monument set up on or near a battlefield immediately after the conflict (for a full survey see Pritchett 1974, 246 ff.), nor indeed the countless dedications of real arms and armour, nor offerings of many different forms paid for from the proceeds of battle spoils. My purpose is to consider a few permanent commemorative monuments of victory: public memorials set up in sanctuaries for their propaganda value, monumental tombs honouring the war dead,[1] and some dedications celebrating naval victories. Some of these monuments are relatively little known, and ought to receive more attention; others are well known, but continue to pose problems and provoke controversy.

There are abundant classical precedents for *tropaia*, dedications of armour, battlefield tombs, memorials in panhellenic sanctuaries, and large public tombs and cenotaphs (above all the *demosion sema* in Athens). The Greeks of the classical period certainly used such monuments as civic propaganda, as the jostling together of dedications in the most prominent areas of sanctuaries makes

[1] When this paper was delivered in February 1990, Fedak 1990 had not yet appeared. His discussion of some of the monumental tombs I consider below does not alter the observations I have made; but in order to avoid duplication I have concentrated more on victory monuments than tombs.

clear. Military dedications were likewise abundant in the hellenistic period.[1] Can any differences in their form be traced over
time?

I take as my starting-point an observation about the difference
between classical and hellenistic 'propagandistic monuments'
made by Pollitt (1986, 19):

> Although [in the classical period] portraits of generals were sometimes
> included in such creations, they were by and large impersonal
> monuments, emphasizing the events and the cities involved but placing
> little or no emphasis on specific personalities. By contrast, the major
> focus of much of the propagandistic art of the Hellenistic period was
> on the personality of the individual ruler who shaped events.

To a certain extent this is true; like all generalizations, it is not
completely true. An emphasis on the royal imagery of a particular
ruler is indeed part and parcel of a broad shift from the generic to
the specific which can be traced in different artistic media during
this period. The development of the genre of portraiture (for
example, the change from a stock type of 'civic *strategos*' figure to
an instantly identifiable individual) is one aspect of this trend; a
change in the method of 'historical representation' is another.
These changes are not, however, progressively 'evolutionary' or
universal.

In the fifth century BC a 'generic' quality can be identified in
most war memorials which consisted of groups of sculpture. An
example is Pausanias' description (10. 10. 1) of the base at Delphi
of one of the Athenian dedications commemorating Marathon. It
contained statues of Athena and Apollo, the general Miltiades,
and eleven legendary heroes. Except for Miltiades, the statues
depicted gods and heroes of special significance to Athens. This
'mythological' type of group monument is typical of those set up
by classical poleis both in the home city and at panhellenic
sanctuaries, as Pausanias' descriptions of Delphi and Olympia
show. This goes hand in hand with the tendency to represent the
contemporary in terms of the legendary; battles of gods and
giants, Greeks and Amazons, Greeks and Persians, Lapiths and

---

[1]   For a survey of such dedications in the hellenistic period, see Launey
1987, 901–1000. A detailed consideration of all of these is far beyond the
scope of this paper.

centaurs are stock motifs in Greek art, symbolizing contemporary struggles of Greek 'civilization' against foreign 'barbarism', whatever form either may take.

Sparta, perhaps surprisingly, seems to have been a partial exception to this rule. Pausanias (3. 11. 3) mentions the Persian Stoa there, built from the spoils of the Persian war, presumably in the second quarter of the fifth century. On it appeared carved statues of the Persian general Mardonios and of Artemisia of Halikarnassos. Vitruvius (1. 1. 6) says that statues of Persians in native dress supported the roof like Caryatids.[1] If statues of individuals were part of the original design (Mardonios and Artemisia would have been famous by repute, and therefore in a special category, like Miltiades on the Delphi Marathon monument), its iconography will have been most unusual for such an early date.

It was also the Spartans who dedicated the most elaborate of the victory monuments known before the age of Alexander, their Aigospotamoi dedication at Delphi, again known from Pausanias (10. 9. 7–10).[2] The Dioskouroi, Zeus, Apollo, and Artemis appeared, along with the general Lysander being crowned by Poseidon. These were surrounded by some thirty-one statues of human participants in the battle, both Spartans and allies, each identified by name. Although Aigospotamoi was indeed a great Spartan victory, it is clear that this monument was different;[3] it was astonishingly large, and it was remarkable for the inclusion of

[1]   The statues and the design of the stoa which Pausanias saw cannot be dated, since he says it was altered in the course of time. Recent British excavations on the Spartan acropolis may shed some light on this structure (see G. B. Waywell and J. J. Wilkes, in French 1989–90, 26). Early reports on the excavation there of a stoa of imperial date have noted the reuse in Byzantine times of archaizing Doric capitals, which (if they belong to the original period of the stoa) may deliberately copy the appearance of a late archaic predecessor, perhaps the Persian Stoa.

[2]   For the most recent discussion of the controversy surrounding its site, see Habicht 1985, 71–7. Whether it was to the right or the left of the sacred way, near the entrance to the sanctuary, its position near the Athenian Marathon base can hardly have been a coincidence.

[3]   Pollitt (1986, 304 n. 1) seems to regard it as belonging to the same 'impersonal' tradition as the Athenian Marathon monuments; I do not agree.

so many mortals. There was nothing like it in scale and conception until the Granikos monument of Alexander (see below).

It is difficult to explain this apparent departure of the Spartans from tradition, but certain specific circumstances may be taken into account. Unlike most Greeks, it was their custom to bury their dead on the field of battle (Pritchett 1985, 249 ff.). If there was not, therefore, a public tomb in the city to serve as a constant reminder of the victory, the Persian Stoa may have been designed using 'specific' rather than 'generic' imagery, in order to recall the particular campaigns of the war. The Aigospotamoi monument is perhaps best seen as part of the previously unparalleled 'cult of personality' that accrued to Lysander in the decades following the Peloponnesian war, when heroic honours, lavish dedications, and so on were bestowed upon him by many Greek cities. Also, it was the custom that Spartans did not dedicate the captured armour of their defeated enemies, although they could set up a dedication from its proceeds (Pritchett 1979, 292–3). Perhaps after their great victory the Spartans felt the need to erect a monument which was especially elaborate, in order to outshine the vast displays of captured armour dedicated by other cities at Delphi.

Monuments associated with Alexander the Great

After the first major battle of Alexander's army against the Persians at the Granikos river, the king ordered the erection of a commemorative battle monument at Dion, the national sanctuary of the Macedonians. Arrian says the following (1. 16. 4): 'On the Macedonian side about twenty-five of the Companions fell in the first shock. Bronze statues of them stand at Dion; Alexander gave the order to Lysippos, the only sculptor he would select to portray himself.' Plutarch (*Alexander*, 16) preserves a similar account, but implies that nine fallen foot-soldiers were also included on the monument. Velleius Paterculus (*History of Rome*, 1. 11. 4) adds that a portrait of Alexander was also part of the group, and that his request to Lysippos specified that the figures were to be life-like portraits (*expressa similitudine*). Although the Spartan Aigospotamoi base at Delphi contained more human figures, there had been nothing on the scale of a monument containing twenty-five bronze equestrian statues (and perhaps others) of mortals; the absence of gods is also a striking feature.

Are there any reasons for the similarities in scale and conception between the Aigospotamoi and Granikos dedications? Both marked important and symbolic victories for their dedicators, and as a king who hardly lacked self-confidence even as a youth, Alexander far surpassed Lysander in the promotion of his person. Another consideration may have been that the dead from neither battle were returned home; Arrian records that Alexander buried his men with their armour at the Granikos, and granted privileges to their dependants. Perhaps there was also a perceived need to publicize at home a victory in foreign lands. The involvement of Lysippos, the leading sculptor of the day, would immediately ensure the fame of the monument, and its erection at an important sanctuary like Dion will have had a propaganda impact on those back home whose menfolk had gone on expedition with their king. We may note that Alexander also sent 300 panoplies of captured armour to Athens in honour of his victory (Arr. 1. 16. 7; Plut. *Alex.* 16).

The Roman general Q. Caecilius Metellus Macedonicus took the Granikos monument to Rome in 146 BC, where it was displayed in the Porticus Metelli.[1] There are few hints as to what it looked like. It has been suggested that there are echoes of it in the main battle scene on the famous 'Alexander sarcophagus' (*Plate 1b*; Pollitt 1986, 43–5). This ornate sarcophagus was found in the royal necropolis at Sidon, and was probably (though not certainly) made for Abdalonymos, the last king of Sidon, installed on his throne by Alexander after the battle of Issos in 333 (the sarcophagus is thought to date from 325–311). The celebration of the exploits of Alexander is surely intended to reflect upon its occupant by association, and it is a reasonable hypothesis that it recalls the most famous and dramatic battle monument erected by Alexander.[2]

[1] Velleius Paterculus 1. 11. 4; Pliny, *Natural History*, 34. 64. Thorough excavation is still in its early stages at Dion, but it is possible that some evidence may emerge for the original location, dimensions, etc., of this monument.
[2] For the difficulties surrounding the iconography of the Alexander sarcophagus, see Ridgway 1990, 37–45; Smith 1991, 190–2. Possible echoes of the Granikos monument have also been seen in a statuette from

In both the Aigospotamoi dedication and the Granikos monument one can identify an emphasis on the 'specific' portrayal of victory, even though a divine context is present in the former case. A similar change can be seen in historical paintings of the late classical period. In the fifth century, battles were commemorated with strong mythological overtones.[1] By the end of the fourth century, battles seem to have been depicted as real historical events. Alexander used painting as well as sculpture to commemorate his exploits, and these historical battle scenes played an important role in early hellenistic painting (see Pollitt 1986, 45–6, for an account of these historical paintings). None of these paintings survives, but it is tempting to suggest (as many have) that one of the famous works which depicted Alexander in combat was the original of which the famous Alexander Mosaic from the House of the Faun in Pompeii is a copy (*Plate 2a*). Although the particular battle cannot be identified, a dominant Alexander is portrayed in a violent clash with a Persian rider who intervenes in his pursuit of Darius.

Let us also recall Alexander's funeral carriage, described by Diodoros (18. 26–8). Within the golden Ionic colonnade which surrounded the tomb proper was a gold net of thick cords, which carried four long, painted tablets, each equal in length to a side of the colonnade (*Fig. 1*). On the first of these tablets was a chariot ornamented with relief work, in which Alexander sat holding a sceptre and surrounded by groups of armed Macedonian and Persian attendants, with armed soldiers in front. The second panel depicted war elephants with their Indian mahouts, arrayed behind the Bodyguard and followed by fully armed Macedonian soldiers. The third tablet showed troops of cavalry in battle formation, and the fourth had ships made ready for naval combat. The specifications of the sizes and positions of these paintings make it clear that they were commissioned for the catafalque. Although it is not

---

Herculaneum (Pollitt 1986, 43; Ridgway 1990, 119), and in a marble group of at least seven armed figures from Lanuvium (ibid. 120; Coarelli 1981).

[1] E.g. in the Marathon painting at the Stoa Poikile in the Athenian agora, the action was presented in a legendary context with gods and heroes lending a helping hand. The only identifiable mortals were the generals Kallimachos and Miltiades (Paus. 1. 15. 4).

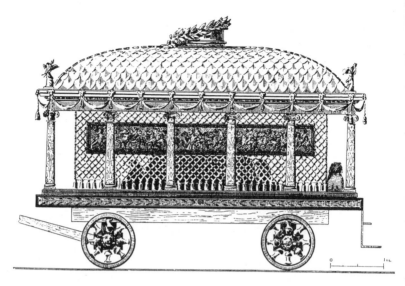

Figure 1 Hypothetical reconstruction of the funeral carriage of Alexander the Great. After H. Bulle.

stated that the court painter Apelles created them, their iconography was surely a true reflection of how Alexander wanted to be depicted; note the commemoration of his international army, his war elephants, his invincible Macedonian cavalry, and his naval prowess.

The medium of historical painting continued to be used to commemorate the military victories of the early hellenistic kings. An Athenian inscription (*IG* ii² 677) records that in 274 BC a supporter of Antigonos Gonatas honoured the king by decorating the stadium at Athens with paintings portraying his deeds against the barbarians, specifically the Gauls whom Antigonos had defeated in 277. Presumably the paintings were historical in character and depicted his specific exploits; there would not have been much point to the honour otherwise.

In so far as we can perceive it through the fragmentary evidence, one trend in the late fourth century and the early hellenistic period was towards the depiction of the military victor in 'specific', individual roles. The 'cult of personality' no doubt hastened this development; although we may see the beginnings of it with

Lysander, it is Alexander and his successors (who publicized their close connections with him in order to ensure the political legitimacy of their rule in areas of his empire) to whom Pollitt's statement most applies (1986, 19):

> the major focus of much of the propagandistic art of the Hellenistic period was on the personality of the individual ruler who shaped events. One of the new tasks that confronted the Hellenistic artist was, therefore, the creation of a royal imagery that would make the nature of these individuals vivid.

Although the kings of the major hellenistic kingdoms quickly developed a pervasive royal imagery which went hand in hand with their imperial propaganda, and although they depended upon military might and success – both publicly proclaimed (this is admirably brought out by Austin 1986) – in order to maintain their position, there is little evidence for any war memorials that might be considered major artistic monuments, other than the famous ones of the Pergamene kings (see below). Were such monuments erected in the other kingdoms, even though no trace survives? Besides the dedications in sanctuaries, attested in ancient literary sources and inscriptions (see n. 1, p. 225) – though the actual forms of these dedications are not recoverable – there is ample evidence for elaborate 'temporary' public commemoration of military victories. The huge parades staged in conjunction with religious festivals in the hellenistic capitals are unmistakable showcases for military propaganda. I have already considered the *pompe* of Ptolemy II Philadelphos in this context (Rice 1983); and other parades for which there is literary evidence reveal precisely analogous features (e.g. the *pompe* of Antiochos IV Epiphanes: Polybios, 30. 25–6). Can it be that there were not also elaborate monuments in Alexandria and Antioch which served as permanent reminders of the claimed victories, places for dedicated armour and captured spoils, and venues for statuary groups representing the victorious and the vanquished? Our literary sources are silent about this, and archaeology has yielded nothing. Although there may yet be hope in Macedonia, where the most important sites are only beginning to be investigated, little is likely to emerge now from continuously inhabited sites like Alexandria.

I follow Austin (1986) in believing that one of the prime aims of hellenistic warfare was the acquisition of booty to enrich the royal coffers. Certainly the kings used some of the proceeds of their military victories to pay for victory dedications – Polybios (30. 26. 9) records that Antiochos IV's parade was paid for partly from the spoils of his war against Egypt – plus grandiose civic benefactions in panhellenic sanctuaries and individual cities; the ample remains of stoas and so on attest to the importance placed by the kings on such public displays of euergetism (H. A. Thompson 1982). The surprising lack of evidence for permanent war memorials may be due to the vagaries of historical survival. We may take Ridgway's discussion of the overall lack of sculptural evidence from the so-called 'empty' third century BC as a case in point. Most of the victory dedications, like honorary statues, were in bronze, which has tended to disappear, and 'the greatest artistic creativity was expended on the production of luxury objects, to provide . . . the trappings of monarchical rule' (Ridgway 1990, 373). To this consideration one might add public relations. It may have been felt that maximum beneficial propaganda could be garnered from the construction of high-profile civic structures which would benefit the largest number of people, or in the staging of festivals which, though brimming with military propaganda as we know the attested parades were, also provided vast crowds of people with a spectacle and with perquisites like free food and wine.

The most famous royal commemorations of victory are of course the series of monuments erected by the Attalid kings of Pergamon to celebrate victories over their various enemies.[1] The bronze statuary groups set up by Attalos I in c.233–228 BC on the acropolis at Pergamon (in so far as they can be reconstructed) showed 'generic' portraits of dead and dying Gauls. These probably included the 'dying trumpeter' and the 'Gaul and his wife', known from famous copies. Cuttings in the long base on which the statues were mounted show that victorious foot-soldiers and mounted cavalry were also present. It is not possible to say whether any of these were individualizing portraits of Attalos I, his generals, and his soldiers, or whether they too were 'generic' victors.

---

[1] These major monuments have a huge bibliography. For a good summary discussion of all the Pergamene groups, see Pollitt 1986, 79–110; Radt 1988, 179–206; Ridgway 1990, 284–96; Smith 1991, 99–104; 155–66.

Other monuments set up on the acropolis at Athens, by Attalos I or II, copies of which are probably to be seen in the so-called 'lesser Attalid group', seem to be largely in the classical 'generic' tradition of presenting contemporary battles in terms of mythological ones. Pausanias (1. 25. 2) says the representations included the war (*sc.* of the gods) against the giants, the battle of the Athenians against the Amazons, their fight against the Persians at Marathon (which had passed into legend even in the fifth century), and the destruction of the Gauls in Mysia. The Gauls identified in Roman copies are, again, 'generic' statues of the defeated barbarian, and were probably meant to be equated with the other defeated barbarians of Greek legend. The famous altar of Zeus, erected on the acropolis of Pergamon by Eumenes II *c.*180 BC after his victories over Bithynia and Pontos, is decorated wholly in the generic fashion with the battle of the gods and the giants.[1]

This continuation of the classical trend of generic representation, in which mythology and heroizing legend play a leading role, is perhaps to be understood in terms of the aspirations of the Attalids to belong to mainstream Greek culture as symbolized by fifth-century Athens. The military victories which they commemorated as the triumph of Greek civilization over barbarism marked their graduation into the 'superpower league' of hellenistic kingdoms. Pergamon, furthermore, came to be seen in the role of protector of Greece against a very real barbarian threat (in the case of the Gauls), and therefore had some pretensions to be the latest champion of the Greek cultural heritage. The Attalids accordingly carried on the classical tradition of civic monuments even while, in other respects, they were as active as the other monarchs in developing a distinctive royal imagery in portraiture and coinage.

Let us now turn to a consideration of a few unusual victory monuments, dedications, and tombs for the military dead. Most were erected by individuals or Greek cities for whom questions of

---

[1] For the date of the Great Altar see Smith 1991, 158, *contra* Callaghan 1981, 115–21. For a full discussion of the propaganda impact of these monuments, and of Pergamene monuments at Delos and Delphi, see Schalles 1985.

royal imagery did not apply; in the other cases, scale and context suggest royal dedications, albeit not attributable.

The Alketas tomb, Termessos

The provinces of Lycia and Pisidia in modern-day Turkey have produced some of the most spectacular tombs and *heroa* with military iconography.[1] The Pisidian mountain city of Termessos was unsuccessfully attacked by Alexander when he passed that way in 333, and reappears in the historical record four years after his death. Antigonos Monophthalmos, in his attempt to gain control over all of Asia, was opposed by (among others) a certain Alketas, a brother of Perdikkas who had served as an infantry general under Alexander (cf. Diod. 18. 44–7). Alketas suffered a defeat, apparently fighting on horseback, in a pitched battle against Antigonos in 319. He escaped to Termessos, followed by Antigonos who demanded his surrender. The population was split between the young men, who wanted to resist Antigonos, and the elders, who inclined to surrender Alketas. The elders agreed in secret to hand him over to Antigonos while the young men were out of the city. Alketas killed himself to avoid capture, and his body was sent to Antigonos. The corpse was degraded for three days, and left decomposing and unburied when Antigonos marched out of Pisidia. The young Termessians recovered the body and gave it a magnificent burial.

In the necropolis area of Termessos, there is one unusual and particularly elaborate tomb which clearly commemorates a military hero (for a full account see Pekridou 1986; Fedak 1990, 94–6). On the projecting cliff over the tomb area is the fine sculpted relief of a mounted warrior (*Plate 2b*). Lower down on the right is a suit of armour (a helmet, a pair of greaves, and a round shield with a sword set diagonally across it), most now badly smashed.

---

[1] The Lycian monuments of the fourth century and later form a whole field of study by themselves, especially the intriguing 'city-taking' reliefs on many tombs (see Childs 1978). I do not consider them here; this iconographic treatment appears to have originated outside the conventions of Greek art proper, although the influence of monumental Lycian tombs spread to Greece by *c.* 300 BC.

There are many notable features about this relief. Firstly, the warrior wears armour identical to that worn by Alexander in the Alexander Mosaic; note the corselet (see *Plate 2a*). Secondly, the relief is juxtaposed to pieces of foot-soldier's armour; this appears inexplicable but for the fact that Alketas is known to have fought both as a horseman and a foot-soldier. The actual tomb is set in an angle of the vertical rock-face; it consists of a stone bench with a ledge above into which the grave was cut (*Plate 3a*). Above is a trellis between columns (perhaps suggesting a canopy; a canopy was constructed over the sarcophagus on Alexander's funeral carriage), topped by an eagle with outspread wings which is holding a snake. The immediate surroundings of the tomb suggest that rites, offerings, or some kind of hero cult may have been observed there. On the left is a 61 cm square rock-cut receptacle with a door carved on the front, perhaps intended for bones, ashes, or offerings. On the right is another square receptacle with a lion's head on the front, two small figures of Hermes and Aphrodite, and a rock-cut round basin 40 cm deep; originally the basin had a lion's head on a panel in front, and it was perhaps intended to hold water, wine, or oil for libations.

The form and iconography of this tomb complex are to my knowledge unparalleled, and the most obvious explanation of its unique design lies in the extraordinary honours paid to the military hero Alketas.

Victory monuments commemorating the great siege of Rhodes

The year-long siege of Rhodes by Demetrios Poliorketes in 305/4 BC ended in a stalemate. The city never fell, but agreed to be an ally of Demetrios except against Ptolemy (it had been the attempt to detach Rhodes from the Ptolemaic alliance that had led to Rhodian resistance and the siege).

The Colossus of Rhodes

When Demetrios finally abandoned the siege, he left behind all of his siege equipment (details of the siege and the various machines are in Diod. 20. 82–8; 91–100). The Rhodians sold the lot, and with the proceeds they commissioned from Chares of Lindos (a pupil of the great Lysippos) a statue of their patron god Helios in thanksgiving for their deliverance. This was, of course, the famous Colossus of Rhodes, considered one of the Seven Wonders of the Ancient World. Pliny (*Natural History*, 34. 41) records that the statue took twelve years to complete and cost 300 talents (a significant sum, although Philo of Byzantion (4. 6) says it cost 500 talents of bronze and 300 of iron). It stood some 33 m tall (for comparison, the Statue of Liberty in New York harbour is 46.3 m tall). Philo gives a complex account of the intricate method by which the statue was cast. It stood until it was toppled (broken at the knees, according to Strabo, 14. 652) by the great earthquake that shook Rhodes in *c*.228 BC. An oracle warned against its re-erection, and so the statue lay where it fell.[1]

Although medieval tradition believed that the statue bestrode the harbour of Rhodes,[2] this is clearly fanciful since the legs would have had to span some 396 m (see *Fig. 2*, no. 1). Because of its great height, the pose of the statue would no doubt have had to be much simpler than in the proposed reconstructions which give it outstretched limbs. It would have had to be fairly columnar in order to stand upright, and one suggested reconstruction is probably along the right lines (see *Fig. 3*).[3]

The site of the statue requires some discussion in the light of recent archaeological discoveries not taken into account by Higgins (1988). He rightly rejects one popular suggestion, namely the east side of the entrance to Mandraki harbour where the fort

---

[1]   Discussions of the Colossus in Higgins 1988; Ekschmitt 1984, 169–81; Gabriel 1932; Maryon 1956; Haynes 1957; Moreno 1973–4, 453–63; Zervoudaki 1975, 1–20.

[2]   It is so depicted in various medieval engravings (see e.g. Higgins 1988, 133; Ehschmitt 1984, 169).

[3]   The Statue of Liberty has a similar columnar shape and one raised arm. Ashton (1988, esp. pl. 15. 1–19) points to an uncommon series of Rhodian didrachmas, dated 304–*c*.265 BC, showing the head of Helios in right profile and wearing a rayed taenia. Since these were produced in parallel with the common Rhodian series (typically depicting Helios in three-quarter profile and bareheaded), and are roughly contemporary with the Colossus, Ashton argues that they are a special issue commemorating the completion of the statue and reflecting the appearance of its head. If so, the colossal head of Helios will have worn a rayed taenia.

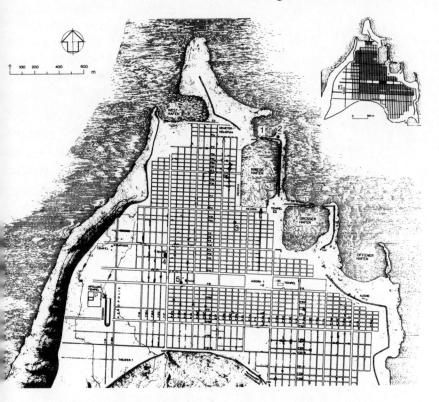

Figure 2 Map of ancient Rhodes, showing grid plan. After Hoepfner and Schwander.

of St Nicholas now stands (*Fig. 2*, no. 2); the problem with this is that one literary source says the Colossus knocked down several houses when it fell over, which could hardly have happened had it stood on a harbour wall.[1] Higgins follows the now popular, and surely correct, view that it stood near the temple of Helios, which recent excavations have almost certainly located on the east side of the acropolis, at the junction of the modern Sophouli and

---

[1] More subjectively, Higgins thinks it unlikely that such an important and valuable piece of land would have been occupied indefinitely by the remains of a fallen statue. Ekschmitt (1984, 180–1) only speculates that the Colossus stood in the middle of the city, perhaps on the acropolis or in the old city of the Knights.

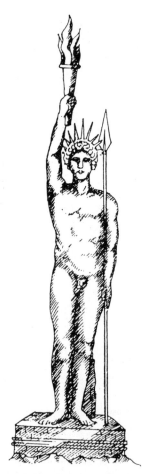

Figure 3 Hypothetical reconstruction of the Colossus of Rhodes. After Clayton and Price.

Cheimarras Streets (*Fig. 2*, no. 4).[1] Archaeological investigation

[1] This corresponds to the junction of the ancient streets P 27 and P 13. For discussion of finds here see Konstantinopoulos 1975; Papachristodoulou 1988, 203; Kontorini 1989, 129–31, with résumé (in French) at p. 195. Higgins had placed the precinct at the top of the medieval Street of the Knights, on the site once occupied by the Church of the Knights (roughly across from the palace of the Grand Masters), where a quantity of ancient masonry and inscriptions was found (*Fig. 2*, no. 3); but it now seems virtually certain that the temple stood *c.*650 m to the sw.

of this area has brought to light dedications to Helios by twelve priests of the god, the earliest of them dating to the mid-third century (Kontorini 1989, nos 53–62); other public and private dedications were found in the area (nos 63–76), of which three (nos 73–4, 76) honour men who have won victories in the games associated with the Halieia, the festival of Helios (Halios in Rhodian dialect). Greek archaeologists have also uncovered the remains of bronze foundries in the area, suggesting that the Colossus was cast here in order to minimize the difficulties of transport to, and assembly at, the sanctuary.[1] In this prime position on the east slope of the acropolis, the Colossus would have been visible from a great distance out to sea, from the lower town below, and from the citadel above. It would thus have served as a landmark to mariners, which would have ensured its fame almost as much as its great size.

The chariot of Helios at Delphi

Pliny (*NH* 34. 63) relates that Lysippos sculpted for the Rhodians a chariot of their patron god Helios (*quadriga cum Sole Rhodiorum*). This is perhaps the chariot of Helios which Cassius Dio (47. 33) says was the only one of the sacred treasures not appropriated from Rhodes by the Roman general Cassius in 43 BC, and the same chariot which Dio Chrysostom (31. 86) says was held in great reverence on the island. This work of Lysippos may alternatively be identical with the golden chariot which, we know

---

[1]   One foundry (*Fig. 2*, no. 5) is at the junction of Diagoridon and Pavlou Mela Streets (which preserve the alignment of the ancient street grid); cf. Doumas 1975, 363. In the basement foundations of a modern building, casting-pits were found, of a size suitable for casting over-life-size bronze statues. (I am grateful to Dr I. Papachristodoulou, Ephor of Antiquities of the Dodecanese, who showed me this site in spring 1984.) Five more casting workshops have recently been found on this E slope of the acropolis, including another on Diagoridon. Rock-cut casting-pits are also reported, and the foundries date to *c.*300–250 BC, which would fit the date of the Colossus. (Information presented in the exhibit 'Forty Years of Rescue Archaeology in Rhodes', Palace of the Grand Masters, spring 1989.)

from an inscription, the Rhodians dedicated at Delphi.[1] This monument, placed upon a high pillar, occupied a prominent position just east of the temple of Apollo, near the famous tripod commemorating the battle of Plataea. (For a full discussion of the chariot see Jacquemin and Laroche 1986; cf. Ridgway 1990, 58.) The style of the dedication is extraordinary in that it was the first pillar monument of such a height, far different in effect from previous dedications elevated on simple, round or triangular bases (Jacquemin and Laroche 1986, 307). In addition, it has been shown that the chariot may be associated with an extraordinary base of pink stone, and with other blocks on which waves were carved, which would symbolize the emergence of the sun from the eastern sea each dawn (*Fig. 4*).[2]

With what event is this monument to be associated? The problems surrounding its date (based on its architectural features as well as on the date of the surrounding monuments in this part of the sanctuary) are highly complex; but the last quarter of the fourth century fits the various pieces of evidence best. The erection of such a spectacular and expensive monument must surely be associated with an event of some importance. If the architectural historians finally conclude that a date at the end of this quarter-century is possible for the Rhodian dedication, then the chariot of Helios is most naturally interpreted as a second glorious victory monument celebrating the lifting of the great siege in 304.

The only other political event of real note in this quarter-century was the expulsion after Alexander the Great's death of the Macedonian garrison which he had imposed upon the island. A dedication associated with this event could still be classed as a victory monument of sorts. Despite the one-time rosy view that Alexander was responsible for the installation of the democratic

---

[1]   A Delphic proxeny decree of 180/79 or 179/8 BC in honour of certain Rhodians specifies that the text is to be written on the 'base of the golden chariot [- - -] by the demos of the Rhodians' (*Fouilles de Delphes*, iii. 3, no. 383. 35–6). The most natural understanding of this incomplete phrase would restore a reference to the chariot of their patron god Helios dedicated by the Rhodian demos.

[2]   Romantics will be disappointed to learn that it is impossible for Helios' horses to be those found at the basilica of San Marco, Venice (see Jacquemin and Laroche 1986, 297; Ridgway 1990, 58).

Figure 4 Hypothetical reconstruction of the Chariot of Helios dedicated by the Rhodians at Delphi. After Jacquemin and Laroche.

constitution at Rhodes, it now seems certain that his garrison was heartily resented by the already democratic Rhodians, and that its removal was a cause for celebration (Fraser 1952). None the less, given the uncertainties of the situation in which all of Asia Minor and the offshore islands found themselves after Alexander's death, it would have been an importunate island that celebrated its apparent – but far from certain – freedom by erecting a striking and extravagant dedication at the leading panhellenic sanctuary of Greece. The lifting of the siege seems a far more likely event.

These two Rhodian victory monuments follow classical custom in terms of their iconography. They are lavish, extravagant, and unmistakably designed for public consumption, fame, and propaganda value; yet their subjects are firmly in the 'generic' tradition. It is the patron god that is the subject of glorification, not the successes of contemporary Rhodians. The same is true of the Nike of Samothrace, which is a Rhodian dedication most probably in commemoration of the naval battles of Side and/or Myonnessos in 190 BC;[1] it is the goddess that is the focus of the monument, even though she is portrayed alighting on the prow of a *trihemiolia*, a type of ship particularly associated with the Rhodian navy. This continuation of the 'generic' tradition in civic contexts co-exists with the 'specific' orientation of some royal practice.

Ship dedications

In the classical period, victories at sea might be commemorated by appropriate naval dedications. Naval spoils that were dedicated might include the detached beak or ram of a captured galley, the whole prow of a ship, the figureheads or name device of a ship, or indeed a whole ship (for these dedication types see Pritchett 1979, 279 ff.). To give just one example of the last type: Thucydides (2. 84) records that the Athenians dedicated a ship to Poseidon on the shore near Rhion, not far from the site of Phormion's victory in the gulf of Corinth during the Peloponnesian war. Since these naval dedications were common (despite the fact that captured ships and equipment did not, by convention, have to be dedicated,

---

[1] See Rice 1991, arguing that the base of Rhodian stone makes it virtually certain that the statue is a Rhodian dedication (*contra* Phyllis and Karl Lehmann).

but could be – and often were – reused by the captors), Pritchett (1979, 285) is no doubt right to consider that these offerings are 'more in the nature of self-glorification on the part of a victorious state or hegemon, that pride has swallowed up piety, and that the dedicated article has become a monument of naval success often set up for purposes of propaganda'. This impression becomes much more marked in the hellenistic period.

The tomb of Alexander the Great's closest companion, Hephaistion (the so-called 'pyre of Hephaistion', fully described by Diod. 17. 115), took the form of a huge stepped pyramid with elaborate decoration on each of six levels. The foundation course was composed of the golden prows of 240 *pentereis*, each manned by statues of a kneeling archer and two armed warriors (*Fig. 5*). Certainly these were not the gilded prows from 240 real ships, but replicas; Alexander hardly had anything like that number of 'disposable' ships. The propaganda value of these 'fake' prows is very striking; such objects might have been fitting on the funeral pyre of a great ancient admiral, but none of Alexander's Companions, nor indeed the king himself, could claim that status.

It has been suggested that these elaborate prow dedications may have been the inspiration for a series of intriguing naval monuments, ranging from coins of Demetrios Poliorketes (depicting a prow surmounted by a figure of Victory) to the elaborate sculpted ship dedications erected throughout the Mediterranean.[1] These survive in the form of representations of a ship or part of a ship, or the bases for such representations, on many sites in the Mediterranean, and vary in date between the fourth century BC and Roman times.[2] The hellenistic Greeks, however, went one better than their classical predecessors in the matter of dedicating entire ships. Not only did they have ships much larger than triremes to dedicate, which will have made an even greater

---

[1] Marcadé 1946, 152. I have discussed elsewhere (Rice 1991) the important Rhodian ship dedications, including the inscribed Lindian base in the form of a *trihemiolia* (*Inscr. Lindos*, 88), the famous rock-cut ship relief on the ascent to the Lindian acropolis (*Inscr. Lindos*, 169), and the Nike of Samothrace whose base is the prow of another *trihemiolia* (see p. 242 above).
[2] For a survey of all these, including the elaborate Cyrene ship monument (of widely disputed date), see Ermeti 1981.

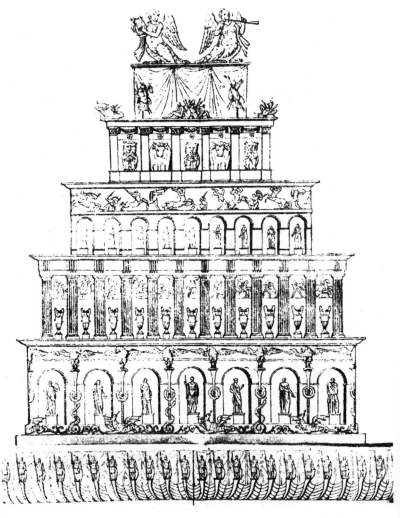

Figure 5 Hypothetical reconstruction of the 'Pyre of Hephaistion' at Babylon. After Quatremère de Quincy.

impression than before, but, as two particular monuments show, the arrangements for ship dedications could involve more elaborate and permanent preparations than simply the beaching and dedicating of a captured ship on the shore adjacent to the site of a naval victory.

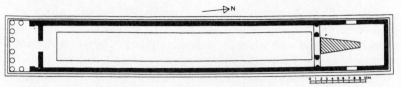

Figure 6 Plan of the Neorion at Delos. After Bruneau and Ducat.

The ship dedication at Delos

A building apparently designed to house a dedicated ship has been discovered on Delos in the sanctuary of Apollo (*Fig. 6*). This is the 'Monument des Taureaux' (so named after a pair of bull *protomai* on a pilaster belonging to the structure), a strikingly unusual building measuring 69.4 × 10.37 m, which, on the basis of its size and design alone, must have been one of the most imposing structures in the sanctuary. (For a full description see Roux 1981, 61–71; Ridgway 1990, 172–5; 204 n. 24). It consists of a monumental Doric porch, leading into a long gallery surrounded by a walkway and decorated with marine sculptures. The centre of this gallery is occupied by a shallow basin measuring 45.65 × 4.48 m. At the north end is a type of antechamber containing a large triangular base.

The shape of this structure and its marine motifs suggest that it held a dedicated ship, and a very large one (the Athenian trireme sheds at the Piraeus measure only 35 × 4.8 m). It is no doubt this building that is referred to in Delian inscriptions as the *neorion* (ship-shed). We may note that Pausanias mentions a ship at Delos, evidently a dedication (1. 29. 1): 'I know that nobody ever conquered the ship in Delos, having as many as nine rowers from the decks.'[1] Perhaps he saw the ship which was housed in this building.

It was suggested a long time ago (Tarn 1910) that the victorious Antigonos II Gonatas dedicated his flagship at Delos after the battle of Kos, one of the few defeats inflicted on the Ptolemaic navy, which took place sometime in the mid-third century.[2] At

---

[1] This enigmatic phrase has caused great difficulty to naval historians (see Casson 1971, 115–16; Morrison 1980, 43–4).
[2] The date of the battle has been much debated, but it probably took place between 262 and 245 BC in the context of the second Syrian war.

this battle Gonatas had a special flagship, the *Isthmia*, which he later dedicated to Apollo. Athenaeus (209 e) describes it as 'a sacred trireme with which he defeated Ptolemy's admirals . . . off Kos, when he vowed the ship to Apollo', which leaves the site of the dedication open. Although some have argued subjectively that Kos would have been a geographically more natural venue for the dedication (Pritchett 1979, 284), a panhellenic sanctuary sacred to Apollo, such as Delos, would certainly have been appropriate. If Delos was the site of Gonatas' dedicated ship, it may have been this ship that Pausanias saw.

The final publication of the 'Monument des Taureaux' in the Delos excavation reports, which has yet to appear, may clarify many of the considerable difficulties involved in its interpretation.[1] At first it seemed obvious to associate the structure with Antigonos' dedication, but detailed study of the construction technique has produced a date at the end of the fourth or the beginning of the third century (Bruneau 1970, 554–7), while the style of the decorative architectural sculptures points to *c*.320–310 at the latest.[2]

Vallois suggests that the building to house the ship dedication was commissioned by Demetrios Poliorketes after his victory at Salamis in 306 – it would be a flamboyant gesture typical of Demetrios – but that it was not finished, and was first used by his son Gonatas (Vallois 1944, 35–6). This may sound like special pleading, but it accords with the otherwise curious fact that the *neorion* is not mentioned in inscriptions of *c*.300–250 BC. This is very odd if it was in use then to house a high-profile dedication by Demetrios I. Furthermore, Roux (1981) observes that the ship that was finally housed in the building seems to have been bigger

---

[1] Pritchett (1979, 283–4) does not fully grasp the nettle in his discussion of this structure, although he could not have known of the observations of Roux (1981).

[2] Marcadé 1946; cf. Bruneau and Ducat 1983, 139. Coupry (1973) suggests that the structure was built *c*.330–315 BC to house an Athenian dedication. While this date may best suit that proposed for the sculpture, it is hard to find a historical context for such an extravagant Athenian naval dedication in this period, and the monument type is foreign to that favoured by Athens.

than the one for which it had been designed.[1] If his line of
reasoning is correct, it would point to the use and adaptation of
the building at a later date, perhaps for the *Isthmia*, Gonatas'
flagship from the victory off Kos.

The ship dedication at Samothrace

The discovery on Samothrace of a building designed to house a
ship dedication was recently announced (McCredie 1987; Catling
1986–7, 50–1). Although the structure has not yet been completely
excavated, rounded keel supports, some evidently *in situ*, along
the length of the building make it clear that it was designed to hold
a ship. Its dimensions are 27.25 × 12 m, so the ship in question
was much shorter than the Delian ship or even a classical
Athenian trireme (unless only the forward part was cut off and
dedicated). An interior colonnade runs along the length of the
structure, so that the width of the ship cannot have exceeded
*c.*4.3 m.

The excavators have dated the building to the first half of the
third century, when Samothrace was under the influence of the
Antigonid kings of Macedonia, and have tentatively associated
the dedication with Gonatas. It seems *prima facie* unlikely that
this is the *Isthmia* (see p. 246); the ship was relatively small and
therefore probably not the king's flagship. It would also be odd
for a ship dedicated to Apollo to be found on Samothrace. The
excavators have suggested that it was a Ptolemaic ship captured
during one of Gonatas' naval victories, either the battle of Kos or
that of Andros (the second occasion on which he defeated the
Ptolemaic navy). This sounds plausible; if he dedicated his
flagship on Delos, or indeed somewhere else, he may well have
dedicated a captured enemy ship at another panhellenic sanctuary. Further speculation must await more details of the find.

[1] He also argues that the N antechamber was originally designed for an
altar, but was remodelled and filled with the curious triangular base
which almost completely obstructs the entrance from the long gallery.
The most reasonable explanation for this anomaly is that the larger ship
that was ultimately dedicated protruded through the door into the N
chamber, where its stern or prow was supported by the improvised base.

Lion monuments

Lion monuments associated with military victories form a special category of war memorial, since they may also serve as tombs or cenotaphs for the dead of the war in question. The lion is a powerful symbol of physical strength, and its connection with valour and military prowess is obvious. In addition, it had chthonic significance from early times and was commonly associated with the cult of the dead (Broneer 1941, 45). Both connotations made it particularly appropriate as a symbol to commemorate the courage, and guard the bodies, of the heroic dead.

Lion monuments are known from the archaic period, and several functioned as war memorials in the classical Greek world. For example, a colossal lion was set up over the tomb of Leonidas at Thermopylai (Herodotos, 7. 225), and another over a *polyandrion* at Thespiai, perhaps after the battle of Delion in 424 BC (Stamatakis 1882; Pritchett 1985, 132–3). A lion which Pausanias (9. 40. 10) says was set up over the tomb of the Thebans who fell at the battle of Chaironeia in 338 was duly discovered in the last century.[1] Several large lions were found in the Piraeus, including the famous one moved to the arsenal at Venice (Panagos 1968, 237–47; Broneer 1941, fig. 31); some of these may have marked tombs. Lion monuments continued to be set up in the later classical and early hellenistic periods, and some of them present intriguing problems of date and context.

The lion monument at Amphipolis

This monument was reconstructed in 1937 near the Strymon river in Thrace (*Plate 3b*; Broneer 1941; Roger 1939; Lawrence 1942). The date and architectural details are disputed, but in the reconstruction a lion is seated on a pedestal above a stepped base.[2]

---

[1] Pritchett 1985, 136; reconstruction in Broneer 1941, figs 34–5.
[2] For the difficulty in reconstructing the base, or associating the monument with blocks preserving engaged Doric half-columns with shields between them, see Miller and Miller 1972, 150–8.

Broneer tries to date the lion to the period shortly after
Alexander's death, interpreting it as a cenotaph-cum-war memorial in honour of one of Alexander's entourage, Laomedon of
Amphipolis. There can be no proof of this, but a date in the late
fourth or early third century seems most likely; that is to say,
contemporary with the lion tomb of Knidos, with which it has
close similarities (Roger 1939, 34–5; Fedak 1990, 78).

The lion of Hamadan

One intriguing monument is the lion from Hamadan in Iran
(Luschey 1968). Hamadan is ancient Ekbatana, capital of the
Medes and later the summer residence of the Achaemenid kings of
Persia. The date of this fragmentary sculpture has been widely
disputed; one main school held it to be a Median monument
dating from the seventh or sixth century BC, the other a Parthian
monument of the early centuries AD. Luschey has shown that the
lion is closely related in size and style to the lions of Chaironeia
and Amphipolis, and differs markedly from known Parthian lions
of a later date.

If the Hamadan lion can be dated to *c*.350–300 BC, a context can
be proposed for the monument to which it originally belonged. In
324, on his return journey from the east, Alexander revisited
Ekbatana (Arr. 7. 14). It was during the festival he staged there
that Hephaistion fell ill and died. Distraught with grief, he
planned an elaborate funeral for his friend at Babylon, involving
the 'pyre' discussed above. Luschey suggests, reasonably, that the
Hamadan lion was erected at Ekbatana by Alexander, as a
cenotaph in memory of his friend in the place where he died.

The lion tomb at Knidos

The famous lion tomb of Knidos stands on a promontory
overlooking the sea east of Knidos town, although its lion now
resides in the British Museum. A hypothetical reconstruction has
been drawn (*Fig. 7*), although certain details remain uncertain
and controversial; the lower portion was square, and ornamented
with engaged Doric columns below a metope and triglyph frieze.

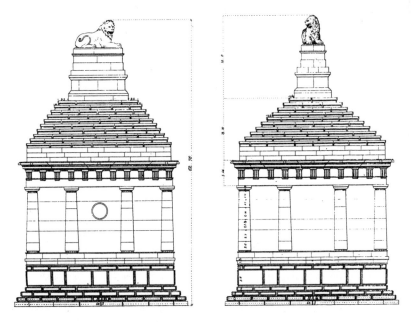

Figure 7 Hypothetical reconstruction of the Lion Tomb at Knidos. After R. P. Pullan, in Newton 1865.

This was topped by a stepped pyramid below a platform for the recumbent lion.[1] The lower portion of the tomb contained a round room with a corbelled roof, and had twelve *loculi* for *ostothekai* around it at ground level. This room is all that remains of the tomb today, but several Doric architectural details lie around (Fedak 1990, 76–8; figs 85–9).

The combination of a lion, the conventional symbol of valour, and the remote position overlooking the sea has suggested that the monument commemorated a naval battle and honoured some of those who died in it (Lawrence 1983, 254). The design of the tomb differs markedly from the rectangular *periboloi* with tombs which occupy the necropolis area between the lion tomb and the city wall, although Newton saw similar tombs nearby (see p. 251). He associated the lion tomb with the great naval action that took

---

[1] Waywell (1980, 5–7) doubts various details, notably the height of the lion's platform, and estimates the overall height as *c*.12.2 m, not the 18.6 m that Newton's architect Pullan estimated (Newton 1865, ii, pl. 23).

place off Knidos in 394, in which the Spartans were defeated by
the Athenian commander Konon (Newton 1863, 493 ff.); but
although dates from 394 to the second century BC have been
suggested, most scholars now opt for the late fourth or early third
century (see especially Waywell 1980, 7; Fedak 1990, 78). This
period was full of naval action, as various of the Successors were
building ever larger 'super-galleys' to outdo their opponents and
win control of the sea (Casson 1971, 137–40). The precise battle,
however, cannot be identified. Knidos, as a wealthy city, may have
wished to commemorate several of her citizens who participated
in one or other of the sea-fights of the Successors. The lion is of
Pentelic marble, which may suggest an Athenian connection (cf.
Fedak 1990, 77).

The monument would have been visible from a great distance,
and even today, in its ruined state, it can be seen from far out to
sea (see *Plate 4a*). Like the Colossus of Rhodes, it would certainly
have served as a landmark to mariners, hence ensuring its
continuing fame. Newton (1863, 502) noted similar tombs along
the rocky Knidian peninsula to the east:[1]

> The manner in which the several tombs are grouped, seems hardly the
> result of chance. Their arrangement would seem to indicate that
> advantage has been taken of the principal eminences, so as to make
> each tomb command a view of the one nearest to it. Thus they may
> have served as a chain of watchtowers, and for the communication of
> signals.

Thus these monuments appear to have had important practical as
well as psychological functions.

The Scylla tomb from Bargylia

The lion tomb of Knidos is assumed to have commemorated naval
dead only because of its position overlooking the sea, and because
of the connotations of lions; there are no specific features of its
iconography which connect it with a sea battle. The decoration of
a little-known tomb from Bargylia in Karia, however, more firmly

[1] In spring 1988 I saw a large, round foundation E of the Lion Tomb,
below the modern road, perhaps one of Newton's tombs.

suggests that it was connected with a naval victory (Waywell 1980, 7–8; 1990).[1] The site of the tomb has not been rediscovered this century, but the Scylla group which crowned it is now in the British Museum (BM 1542), and we have Biliotti's description of his investigation of the site in 1865 (partly published in Waywell 1980). Like the lion tomb, the Scylla tomb stood on a high promontory overlooking the sea, apparently in an isolated position. The tomb was rectangular with engaged Doric columns, probably with a stepped pyramidal roof crowned by the sea monster Scylla. She has a female torso, three foreparts of dogs, and two fishtails spiralling high behind the group.

From the style of the monument, Waywell suggests a date in the late third or early second century BC. Quite apart from the importance of this sculpted group (it may be the earliest monumental treatment of a theme that became popular in later hellenistic and Roman times), its presence on a monumental tomb is intriguing and not readily explicable. Might the tomb have been designed to commemorate a sea battle, represented in dramatic and symbolic fashion? It is worth noting that Bargylia was close to Rhodian territory, which at this date included parts of Karia. Rhodes had one of the strongest navies in the Mediterranean at this time, and had taken over from the Ptolemaic navy the role of policing the seas and ridding them of pirates. There were probably several naval actions, minor if not major, in waters not far from Bargylia.

The Turgut tomb

One construction which is related to pyramidal mausolea as well as to lion monuments is a little-known tomb in the Rhodian *peraia* in south-west Turkey, located near the modern village of Turgut (first noted by Fraser and Bean 1954, 44–5). The tomb stands on an outcrop on a prominent hill; it is a square chamber tomb with a steep pyramidal roof (*Plate 4b*); at some time it was

---

[1] I am extremely grateful to Professor Waywell for an advance copy of the latter text. Discussion of the tomb must be provisional until his full publication of the Scylla group in the British Museum appears. Suggested reconstruction of the tomb: Waywell 1990, 387, fig. 1.

converted by the local inhabitants into an Islamic shrine. A largely effaced metrical inscription of hellenistic date on the lintel over the door records that this was the tomb of Diagoras and his wife Aristomacha (the name Diagoras was common in the most famous classical family on Rhodes, the Diagoridai). The poem relates that a pair of lions stood beside the door,[1] and a statue of Diagoras on the summit of the pyramid. The elaborate tomb, which is to my knowledge unique, plus the guardian lions are no doubt to be explained by the fact that Diagoras was 'renowned in war', as the epitaph says. Like the Alketas tomb at Termessos, the unusual iconography is no doubt to be explained by the particular circumstances of the deceased.

Conclusion

Observations about such a disparate group of monuments cannot be organized into any neat conclusions. Comments have been made above about the general trend towards specific representations of historical events in the late classical period, which can be seen in the Spartan Aigospotamoi monument and those associated with Alexander. The lack of evidence about any major artistic commemorative monuments (if any ever existed) erected by the kings of Macedonia, Egypt, and Syria precludes any observations about the iconographic direction they may have taken, although the kings' victory parades and traditions of royal portraiture would lead most naturally to the hypothesis of 'specific' imagery. (The Raphia stele is an extraordinary example that bears this out. In a relief carving atop a trilingual text celebrating his victory at the battle of Raphia in 317, Ptolemy IV is depicted in full Macedonian battledress in a scene which is otherwise Egyptian in style.)[2]

The epigraphic evidence for royal dedications also supports the hypothesis of 'specific' iconography. As Austin has noted (1986,

[1]   A damaged marble lion is reported to have been in the garden of the house nearest to the tomb (Fraser and Bean 1954, 45); I did not see it in 1989 (there is no house very near to the tomb).
[2]   For this stele and its iconography see D. J. Thompson 1988, 117–18; pl. 6. The Greek text is *SEG* viii. 504 *a*.

458), classical war memorials emphasize the glory due to the polis and its citizens, whereas hellenistic dedications give the glory to the king: 'The glory of victory belonged to the king himself, usually exclusively, except when a king acted together with allies whose contribution had to be acknowledged.' This is true also of the texts inscribed on the Pergamene monuments, which artistically belong more to the classical generic tradition, seen in fifth-century Athens and in independent hellenistic cities like Rhodes. Possible reasons for this iconographic difference have been indicated above.

Many commemorations of victory are also closely linked with the study of monumental tombs. Fruitful lines of further enquiry might include the ways in which the increasing diversity and individuality of tomb design in the hellenistic age allowed specific, naturalistic representations of military conflict, defeat, and victory to be portrayed. The special category of naval monuments might also be studied for information about the design of ancient warships, concrete evidence for which is so badly needed.[1] Finally, a separate study is needed of ways in which hellenistic commemorations of victory influenced Roman victory monuments in particular, and the tradition of Roman historical narrative art in general.[2]

---

[1] This has been done with Octavian's naval memorial at Nikopolis, erected after Actium (see Murray and Petsas 1989). The results of the study promise to have far-reaching importance.

[2] E.g. after the battle of Pydna (168) the Roman general L. Aemilius Paullus commandeered a half-finished quadrangular pillar which was being erected as the base for a portrait of Perseus at Delphi, in front of the temple, and had it turned into a memorial for himself and his victory. It bore a bronze equestrian portrait of himself and a Greek-style frieze of a battle between Romans and Macedonians – i.e. a real rather than a mythological battle. By the second century this would have been a familiar type of monument in Greece, but 'from the Roman point of view it was a landmark, . . . perhaps the first of the great tradition of historical reliefs in Roman art' (Pollitt 1986, 155–8, at 157–8; see also Smith 1991, 185–6; Kähler 1965). Pollitt (p. 155) stresses the importance of Paullus' hiring the Athenian Metrodoros to create paintings for his triumph (Pliny, *HN* 35. 135); he thereby adopted a second Greek artistic medium, historical painting, and transferred it to a Roman context. On Greek honours and their gradual adaptation by Romans, see Wallace-Hadrill 1990, 150–6; 169.

The glorious dead 255

Bibliography

Ashton, R. (1988), 'Rhodian coinage and the Colossus', *Revue numis-matique* (6th ser.), 30: 75–90.
Austin, M. M. (1986), 'Hellenistic kings, war and the economy', *CQ* 80 (n.s. 36): 450–66.
Broneer, O. (1941), *The Lion Monument at Amphipolis* (Cambridge, Mass.).
Bruneau, P. (1970), *Recherches sur les cultes de Délos à l'époque hellénistique et à l'époque impériale* (Paris).
—— and Ducat, J. (1983), *Guide de Délos* (3rd edn, Ecole Française d'Athènes).
Bulle, H. (1906), 'Der leichenwagen Alexanders', *Jahrbuch des Deutschen Archäologischen Instituts*, 21: 53–73.
Callaghan, P. J. (1981), 'On the date of the Great Altar of Zeus at Pergamon', *Bulletin of the Institute of Classical Studies*, 28: 115–21.
Casson, L. (1971), *Ships and Seamanship in the Ancient World* (Princeton).
Catling, H. W. (1986–7), 'Archaeology in Greece 1986–7', *AR* 33: 3–61.
Childs, W. A. P. (1978), *The City-reliefs of Lycia* (Princeton).
Clayton, P. A., and Price, M. J. (eds 1988), *The Seven Wonders of the Ancient World* (London, etc.).
Coarelli, F. (1981), 'Alessandro, i Licinii e Lanuvio', in *L'Art décoratif à Rome à la fin de la république et au début du principat* (Collection de l'Ecole Française de Rome, 55; Rome).
Coupry, J. (1973), 'Autour d'une trière', in *Etudes Déliennes* (*BCH* suppl. 1), pp. 147–56.
Doumas, Ch. (1975), 'Archaiotites kai mnimeia Dodekanison', *AD* 30, Chron. 361–72 (in Greek).
Ekschmitt, W. (1984), *Die sieben Weltwunder: ihre Erbauung, Zerstör-ung und Wiederentdeckung* (Kulturgeschichte der Antiken Welt; Mainz am Rhein).
Ermeti, A. L. (1981), *L'agorà di Cirene*, iii. 1: *Il monumento navale* (Rome).
Fedak, J. (1990), *Monumental Tombs of the Hellenistic Age* (Phoenix, suppl. 27; Toronto).
Fraser, P. M. (1952), 'Alexander and the Rhodian constitution', *Parola del passato*, 7: 192–206.
—— and Bean, G. E. (1954), *The Rhodian Peraea and Islands* (Oxford).
French, E. B. (1989–90), 'Archaeology in Greece 1989–90', *AR* 36: 3–82.
Gabriel, A. (1932), 'La construction, l'attitude, et l'emplacement du Colosse de Rhodes', *BCH* 56: 331–59.
Habicht, C. (1985), *Pausanias' Guide to Ancient Greece* (Berkeley, etc.).
Haynes, D. E. L. (1957), 'Philo of Byzantium and the Colossus of Rhodes', *JHS* 77: 311–12.
Higgins, R. A. (1988), 'The Colossus of Rhodes', in P. A. Clayton and

M. J. Price (eds), *The Seven Wonders of the Ancient World* (London, etc.), pp. 124–37.

Hoepfner, W., and Schwandner, E.-L. (1986), *Haus und Stadt im klassischen Griechenland* (Wohnen in der klassischen Polis, 1; Munich).

Jacquemin, A., and Laroche, D. (1986), 'Le char d'or consacré par le peuple rhodien', *BCH* 110: 285–307.

Kähler, H. (1965), *Der Fries vom Reiterdenkmal des Aemilius Paullus in Delphi* (Berlin).

Konstantinopoulos, G. (1975), 'Anaskaphai eis Rodon', *Praktika tis en Athinais Archaiologikis Etaireias*, part 1, pp. 238–48 (in Greek).

Kontorini, V. (1989), *Anekdotes epigraphes Rodou*, ii (in Greek with French summary) Athens.

Launey, M. (1987), *Recherches sur les armées hellénistiques*, ii (2nd edn, rev. Y. Garlan, P. Gauthier, and C. Orrieux; BEFAR 169; Paris).

Lawrence, A. W. (1942), review of Broneer (1941), *JHS* 62: 101–2.

—— (1983), *Greek Architecture* (rev. R. A. Tomlinson; London).

Luschey, H. (1968), 'Der Löwe von Ekbatana', *Archäologische Mitteilungen aus Iran*, n.s. 1: 115–22.

McCredie, J. (1987), 'A ship for the Great Gods: excavations in Samothrace, 1986' (abstract), *AJA* 91: 270.

Marcadé, J. (1946), 'Sur une base lindienne en forme de proue', *Revue archéologique*, 6th ser., 26: 147–52.

Maryon, H. (1956), 'The Colossus of Rhodes', *JHS* 76: 68–86.

Miller, Stella Grobel and Miller, Stephen G. (1972), 'Architectural blocks from the Strymon', *AD* 27, Mel. 140–69.

Moreno, P. (1973–4), 'Cronologia del Colosso di Rodi', *Archeologia classica*, 25–6: 453–63.

Morrison, J. S. (1980), *The Ship*, ii: *Long Ships and Round Ships: Warfare and Trade in the Mediterranean, 3000 BC–500 AD* (National Maritime Museum; London).

Murray, W. M., and Petsas, Ph. M. (1989), *Octavian's Campsite Memorial for the Actian War* (Transactions of the American Philosophical Society, 79. 4; Philadelphia).

Newton, C. T. (1863), *A History of Discoveries at Halicarnassus, Cnidus, and Branchidae*, ii. 2 (London).

—— (1865), *Travels and Discoveries in the Levant* (London).

Panagos, Ch. Th. (1968), *Le Pirée* (Athens).

Papachristodoulou, I. (1988), 'Recent investigations and activities carried out by the Archaeological Service of the Dodecanese', in S. Dietz and I. Papachristodoulou (eds), *Archaeology in the Dodecanese* (Copenhagen), pp. 200–9.

Pekridou, A. (1986), *Das Alketas-Grab in Termessos* (Tübingen).

Pollitt, J. J. (1986), *Art in the Hellenistic Age* (Cambridge).

Pritchett, W. K. (1974), *The Greek State at War*, ii (Berkeley, etc.).

—— (1979), *The Greek State at War*, iii: *Religion* (Berkeley, etc.).

—— (1985), *The Greek State at War*, iv (Berkeley, etc.).

Quatremère de Quincy, A. C. (1829), *Monuments et ouvrages de l'art antiques* (Paris).

Radt, W. (1988), *Pergamon: Geschichte und Bauten, Funde und Erforschung einer antiken Metropole* (DuMont Dokumente; Köln).

Rice, E. E. (1983), *The Grand Procession of Ptolemy Philadelphus* (Oxford).

—— (1991), 'The Rhodian navy in the hellenistic age', in W. R. Roberts and J. Sweetman (eds), *New Interpretations in Naval History: Selected Papers from the 9th Naval History Symposium* (Annapolis, Md.), pp. 29–50.

Ridgway, B. S. (1990), *Hellenistic Sculpture*, i: *The Styles of ca. 331–200 BC* (Madison, Wis.).

Roger, J. (1939), 'Le monument au lion d'Amphipolis', *BCH* 63: 4–42.

Roux, G. (1981), 'Problèmes déliens', *BCH* 105: 41–78.

Schalles, H.-J. (1985), *Untersuchungen zur Kulturpolitik der pergamenischen Herrscher im 3. Jh. v. Chr.* (Istanbuler Forschungen, 36; Tübingen).

Smith, R. R. R. (1991), *Hellenistic Sculpture* (London).

Stamatakis, P. (1882), 'Ekthesis peri ton en Boiotia ergon', *Praktika tis en Athinais Archaiologikis Etaireias*, 67–74 (in Greek).

Tarn, W. W. (1910), 'The dedicated ship of Antigonus Gonatas', *JHS* 30: 209–22.

Thompson, D. J. (1988), *Memphis under the Ptolemies* (Princeton).

Thompson, H. A. (1982), 'Architecture as a medium of public relations among the successors of Alexander', in B. Barr-Sharrar and E. N. Borza (eds), *Macedonia and Greece in Late Classical and Early Hellenistic Times* (Studies in the History of Art, 10; Washington, DC), pp. 173–89.

Vallois, R. (1944), *L'architecture hellénique et hellénistique à Délos*, i (Paris).

Wallace-Hadrill, A. (1990), 'Roman arches and Greek honours: the language of power at Rome', *PCPS* 216 (n.s. 36): 143–81.

Waywell, G. B. (1980), 'Mausolea in south-west Asia Minor', *Yayla*, 3: 5–11.

—— (1990), 'The Scylla monument from Bargylia: its sculptural remains', in *Akten des 13. Internationalen Kongresses für klassische Archäologie, Berlin 1988* (Mainz am Rhein).

Zervoudaki, E. (1975), 'Helios kai Helieia', *AD* 30, Mel. 1–20 (in Greek).

Index

Compiled by Graham Shipley
and Helen Parkins